T0135133

Present and Ulterior Software Engineering

Manuel Mazzara • Bertrand Meyer
Editors

Present and Ulterior Software Engineering

Springer

Editors
Manuel Mazzara
Innopolis University
Innopolis, Russia

Bertrand Meyer
Chair of Software Engineering
ETH Zürich
Zürich, Switzerland

ISBN 978-3-319-88429-5   ISBN 978-3-319-67425-4   (eBook)
https://doi.org/10.1007/978-3-319-67425-4

Printed on acid-free paper

This Springer imprint is published by Springer Nature
The registered company is Springer International Publishing AG
The registered company address is: Gewerbestrasse 11, 6330 Cham, Switzerland

Preface

The PAUSE symposium took place from the 16th to the 19th of December 2015. It was the first scientific event in the elegant Château of Villebrumier, in the Southwest of France, newly equipped to serve as a conference center for technical meetings, with a particular focus on information technology.

The aim of PAUSE was to mark the completion of 14 years of work at the Chair of Software Engineering at ETH Zurich. The participants were former members of the Chair and colleagues from every part of the world who had the opportunity to collaborate with it over the years.

In this inspiring context, extensive discussions about the past, present, and future of software engineering took place between some of the best minds in the field. This volume includes some of the presentations given at Villebrumier, edited and extended into full chapters.

The content of this volume can be considered an effective synthesis of the current state of the art in software engineering with a projection into the future of the discipline.

Innopolis, Russia   Manuel Mazzara
Zürich, Switzerland   Bertrand Meyer
28 April 2017

Contents

Engineering by Software: System Behaviours as Components

Michael Jackson

Abstract *Software engineering* means developing software for a purpose. For systems that interact with a physical *problem world*, the proximate purpose is a desired behaviour of that problem world: the fundamental engineering task is to develop the system behaviour and specify the software that will evoke it. This chapter sketches a discipline for this task, in which behaviours are always understood as the result of interactions of a software machine and a physical problem world. Complex behaviour is designed in terms of simple constituent behaviours. The running behaviour instances form a dynamic tree in which control of the tree is exercised by the software machines at the nodes.

Some salient concepts, principles, practices and concerns of this discipline are discussed. After an introductory section, the development of a simple behaviour is clarified, and the iterative relationship between behaviour and requirements is illustrated. Requirements state the benefits expected from the system behaviour. An abstract goal behaviour is proposed, intended to satisfy the requirements. After elaboration into a concrete behaviour of the physical problem world, it is again evaluated against the requirements. The nature and development of complex behaviour is discussed. Development is partly top-down and partly bottom-up: top-down development decomposes a well-understood function into subfunctions; bottom-up development combines disparate functions springing from distinct requirements. In both, the identification and design of constituent behaviours is distinguished from their combination into a complex whole. The chapter ends with some general observations on the principles embodied in the approach described.

1 Introduction

1.1 Two Faces of Software Engineering

We distinguish the engineering *of* software from engineering *by* software. The first looks inward at the computer, inventing, structuring, elaborating and transforming

M. Jackson (✉)
The Open University, Milton Keynes, UK
e-mail: jacksonma@acm.org

© Springer International Publishing AG 2017
M. Mazzara, B. Meyer (eds.), *Present and Ulterior Software Engineering*,
https://doi.org/10.1007/978-3-319-67425-4_1

programs for efficient execution and correct computation. The second looks outward at the problem world with which the computer interacts, specifying software whose execution will produce desired behaviours in that world.

If the problem—for example, factorising a large integer or solving a set of equations—is located in an abstract and timeless world, then engineering *by* software makes little sense: in a timeless world, the computer can produce no effects and evoke no behaviour. By contrast, the world of a physical problem can be affected and even controlled. Achieving the desired effects and control is an engineering problem: if it can be solved by introducing an appropriately programmed computer into the world, it becomes a problem of engineering *by* software. This chapter is concerned with problems of this kind. More specifically, it is concerned with the development of *embedded* or *cyber-physical* systems. These systems have the potential to bring dramatic benefits to society, but it will not be possible to realise those benefits—especially in critical applications—unless software becomes more dependable [1].

1.2   The System and the Project

For embedded or cyber-physical software, the system comprises both the software and the problem world—those parts of the natural, engineered and human physical world—whose behaviour it must control.

The most important *requirements* are desired properties and effects of this behaviour. It is a common mistake to identify the requirements with the system behaviour itself. The behaviour itself is the product of a design activity, while the requirements should identify the benefits that the behaviour must bring. A behaviour cannot be specified exactly by enumerating its intended benefits, because the same set of benefits can be provided by different system behaviours. Some organisations, aiming to state their requirements exactly, try to cast them in the form of stimulus-response pairs, describing the software's required response to each of the myriad events that may happen in the problem world. One company proudly announced at a requirements workshop that a certain product line had 200,000 requirements. Such an approach fails on both scores: it neither specifies the behaviour exactly—or even consistently—nor captures its intended benefits explicitly.

We identify these conceptual parts of a development problem:

- The *machine*: the part of the system executing the software
- The *problem world*: the physical world monitored and controlled by the machine
- The *system behaviour*: the behaviour of the problem world resulting from its interaction with the software
- The *requirements*: the benefits that the system behaviour must provide—some directly observable in the problem world and others due to more remote effects and consequences of the behaviour

We also identify these two roles in a development project:

- The *stakeholders*: the people and organisations who have legitimate interests in the system and a proper expectation that it will satisfy their needs and purposes as expressed in the requirements; some stakeholders may themselves participate in the system behaviour.
- The *developers*: the software engineers who will design the system behaviour, specifying the software that will evoke it, and working with the stakeholders to validate the behaviour—that is, to confirm that their expectations will be satisfied.

These roles are merely conceptual: the stakeholders have needs; the developers design the system to satisfy them. In practice, the roles may overlap, they may be structured into many specialisms, and the same person may play more than one role.

2 Simple Behaviour

2.1 A Simple System: Zoo Visitor Control

Realistic systems have complex behaviours. Complex behaviour emerges from a combination of simple behaviours and the interactions among them. To address complexity, one must have a clear understanding of simplicity. So we begin here with a very simple system whose purpose is to control visitor entry to a small zoo. The system can be depicted in a schematic diagram in Fig. 1.

The striped box represents the machine. The other boxes represent the *problem domains* of the problem world. These are the identified relevant components in which the system behaviour will be evoked: the Coin Acceptor, the Barrier, the Stop Button, the Manager and the Visitors. The labelled connecting lines represent interfaces of shared phenomena between system components: at interfaces e and f, the Visitors can operate the Coin Acceptor and the Barrier; at interface d, the Manager can operate the Stop Button; at interfaces a, b and c, the machine interacts with the Stop Button, Coin Acceptor and Barrier.

Fig. 1 A simple system

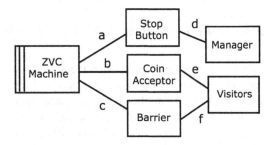

The requirements, as initially stated by the stakeholders, are as follows:

1: No entry without payment (one coin).
2: No visitor is harmed by the system.
3: The system is easy and convenient to use.
4: The system positively attracts new customers.
5: The system speeds entry and so improves zoo profits.

2.2   Abstract Goal Behaviour

Requirement 1 seems most directly significant, stating a *goal* (in the KAOS [2] sense) apparently satisfiable by a suitable system behaviour. The developers propose an *Abstract Goal Behaviour* AGB1: (*acceptCoin;admitVisitor*)*. The behaviour is *abstract* in the sense that events '*acceptCoin*' and '*admitVisitor*' are commonsense abstractions: they are not known to be elements in the alphabets of the Coin Acceptor and Barrier at the interfaces b and c or e and f. However, after briefly examining the properties of the devices, the developers have decided that the behaviour AGB1 is *feasible*. That is, they are confident that they can specify executable software behaviour at b and c that will realise the abstract events sufficiently reliably and will enforce the alternating pattern of AGB1.

Wisely, instead of proceeding immediately to develop the system behaviour and software for AGB1, the developers present it to the stakeholders for confirmation that it will satisfy their requirements. The stakeholders soon discover a previously unrecognised difficulty. Teachers who bring groups of schoolchildren to the zoo would like to insert the coins for the group without being constrained by the strict alternation of AGB1: for them, Requirement 3 is not satisfied.

It is therefore agreed that a better behaviour would be AGB2: (*acceptCoin | admitPaidVisitor*)*: the abstract events '*acceptCoin*' and '*admitVisitor*' can occur in any order provided only that the cumulative number of admissions never exceeds the cumulative number of inserted coins. Whenever the numbers of admissions and coins are equal, the next event must be insertion of a coin.

2.3   Concrete System Behaviour

The developers are confident that the abstract events '*acceptCoin*' and '*admitVisitor*' can be realised by suitable procedures built from phenomena in the alphabets of the Coin Acceptor and Barrier at interfaces b and c, respectively. Demands for each are recognised by the machine at the same interfaces b and c.

To specify the machine's software (M) to enforce AGB2, formal models (W) of the problem domains' intrinsic given properties and behaviours must be developed. The system, as depicted in Fig. 1, is a physical contrivance, and the necessary reasoning for software specification is primarily causal. The problem domain models describe each domain's potential behaviour that will be constrained by its interactions with the machine and with other domains at each of its interfaces. These models may be expressed, for example, as state machines with inputs and with outputs and states (some hidden, some shared at an interface). Execution of the specified machine software M, in parallel with the problem domain behaviours W of the Visitors, Manager, Stop Button, Coin Acceptor and Barrier, produces the *concrete system behaviour* CSB. That is, CSB = M || W. The alphabet of CSB is the union of the alphabets of M and W. The alphabet of M may include phenomena that are not shared by W. For example, a machine M designed to enforce AGB2 must have a local variable *sc* in which it records the current surplus of coins over entries. This local variable is an element of the internal state of M.

Evoking the concrete system behaviour CSB relies on given mechanisms in the problem domains, identified and described in W. Some of these mechanisms will involve hidden internal phenomena of the domains. In general, therefore, the concrete system behaviour will be more elaborate, and of finer granularity, than the abstract goal behaviour that originally motivated it. Furthermore, the relationship between the abstract alphabet of AGB and the concrete alphabet of CSB, both hidden and visible at the interfaces, may be far from obvious. This is a complication likely—perhaps almost certain—to appear in any development which starts from abstract concepts and aims to realise them in the physical world. The complication arises because the abstract concept must be realised in some physical procedure comprising multiple concrete phenomena, and any particular execution of the procedure may be in some way imperfect or incomplete. Developers of the formal model, their choice of abstractions and their design of the concrete realisations must take care lest this complication cause a major inconsistency between the model and the concrete reality.

2.4   Concrete System Behaviour: Problem Concerns

The machine specification M is designed to ensure that CSB, the concrete system behaviour which it evokes, satisfies the requirements. For example:

- Its design being motivated by AGB2, CSB should satisfy 'no entry without payment'.
- Its design being motivated by AGB2 rather than by AGB1, CSB should satisfy 'easy and convenient to use'.
- The operation of the Barrier by M should avoid harming any Visitor.
- The causal chains by which M evokes CSB should respect the stipulated operating protocols for the Coin Acceptor and Barrier, to avoid damage to the equipment.

The first three of these are explicit stakeholder requirements; but the fourth is an example of what we may call *a standard problem concern*. The idea of a standard concern is familiar in programming. A program must avoid arithmetic overflow and underflow, storage leaks, using the value of an uninitialised variable, dereferencing a null pointer, and so on. Design of a simple system behaviour similarly demands attention to a standard repertoire of concerns. Here are some examples:

- *Breakage:* the behaviour evoked by the software must not break or maltreat any problem domain.
- *Initialisation:* if the designed behaviour assumes an initial state of the problem world, the designer must make this constraint on the possible activations of its machine fully explicit.
- *Abortion:* if pre-emptive termination of the behaviour can leave the problem world in a dangerous state—for example, if the machine is unexpectedly switched off—the designer must make this danger fully explicit.
- *Creep:* a continuous physical value cannot be exactly represented by a software variable; for a particular physical domain, a to-and-fro translation—for example, *moveArmTo(v)*; $v: = senseArmPosition()$—may tend to increase v more often than reduce it; repeated to-and-fro translations will cause excessive undesired creep in the physical value and must be avoided.
- *Resources:* all physical resources are limited; behaviour design must take explicit account of the possibility of resource exhaustion.
- *Termination:* the behaviour—if not pre-emptively terminated—must reach an orderly termination.

Standard concerns such as these are particularly important in designing a concrete system behaviour to satisfy an abstract goal behaviour. In general, a concrete behaviour has complexities of which the stakeholders are unaware and therefore cannot mention in their initial requirements which motivate the abstract goal behaviour. Standard concerns help developers to address the full requirements of a concrete behaviour.

2.5   Formalisation and Correctness

Developing a system behaviour is a design activity, proposing and evaluating successive versions. Requirements are rarely exact and never complete and so cannot be treated as formal specifications: instead, each proposed complete behaviour must be evaluated against largely informal requirements.

However, even in the absence of a formal specification, the designed behaviour CSB must be *dependable*: that is, we must be able to determine whether a particular set of putative traces can, or cannot, be evoked by the software. This reasoning must be formal, based on formal models of the machine (M) and of the given properties (W) of the problem world domains, and the possibility of calculating CSB = M || W. The model M captures the behaviour of the machine at its interface with the problem world, and W captures enough of the given properties of the problem domains for the calculation of CSB.

We must therefore (a) exclude from the problem world anything that defies adequate formalisation and (b) include everything necessary for the formal calculation. These rules apply both to the problem domains and to the elements of their models' alphabets. Human participants in the system behaviour must be included as problem domains. People play many roles in system behaviours, as customers, informants, advisers, players, patients, operators, drivers, passengers, and so on: they must be included because their contributions to the behaviour cannot be attributed to any other problem domain.

For most systems, and in programming generally, it is acceptable to treat the machine as a formal system exactly modelled by the programming language. We know that in reality it is a physical system and therefore subject to decay and failures, invalidating any formal model; but computers can be engineered well enough for this limitation to be ignored except in the most critical systems. The non-formal nature of the problem world, by contrast, is not so easily ignored. Formalisation of non-formal domains is a vital but largely neglected discipline in software engineering. Here we observe only that a formal model of a problem domain to be used in the development of a behaviour is contingent: it is required to be adequate only for the purpose for which it is used and under conditions stipulated by the developer.

2.6   The Operating Envelope of a System

The contingent nature of a formal model has two aspects. First, it is required only to model the given behaviour and properties of the domain that are relevant to the behaviour in question—that is, relevant to its participation in the CSB for a given machine M and the other participating problem domains. Second, the system and its CSB are always designed for a restricted *operating envelope*. The idea of an operating envelope is familiar from devices for which such operating conditions as ambient temperature, power supply and maximum loading are stipulated. Here we use an extended notion of the operating envelope, including all the environmental conditions outside the system on which the fidelity of the problem world model W may depend.

The designed behaviour therefore depends on two levels of assumption. First, it is unavoidably assumed that the explicit formal machine and problem world models adequately represent the non-formal reality. Second, this first assumption depends on the larger assumption that the system is operating within its specified operating envelope—for example, that the ambient conditions are within stipulated limits, that the equipment has been properly maintained, that no external destructive force damages any problem domain, that a human participant is not malicious, and so on. This larger assumption is chiefly informal, but must not be ignored.

We note here that in principle neither assumption can be checked by the system itself: if the system checks it, it's not an assumption of the system. If the operating envelope is considered to be structured as a set of nested and overlapping *regions*, then the assumptions of one region can, of course, be checked by a part of the system operating in a larger enclosing region. For a trivial system, such as a toy radio-controlled car, the whole operating envelope may be one very small region: if the car is operated outside this small envelope, there can be no complaint if it fails. A very large and complex operating envelope is characteristic of critical systems. In a famous tragic example, a power station was designed to operate dependably in the presence of an earthquake and also to operate dependably in the presence of a tsunami. The assumed operating envelope had three regions: earthquake, tsunami and neither. Tragically, the remarkable and exceptional simultaneous occurrence of an earthquake and a tsunami revealed a deficiency in the operating envelope: the lack of a fourth region for simultaneous earthquake and tsunami. In this fourth region, the assumed operating conditions did not apply; the problem world properties did not conform to the model W, and the unpredicted behaviour of the system was catastrophic.

2.7   Criteria of Simplicity

The zoo entry system is unrealistically simple, even if we address the problem concerns that have been neglected here. Behaviour of a realistic system is far more complex, and that complexity must be effectively addressed. Following Descartes' rule of dividing difficulties into many parts, the discipline described here aims to understand complex behaviours as designed combinations of simple behaviours. However, as Leibniz pointed out, 'by dividing his problem into unsuitable parts, the inexperienced problem-solver may increase his difficulty'. Any approach to complexity that rests on division into parts should possess explicit criteria of simplicity. The zoo entry system—as we have discussed it so far—illustrates the following criteria:

- *Simple Abstract Goal Behaviour:* the two versions AGB1 and AGB2 are simple in the sense that they are easily understood to achieve the goal 'No entry without payment'. This is an informal but vital criterion.
- *Constant Domain Properties:* the problem world model W comprises models of the given properties of the CoinAcceptor and Barrier domains. These domain properties are *constant* in the sense that for each domain they hold throughout the system behaviour.
- *Constant Domain Roles:* throughout the system behaviour, each participating problem domain plays a constant role in its interactions with other domains.
- *Unbroken Time Span:* the machine remains constantly connected to, and inter-acting with, the problem world throughout the behaviour—multiple distinct instantiations of the whole system behaviour may occur, but the behaviour machine carries nothing over from one instance to the next.

- *Single Regular Control Flow:* the control flow of the software executed by the machine is essentially a single regular expression—that is, there is no structure clash (in the JSP sense) in the control flow.
- *Closed Problem:* the system is closed in the sense that external interactions with parts of the world outside the problem world are excluded; any external interaction is internalised by regarding the locus of the interaction as an internal phenomenon only of each participating problem world domain independently, controlled solely by that domain and constrained only by its given properties.

These criteria aim to capture the essential characteristics of a behaviour that is humanly comprehensible. They are not formalised, because any formalisation is fragile if detail is added. For example, a single local variable added to a regular control flow can destroy its strictly regular character: strict regularity of AGB2 was vitiated by introducing the variable *sc*, but in applying the simplicity criteria judgment is essential.

3   Complex Behaviours

3.1   An Approach to Complexity

We regard a complex behaviour as a combination of simple *constituent behaviours*. Modern cars illustrate the idea: the behaviour of a car moving on a highway under driver control may comprise many constituent behaviours. For example:

- *Cruise Control* is maintaining the driver's currently chosen speed.
- *Lane Departure Warning* is watching the lane markings.
- *Speed Limiting* is preventing the driver from exceeding 110 kph.
- *Hybrid Control* is monitoring and managing drive torque.
- *Digital Suspension Control* is monitoring and adjusting the car's attitude.
- *ABS* is monitoring wheel speeds and brake pressure.

Other constituent behaviours may have no currently active instance—for example, *Air Conditioning*, *Automatic Parking* and *Stop-Start*. Some constituent behaviours are coterminous with the ignition cycle: that is, an instance of the behaviour is created and activated when the ignition is turned on and terminated when it is switched off. This may be true of *Hybrid Control, Digital Suspension Control* and *ABS*. For some, instances are activated and created in response to driver commands. This is true of *Cruise Control, Speed Limiting, Lane Departure Warning* and *Automatic Parking*.

Our approach will be to identify simple candidate constituent behaviours and design them in isolation, then, and only then, to consider how they are to be combined. This discipline has an obvious rightness: it makes sense to know what parts are to be combined before designing their combination. Relationships among constituent behaviours are a central topic of behaviour design. For example, *Speed*

Limiting can conflict with *Cruise Control*. How should this conflict be resolved? Perhaps one should take precedence, or perhaps instances of the two constituents are mutually exclusive. Conflict may be less obvious. For example, instances of *Air Conditioning* and *Stop-Start* cannot coexist in a petrol or diesel car, because the high battery drain imposed by *Air Conditioning* endangers the ability to restart an engine temporarily stopped by *Stop-Start*.

3.2   Zoo Visitor Control: Top-Down Development

As the car illustration suggests, identification of constituent behaviours will proceed largely bottom-up. However, top-down also has a place, and it finds an illustration in the zoo entry system.

The stakeholders, we will suppose, have reconsidered their acceptance of AGB2: the developers have now said that they expect each *acceptCoin* or *admitVisitor* event to monopolise the machine for a significant time, during which nothing else can happen. Impatient visitors will consider the system inconvenient, and the zoo manager will no longer agree that the system increases profits by speeding entry. Evidently, a new abstract goal behaviour, AGB3, is needed, which will permit concurrent operation of the CoinAcceptor and the Barrier. AGB3 is therefore (*acceptCoin** | | *admitPaidVisitor**). The events of the multiple *acceptCoin* and multiple *admitPaidVisitor* procedure executions must be somehow interleaved to accommodate all possible relationships between them. This demand cannot be satisfied by software with a single regular control flow. The two concurrent processes ZCA (*acceptCoin**) and ZB (*admitPaidVisitor**) will therefore form distinct constituent behaviours that must be first designed and then combined.

The behaviours ZCA (*acceptCoin**) and ZB (*admitPaidVisitor**) are parallel: neither is a subfunction of the other. Their activation and termination must therefore be *governed* by a third behaviour Z. Z is the residual behaviour of the whole system after direct management of the *acceptCoin* and *admitVisitor* procedures has been delegated to ZCA and ZB, respectively: it responds to the event on which the Manager presses the Stop Button. When we speak in this way of one behaviour governing another, we mean, of course, that the machine of the one governs the machine of the other. Government of a behaviour is exercised through a standard protocol. Essentially, the governing machine instantiates and activates the governed machine, possibly passing references to problem domains for the governed behaviour. It can detect current and final states of execution; it can abort execution arbitrarily; it can detect designed termination; it can command termination at the next stable state encountered.

The question arises: how are the behaviours ZCA and ZB to communicate? In the software for AGB2, the machine for managing the Coin Acceptor and managing the Barrier required a local variable *sc*, which recorded the current surplus of coins over entries. To preserve the closed problem world of behaviour design for ZCA and ZB, this variable is promoted to a problem domain that can be shared between ZCA and

ZB. Like the local variable *sc*, this domain must be *designed*: we therefore call such a domain a *designed domain*. For each behaviour that uses it to communicate, it is a domain of the problem world, along with the behaviour's *given problem domains*. For the behaviour that governs their activation and termination, it is a promoted local variable of that behaviour's machine, passed as a parameter when the governed machine is activated.

3.3 The Behaviour Machine Tree

We stipulate that a behaviour instance can be governed only by the instantiating behaviour. The governed relationship therefore forms a tree of behaviour instances, represented by their machines. The tree also includes the designed domains instantiated by each machine; other than these designed domains, the tree includes no problem domains.

Figure 2 shows the behaviour machine tree for the zoo entry system.

The root of the tree is the top-level machine of which a single execution constitutes one complete execution of the system behaviour. Evidently, a software machine cannot activate itself: to do so, it would necessarily be already activated in order to monitor the activation command or condition. This is why the Zoo entry machine has no Start Button, but only a Stop Button. For the top-level machine, activation must be performed by an external agent, by non-software means. If activation were performed by software, then the activating software would itself be the top-level machine.

These apparently puristic considerations have an important consequence in the design of large system behaviour with a highly extended duty cycle of machine control of the problem world. If the top-level behaviour is executed more than once, then each execution is in principle independent: the behaviour is not a tree, but a forest of independent trees. There is no top-level machine in the tree to govern the instantiation of the successive executions or to allow communication between them by instantiating a designed domain that can be recognised as a local variable of this higher-level machine. In common practice, both of these responsibilities—if, indeed, they are recognised as responsibilities—are commonly

Fig. 2 A behaviour machine tree

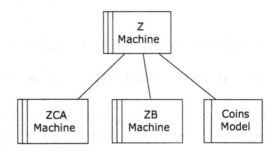

assigned to manual procedures, with all the vulnerability to failure that this implies. A database of any kind is in principle a designed domain: it is a local variable of some software machine. The machine may be the root of a large and complex behaviour subtree, and the database structure also will then be large and complex. If the machine is not explicitly present and specified in the behaviour design, then the database is orphaned. A database orphaned in this way is vulnerable to uncontrolled interference and manipulation outside the system, possibly resulting in failure of the system in its next duty cycle.

3.4   Developing Complex Behaviour

Development of complex behaviour must be largely bottom-up. The reason is clear from the car illustration of a complex behaviour. There is no intelligible top-level requirement that can be decomposed top-down into constituent behaviours. Rather, there is a heterogeneous set of constituent behaviours to be identified, designed and incrementally combined into the whole complex behaviour. It is a compelling, but much neglected, principle that before combining parts into a whole one must first identify and study the parts. The zoo entry system could be developed top-down because we began with a simple requirement from which we derived a simple abstract goal behaviour. The decomposition into Z, ZCA and ZB came only when we recognised that simplicity demanded separate constituent behaviours for coin acceptance and visitor admission.

In practising both bottom-up and top-down development, it is necessary to develop the identified constituent behaviours in two clear stages. First, a candidate constituent is considered in isolation, ignoring its possible eventual interactions with other behaviours. Only when the constituent behaviour has been designed in this simple form should we move on to design its interactions with other behaviours that have already been similarly treated. In the zoo entry system, for example, we should develop ZCA and ZB in isolation, respectively, writing and reading the Coins Model designed domain, and treated as non-terminating processes. Only then do we consider the (easy) *combination concern* of assuring mutual exclusion in accessing the Coins Model and the (harder) concern of achieving orderly termination when the Manager presses the Stop Button.

4   General Development Principles

4.1   Identifying and Developing Constituent Behaviours

System behaviour is developed incrementally. The texture of the development is loose in more than one way. Functional requirements suggest candidate constituent behaviours for which simple abstractions appear useful. For example, in a passenger lift system, we might decide that NormalLiftService (NLS) is a good candidate constituent behaviour. We might propose an Abstract Goal Behaviour: the lift car simply makes repeated unconditional round trips between the ground and top floor, stopping at every floor. An iterative process similar to the development of the zoo entry system reveals inadequacies in this and several succeeding AGB proposals; it also reveals various complications. In general [3], the process depends on alternating consideration of requirements and behaviours.

An early abstraction may have assumed that the abstract operations of opening and closing the doors can be regarded as atomic and fully reliable. In fact, they may fail because of wilful or accidental obstruction or because of equipment failure. Since the lift car should not move while opening or closing the doors, these operations can be identified as constituent behaviours ODN and CDN (OpenDoorsNormal and CloseDoorsNormal) governed by NLS.

Examination of the floor sensor equipment and the lift motor control shows that failure is possible here too. Detection and diagnosis of equipment failure is complex enough to demand a dedicated constituent behaviour LFM (Maintain Lift Fault Model) to build and maintain a model in the form of a designed domain. The treatment of requests for lift service also demands a dedicated constituent behaviour NQM (Maintain Normal Requests Model). Whereas instances of ODN and CDN are nested within an instance of NLS, it is less clear how instances of NLS, LFM and NQM are related.

4.2   Developing the Behaviour Machine Tree

Temporal and other relationships among candidate constituent behaviours, and the design and implementation of those relationships, are the core concern in bottom-up behaviour design. Interactions among constituent behaviours may raise combination concerns. For example, two potentially concurrent behaviours having a common problem domain may require *mutual exclusion*. Another common combination concern is *switching*: one behaviour is to be terminated and another to be instantiated and activated. For example, if fire breaks out, NormalLiftService must be terminated and replaced by FLS (FirefighterLiftService). The switchover may demand an additional behaviour that properly belongs neither to NLS nor to FLS: this transitional behaviour may be required to bring the lift passengers directly to the ground floor and park the lift car there with the doors open.

Broadly, bottom-up development of complex behaviour is motivated by the need to embody a multiplicity of disparate constituent behaviours, instantiating and governing them according to changing demands and circumstances. This motivation can be seen at multiple levels of the behaviour machine tree for a large system: for the root machines of many subtrees, no useful goal behaviour can be identified beyond accommodating and governing its constituent behaviours at the next level.

4.3 Particular and General in Behaviour Design

It may be thought that development should aim at a high degree of abstraction and generality to increase the utility—and hence the value—of the product. However, this advice must be treated with caution. Abstraction and generalisation are, in a sense, combining what would otherwise be distinct parts into a seamless whole: the principle mentioned earlier, that combination should be preceded by careful identification and study of the parts to be combined, applies with full force.

NormalLiftService and FirefighterLiftService provide an illustration. At first sight, it may seem that both behaviours are designed to transport people from floor to floor in accordance with their demands: it must be economical to develop a single more general behaviour embodying variations of detail at the points at which NLS and FLS differ. This would be a mistake. Careful examination shows that the differences dominate the similarities:

- FLS ignores requests from buttons on the floors, responding only to the buttons in the lift car. NLS responds to both.
- NLS opens and closes the doors automatically when it stops at a floor. FLS opens and closes the doors only in response to the door command buttons in the lift car.
- NLS remembers and responds to multiple floor requests. FLS responds only to the most recent.
- NLS respects access restrictions to certain floors. FLS ignores all access restrictions.
- If primary power fails, NLS moves under emergency backup power to the nearest floor and parks there. If primary power fails, NLS continues operation under emergency power.
- NLS satisfies the requirement that the doors are always closed unless the lift car is stationary at a floor. FLS does not.

When we add further differences between OpenDoorsNormal and OpenDoorsFirefighter, and between CloseDoorsNormal and CloseDoorsFirefighter, it is clear that NLS and FLS must remain distinct. There is no useful generalisation.

4.4 Behaviours and Use Cases

Originally, a *use case* was understood as an episode of interaction between a *user* and the *system*, originated by the user to achieve some goal [4]. The description, or specification, of a use case was a scenario of alternating actions by the user and the system, describing how the system must respond to each user action. (More recently, some researchers and practitioners have generalised this quite specific idea in many directions to allow all functional requirements to be understood as use cases [4]. Here we will refer only to the original idea, relating it to our notion of a system behaviour.)

One difference between use cases and system behaviours is that in a use case the user is assumed to be an agent external to the system rather than a participant problem domain within the system. Another difference is that a use case is always activated by the user to achieve a user goal, the system's role being chiefly to react appropriately. Some behaviours are like this, but most are not.

The difference between NormalLiftService and FirefighterLiftService is illuminating. FirefighterLiftService behaviour is close in concept to a use case. A firefighter, or a group of firefighters, takes possession of the lift car; pressing a request button inside the car is effectively a command, and the lift car obediently travels to the requested floor; opening and closing the doors is similarly commanded; so too is departure from a floor by requesting another floor from within the car. Effectively, the firefighters are acting as operators, and the system—in which they are participants—behaves accordingly.

NormalLiftService behaviour, by contrast, does not treat the intending and actual passengers as operators. Like a train or bus service, its purpose is to execute a common behaviour for the benefit of many potential users, affording each individual opportunities for its use. This common behaviour cannot be described in a set of use cases—although a set of use cases may form an important subset of the behaviour's requirements. Each use-case description has the status of a requirement on the behaviour: the system behaviour must be such that a person who follows the procedure described in the use case is assured of being carried eventually to their destination.

4.5   The Products of Behaviour Design

Because we are concerned with *engineering by software* rather than *engineering of software*, our lowest-level behavioural component is what we have called a *system behaviour*: this is the behaviour of a problem world and a machine, interacting at their specification interface. Behaviours are combined in a tree structure of their machines, in which each parent node is a machine instantiating and governing the machines of its immediate constituent behaviours. Relationships and constraints among behaviours result from their governance within this tree and also from shared problem domains. A shared problem domain is, in effect, a shared variable, participating in the problem world of more than one behaviour. Where sharing by multiple behaviours must be engineered, the machine of a common ancestor instantiates a designed domain that participates in the behaviours' problem worlds.

The primary aim of this approach to behaviour design is clarity and simplicity. The behaviour tree forms a system software specification. The design of each constituent behaviour specifies a software machine and elucidates the problem world behaviour resulting from its activation and execution. The problem domain models formalise the properties of the relevant physical realities on which the behaviour design explicitly rests. The granularity of a simple constituent behaviour is chosen to match stakeholders' functional requirements, enabling developers and stakeholders to assess how well the behaviour satisfies those requirements.

The approach relegates other legitimate aims of development to a lower priority or postpones them to a later stage. The behaviour machine tree is a kind of software architecture, but it is not designed for efficient execution on a particular configuration of computing equipment—or, perhaps, at all. The formal modelling of problem domains, both given and designed, makes no attempt to avoid redundancy or repetition. A physical given domain that participates in many constituent behaviours must have many formal models. This multiplicity is inevitable because different behaviours will rely on different properties: for example, the formal model of the lift equipment for NormalLiftService cannot be the same as the formal model for MaintainLiftFaultModel.

5   Concluding Remarks

The separation defined here of requirements from system behaviour is not commonly practised. A widespread practice is to treat the specification of system behaviour as an output of requirements work, often in the form of fragmented stimulus-response pairs: 'when such-and-such an event or state change occurs in the problem world, the system response shall be such-and-such'. To some extent, the difference is a matter of mere nomenclature, attributing a different meaning to the term *requirement* than has been adopted here. But the difference runs deeper in at least two respects.

First, the system behaviour is the essential product of software execution. If the system is to be dependable, its behaviour must be well understood by the developers and comprehensible to the human participants who play the roles of operators and users. Comprehension, as Dijkstra pointed out nearly 50 years ago in the famous 'GO-TO letter' [5], depends on a clear relationship between the behaviour execution and its readable description. Fragmentation into stimulus-response pairs removes the readable structure that makes human comprehension possible.

Second, a fundamental goal of the separation defined here is to ensure that the system behaviour can be formally calculated from the machine specification and the formal model of the problem world. Because many stakeholder needs and purposes defy formalisation, non-formal elements cannot and should not be avoided in requirements; but they can and should be excluded from the formal work of behaviour design and calculation.

The approach to development sketched in this chapter can be characterised as a *pre-formal* approach. Formal modelling, calculation and proof are essential tools for developing dependable systems, but they cannot be self-sufficient. As Henri Poincaré wrote [6], 'it is by logic one demonstrates; by intuition one invents'. Before formal tools can be usefully deployed, we must do the pre-formal work of inventing conceptual structures to reveal what we must model, what calculations are to be made and what must be proved. Rushing to formalise is no more sensible than rushing to write program code.

References

1. Software for Dependable Systems: Sufficient Evidence? Report of the National Research Council Committee on certifiably dependable software systems. In: Jackson, D., Thomas, M., Millett, L.I. (eds.) (2007)
2. van Lamsweerde, A.: Requirements Engineering: From System Goals to UML Models to Software Specifications. Wiley, Hoboken (2009)
3. Nuseibeh, B.: Weaving together requirements and architecture. IEEE Comput. **34**(3), 115–119 (2001)
4. Jacobson, I., Booch, G., Rumbaugh, J.: The Unified Software Development Process. Addison-Wesley, Boston (1999)
5. Dijkstra, E.W.: A Case Against the Go To Statement, EWD 215, published as a letter to the Editor (Go To Statement Considered Harmful): CACM 11, 3, pp. 147–148 (1968)
6. Poincaré, H.: Science et Methode; Chapter II Mathematical Definitions and Teaching, Section 9. Tr George Bruce Halsted. The Science Press, New York (1913)

What Is a Procedure?

Eric C.R. Hehner

Abstract Whether the meaning of a procedure is given by its specification or by its implementation has consequences for scalability of analysis, for localization of errors, for loop semantics, for program translation, and even for the halting problem.

1 Question and Answers

The simple question "What is a procedure?" is not so simple to answer, and its answer has far-reaching consequences throughout computer science. By "procedure" I mean any named, callable piece of program; depending on the programming language, it may be a procedure, or function, or method, or something else. To illustrate my points, I will use the Pascal programming language, designed at ETH Zürich 40 years ago by my academic grandfather, Niklaus Wirth. I think it is an appropriate choice for celebrating the history of software engineering at ETH. But the points I make apply to any programming language.

Here are two Pascal procedures.

```
procedure A; {this procedure prints 'A'}
begin
    print ('B')
end;
procedure AA; {this procedure prints 'AA'}
begin
    A; A
end
```

What is the meaning of procedure A? Is it a procedure that prints 'A' as its specification (the comment) says, or is it a procedure that prints 'B' as its implementation (the body) says? Perhaps I should instead ask: Is A implemented correctly? Clearly it is not, though we cannot say whether the specification or the

E.C.R. Hehner (✉)
University of Toronto, Toronto, ON, Canada
e-mail: hehner@cs.utoronto.ca

© Springer International Publishing AG 2017
M. Mazzara, B. Meyer (eds.), *Present and Ulterior Software Engineering*,
https://doi.org/10.1007/978-3-319-67425-4_2

implementation is at fault. Is *AA* implemented correctly? This time I want to say yes: its specification says it prints 'AA', and to do so it twice calls a procedure whose specification says it prints 'A'. The error is in procedure *A*, not in procedure *AA*.

Now consider this example.

function *binexp* (*n*: **integer**): **integer**; {for $0 \leq n < 31$, *binexp* (*n*) = 2^n}
procedure *toobig*; {if 2^{20} > 20000, print 'too big' ; otherwise do nothing}
begin
   if *binexp* (20) > 20000 **then** *print* ('too big')
end

Only the header and specification of function *binexp* appear; the body is missing. But *toobig* is there in its entirety. Now I ask: Is *toobig* a Pascal procedure? And I offer two answers.

Program Answer   No. We cannot compile and execute *toobig* until we have the body of *binexp*, or at least a link to the body of *binexp*. *toobig* is not a procedure until it can be compiled and executed. (We may not have the body of *print* either, and it may not even be written in Pascal, but the compiler does have a link to it, so it can be executed.) Since *toobig* calls *binexp*, whose body is missing, we cannot say what is the meaning of *toobig*. The specification of *binexp*, which is just a comment, is helpful documentation expressing the intention of the programmer, but intentions are irrelevant. We need the body of *binexp* before it is a Pascal function, and when we have the body of *binexp*, then *toobig* will be a Pascal procedure.

Specification Answer   Yes. *toobig* conforms to the Pascal syntax for procedures. It type checks correctly. To determine whether *binexp* is being called correctly within *toobig*, we need to know the number and types of its parameters, and the type of result returned; this information is found in the header for *binexp*. To determine whether *print* is being called correctly, we need to know about its parameters, and this information is found in the list of built-in functions and procedures. To understand *toobig*, to reason about it, to know what its execution will be, we need to know what the result of *binexp* (20) will be, and what effect *print* ('too big') will have. The result of *binexp* (20) is specified in the comment, and the effect of *print* ('too big') is specified in the list of built-in functions and procedures. We do not have the body of *binexp*, and we probably cannot look at the body of *print*, but we do not need them for the purpose of understanding *toobig*. Even if we could look at the bodies of *binexp* and *print*, we should not use them for understanding and reasoning about *toobig*. That's an important principle of software engineering; it allows programmers to work on different parts of a program independently. It enables a programmer to call functions and procedures written by other people, knowing only the specification, not the implementation. There are many ways that binary exponentiation can be computed, but our understanding of *toobig* does not depend on which way is chosen. Likewise for *print*. This important principle also enables a programmer to change the implementation of a function or procedure, such as *binexp* and *print*, but still satisfying the specification, without knowing where and why the function or procedure is being called. If there is an error in implementing *binexp* or *print*, that error should not affect the understanding of and reasoning about *toobig*. So, even without the bodies of *binexp* and *print*, *toobig* is a procedure.

The semantics community has decided on the Program Answer. For them, the meaning of a function or procedure is its body, not its specification. They do not assign a meaning to *toobig* until the bodies of *binexp* and *print* are provided.

Most of the verification community has decided on the Program Answer. To verify a program that contains a call, they insist on seeing the body of the procedure or function being called. They do not verify that 'too big' is printed until the bodies of *binexp* and *print* are provided.

I would like the software engineering community to embrace the Specification Answer. That answer scales up to large software; the Program Answer doesn't. The Specification Answer allows us to isolate an error within a procedure (or other unit of program); the Program Answer doesn't. The Specification Answer insists on having specifications, which are the very best form of documentation; the Program Answer doesn't.

2 Theory of Programming

In my theory of programming [1] (sometimes called "predicative programming," sometimes called UTP), we do not specify programs; we specify computation, or computer behavior. The nonlocal (free) variables of the specification represent whatever we wish to observe about a computation (initial state, final state, all states, interactions, execution time, space occupied). Observing a computation provides values for those variables. A specification is a binary (i.e., Boolean) expression because, when you instantiate its variables with values obtained from observing a computation, there are two possible outcomes: either the computation satisfies the specification or it doesn't. If you write anything other than a binary expression as a specification, you must say what it means for a computation to satisfy a specification, and to do that formally, you must write a binary expression anyway.

A program is an implemented specification. It is a specification of computer behavior that you can give to a computer and get the specified behavior. I also refer to any statement in a program, or any sequence or structure of statements, as a program. Since a program is a specification, and a specification is a binary expression, therefore a program is a binary expression. For example, if the state (or program) variables are x and y, then the program $x := x + y$ is the binary expression $x' = x + y \wedge y' = y$, where unprimed variables represent the values of the state variables before execution of the assignment and primed variables represent the values of the state variables after execution of the assignment.

$$x := x + y \;=\; x' = x + y \wedge y' = y$$

Similarly for a conditional program

if b **then** P **else** $Q = b \wedge P \vee \neg b \wedge Q$
$$= (b \Rightarrow P) \wedge (\neg b \Rightarrow Q)$$

Sequential composition is a little more complicated

$P;Q = \exists x'', y''$ (in P substitute x'', y'' for x', y')
$$\wedge \text{ (in } Q \text{ substitute } x'', y'' \text{ for } x, y)$$

but fortunately we can prove the Substitution Law, which doesn't involve quantification:

$x := e \, ; P = $ (for x substitute e in P)

For example,

$x := x + y \, ; x + y < 5 \ = \ (x + y) + y < 5$

To say "specification P refines specification Q" means that all behavior satisfying P also satisfies Q. Formally, that's just implication: $P \Rightarrow Q$. For example,

$x' < x \ \Leftarrow \ x := x - 1$

says that specification $x' < x$ is implied by or refined by or implemented by program $x := x-1$, and it is trivial to prove. As a second example,

$x' \leq x \Leftarrow$ **if** $x > 0$ **then** $x' < x$

From those two examples, we conclude:

$x' \leq x \Leftarrow$ **if** $x > 0$ **then** $x := x - 1$

and that's how stepwise refinement works.

A complete explanation can be found in the book *A Practical Theory of Programming* [1] and the online course Formal Methods of Software Design [2].

3   Loop Semantics

Equating programs with binary expressions gives meaning to straight-line and branching programs; but how shall we give meaning to loops? There are two answers: the Program Answer and the Specification Answer. The Program Answer is the standard answer: by a construction axiom and an induction axiom, also known as a least-fixed-point.

while-construction (fixed-point) axiom:
    while a **do** $B = $ **if** a **then begin** B; **while** a **do** B **end**

while-induction (least-fixed-point) axiom (σ is the prestate and σ' is the poststate):
    $(\forall \sigma, \sigma' \cdot S = $ **if** a **then begin** B; S **end**$) \Rightarrow (\forall \sigma, \sigma' \cdot S \Rightarrow$ **while** a **do** $B)$

Construction says that a **while**-loop equals its first unrolling. Induction says that of all specifications satisfying the construction axiom, the **while**-loop is the weakest (least deterministic). Least-fixed-points are difficult to use for program verification, so the verification community has gone part way toward the Specification Answer, by using invariants.

The Specification Answer requires an implementable specification. Specification S is implementable if $\forall\sigma\cdot\exists\sigma'\cdot S$. The refinement means

$S \Leftarrow$ **while** a **do** B

or is an alternate notation for

$S \Leftarrow$ **if** a **then begin** B; S **end**

In this unrolling, following the body B, we do not have the **while**-loop, but rather the specification S. Any refinement is a sort of small procedure, and this refinement is a small procedure with a recursive call, just like

procedure S; **begin if** a **then begin** B; S **end end**

and its execution is just like

S: **if** a **then begin** B; **goto** S **end**

For the recursive call, according to the Specification Answer, we take the meaning of the procedure to be the specification. And so also for loops, with the same benefits. Here is an example in one integer state variable x. To prove

$x{\geq}0 \Rightarrow x'{=}0 \Leftarrow$ **while** $x{>}0$ **do** $x:= x{-}1$

prove instead

$x{\geq}0 \Rightarrow x'{=}0 \Leftarrow$ **if** $x{>}0$ **then begin** $x:= x{-}1$; $x{\geq}0 \Rightarrow x'{=}0$ **end**

That means proving

$$x \geq 0 \Rightarrow x' = 0 \ \Leftarrow\ x > 0 \wedge (x:= x-1; x \geq 0 \Rightarrow x' = 0) \vee x \leq 0 \wedge x' = x$$

Inside the parentheses, we use the Substitution Law and get

$$x \geq 0 \Rightarrow x' = 0 \ \Leftarrow\ x > 0 \wedge (x-1 \geq 0 \Rightarrow x' = 0) \vee x \leq 0 \wedge x' = x$$

Now we have no more programming notations; the proof is just binary and number laws.

For proof purposes, the Specification Answer is much easier to use than the Program Answer. But the biggest advantage of the Specification Answer is during programming. We start with a specification, for example, $x \geq 0 \Rightarrow x' = 0$, and we refine it. The obvious refinement is

$$x \geq 0 \Rightarrow x' = 0 \ \Leftarrow\ x := 0$$

but to obtain the same computation as in the preceding paragraph, we can refine it as

$x{\geq}0 \Rightarrow x'{=}0 \Leftarrow$ **if** $x{>}0$ **then** $x{>}0 \Rightarrow x'{=}0$ **else** $x{=}0 \Rightarrow x'{=}0$

Now we have two more specifications to refine.

$x{>}0 \Rightarrow x'{=}0 \Leftarrow x{:}{=} x{-}1;\ x{\geq}0 \Rightarrow x'{=}0$
$x{=}0 \Rightarrow x'{=}0 \Leftarrow$ **begin end**

And we're done. We never refine to a loop construct, so we never need any fixed-points, nor any proof rules concerning loops, nor any invariants. But we form loops by reusing specifications.

For execution time, we just add a time variable t and increase it wherever we need to account for the passage of time. To count iterations, we place $t{:}{=} t + 1$ inside the loop. And we can write specifications about execution time. For example,

$x{\geq}0 \Rightarrow t'{=}t{+}x \Leftarrow$ **while** $x{\neq}0$ **do begin** $x{:}{=} x{-}1;\ t{:}{=} t{+}1$ **end**

which means, according to the Specification Answer,

$x{\geq}0 \Rightarrow x'{=}t{+}x \Leftarrow$ **if** $x{\neq}0$ **then begin** $x{:}{=} x{-}1;\ t{:}{=} t{+}1;\ x{\geq}0 \Rightarrow x'{=}t{+}x$ **end**

That means proving

$$x \geq 0 \Rightarrow x' = t + x \Leftarrow x \neq 0 \wedge (x := x-1; t := t+1; x \geq 0 \Rightarrow x' = t + x) \vee x = 0 \wedge$$
$$x' = x \wedge t' = t$$

Inside the parentheses we use the Substitution Law twice, and get

$$x \geq 0 \Rightarrow x' = t + x \Leftarrow x \neq 0 \wedge (x-1 \geq 0 \Rightarrow x' = t + 1 + x - 1) \vee x = 0 \wedge x' = x \wedge$$
$$t' = t$$

Now we have no more programming notations; the proof is just binary and number laws.

We can just as easily prove

$x{<}0 \Rightarrow t'{=}\infty \Leftarrow$ **while** $x{\neq}0$ **do begin** $x{:}{=} x{-}1;\ t{:}{=} t{+}1$ **end**

which means

$x{<}0 \Rightarrow t'{=}\infty \Leftarrow$ **if** $x{\neq}0$ **then begin** $x{:}{=} x{-}1;\ t{:}{=} t{+}1;\ x{<}0 \Rightarrow t'{=}\infty$ **end**

That means proving

$$x < 0 \Rightarrow t' = \infty \Leftarrow x \neq 0 \wedge (x := x-1; t := t+1; x < 0 \Rightarrow t' = \infty) \vee x = 0 \wedge x' =$$
$$x \wedge t' = t$$

Inside the parentheses we use the Substitution Law twice, and get

$$x < 0 \Rightarrow t' = \infty \Leftarrow x \neq 0 \wedge (x-1 < 0 \Rightarrow t' = \infty) \vee x = 0 \wedge x' = x \wedge t' = t$$

Now we have no more programming notations; the proof is just binary and number laws.

The Specification Answer is a general recipe for all kinds of loops. Departing momentarily from Pascal, here is a more complicated structure using one- and two-level exits.

```
loop
  A;
  exit 1 when b;
  C;
  loop
    D;
    exit 2 when e;
    F;
    exit 1 when g;
    H
  end;
  I
end
```

The Specification Answer requires a specification for each loop. If they are P and Q for these two loops, then what we must prove is

$P \Leftarrow A$; **if not** b **then begin** C; Q **end**
$Q \Leftarrow D$; **if not** e **then begin** F; **if not** g **then begin** H; Q **end**
                             else begin I; P **end**
            end

Note that specifications P and Q are used, rather than the loop constructs, on the right sides of these reverse implications; that's the Specification Answer.

The literature on loop semantics is large, and entirely according to the Program Answer. But the Specification Answer has advantages: it makes proofs much easier, and program derivation much much easier. If we include time, we have more than total correctness, without any least-fixed-points or invariants.

4 Halting Problem

The halting problem [3] is widely considered to be a foundational result in computer science. Here is a modern presentation of it. We have the header and specification of function *halts*, but not its body. Then we have procedure *diag* in its entirety, and *diag* calls *halts*. This is exactly the situation we had with function *binexp* and procedure *toobig*. Usually, *halts* gives two possible answers: 'yes' or 'no'; for the purpose of this chapter, I have added a third: 'not applicable'.

function *halts* (p, i: **string**): **string**;
{return 'yes' if p represents a Pascal procedure with one string input parameter}
{   whose execution terminates when given input i;}
{return 'no' if p represents a Pascal procedure with one string input parameter}
{   whose execution does not terminate when given input i;}
{return 'not applicable' if p does not represent a Pascal procedure}
{   with one string input parameter}

procedure *diag* (*s*: **string**); {execution terminates if and only if *halts* (*s*, *s*) $\neq$ 'yes'}
begin
   if *halts* (*s*, *s*) = 'yes' **then** *diag* (*s*)
end

We assume there is a dictionary of function and procedure definitions that is accessible to *halts* so that the call *halts* ('*diag*', '*diag*') allows *halts* to look up '*diag*', and subsequently '*halts*', in the dictionary and retrieve their texts for analysis. Here is the "textbook proof" that *halts* is incomputable.

Assume the body of function *halts* has been written according to its specification. Does execution of *diag* ('*diag*') terminate? If it terminates, then *halts* ('*diag*', '*diag*') returns 'yes' according to its specification, and so we see from the body of *diag* that execution of *diag* ('*diag*') does not terminate. If it does not terminate, then *halts* ('*diag*', '*diag*') returns 'no', and so execution of *diag* ('*diag*') terminates. This is a contradiction (inconsistency). Therefore the body of function *halts* cannot have been written according to its specification; *halts* is incomputable.

The "textbook proof" begins with the computability assumption: that the body of *halts* can be written, and has been written. The assumption is necessary for advocates of the Program Answer to say that *diag* is a Pascal procedure, and so rule out 'not applicable' as the result of *halts* ('*diag*', '*diag*'). If we suppose the result is 'yes', then we see from the body of *diag* that execution of *diag* ('*diag*') is nonterminating, so the result should be 'no'. If we suppose the result is 'no', then we see from the body of *diag* that execution of *diag* ('*diag*') is terminating, so the result should be 'yes'. Thus all three results are eliminated, we have an inconsistency, and advocates of the Program Answer blame the computability assumption for the inconsistency.

Advocates of the Program Answer must begin by assuming the existence of the body of *halts*, but since the body is unavailable, they are compelled to base their reasoning on the specification of *halts* as advocated in the Specification Answer, contrary to the Program Answer.

Advocates of the Specification Answer do not need the computability assumption. According to them, *diag* is a Pascal procedure even though the body of *halts* has not been written. What does the specification of *halts* say the result of *halts* ('*diag*', '*diag*') should be? The Specification Answer eliminates 'not applicable'. As before, if we suppose the result is 'yes', then we see from the body of *diag* that execution of *diag* ('*diag*') is nonterminating, so the result should be 'no'; if we suppose the result is 'no', then we see from the body of *diag* that execution of *diag* ('*diag*') is terminating, so the result should be 'yes'. Thus all three results are eliminated. But this time there is no computability assumption to blame. This time, the conclusion is that the body of *halts* cannot be written due to inconsistency of its specification.

Both advocates of the Program Answer and advocates of the Specification Answer conclude that the body of *halts* cannot be written, but for different reasons. According to advocates of the Program Answer, *halts* is incomputable, which means that it has a consistent specification that cannot be implemented in a Turing-Machine-equivalent programming language like Pascal. According to advocates of the Specification Answer, *halts* has an inconsistent specification, and the question of computability does not arise.

5 Simplified Halting Problem

The distinction between these two positions can be seen better by trimming away some irrelevant parts of the argument. The second parameter of *halts* and the parameter of *diag* play no role in the "textbook proof" of incomputability; any string value could be supplied, or the parameter could be eliminated, without changing the "textbook proof." The first parameter of *halts* allows *halts* to be applied to any string, but there is only one string we apply it to in the "textbook proof"; so we can also eliminate it by redefining *halts* to apply specifically to '*diag*'. Here is the result.

function *halts*: **string**;
{return 'yes' if *diag* is a Pascal procedure whose execution terminates;}
{return 'no' if *diag* is a Pascal procedure whose execution does not terminate;}
{return 'not applicable' if *diag* is not a Pascal procedure}

procedure *diag*; {execution terminates if and only if *halts* $\neq$ 'yes'}
begin
   if *halts* = 'yes' **then** *diag*
end

The "textbook proof" that *halts* is incomputable is unchanged.

Assume the body of function *halts* has been written according to its specification. Does execution of *diag* terminate? If it terminates, then *halts* returns 'yes' according to its specification, and so we see from the body of *diag* that execution of *diag* does not terminate. If it does not terminate, then *halts* returns 'no', and so execution of *diag* terminates. This is a contradiction (inconsistency). Therefore the body of function *halts* cannot have been written according to its specification; *halts* is incomputable.

Function *halts* is now a constant, not depending on the value of any parameter or variable. There is no programming difficulty in completing the body of *halts*. It is one of three simple statements: either *halts*:= 'yes' or *halts*:= 'no' or *halts*:= 'not applicable'. The problem is to decide which of those three it is. If the body of *halts* is *halts*:= 'yes', we see from the body of *diag* that it should be *halts*:= 'no'. If the body of *halts* is *halts*:= 'no', we see from the body of *diag* that it should be *halts*:= 'yes'. If the body of *halts* is *halts*:= 'not applicable', advocates of both the Program Answer and the Specification Answer agree that *diag* is a Pascal procedure, so again that's the wrong way to complete the body of *halts*.

The specification of *halts* is clearly inconsistent; it is not possible to conclude that *halts* is incomputable. The two parameters of *halts* served only to complicate and obscure.

6   Printing Problems

The "textbook proof" that halting is incomputable does not prove incomputability; it proves that the specification of *halts* is inconsistent. But it really has nothing to do with halting; any property of programs can be treated the same way. Here is an example.

function *WhatTwistPrints*: **string**;
{return 'yes' if *twist* is a Pascal procedure whose execution prints 'yes';}
{return 'no' if *twist* is a Pascal procedure whose execution does not print 'yes';}
{return 'not applicable' if *twist* is not a Pascal procedure}

procedure *twist*; {if *WhatTwistPrints* = 'yes' then print 'no'; otherwise print 'yes'}
begin
   if *WhatTwistPrints* = 'yes' **then** *print* ('no') **else** *print* ('yes')
end

Here is the "textbook proof" of incomputability, adapted to function *WhatTwist-Prints*.

Assume the body of function *WhatTwistPrints* has been written according to its specification. Does execution of *twist* print 'yes' or 'no'? If it prints 'yes', then *WhatTwistPrints* returns 'yes' according to its specification, and so we see from the body of *twist* that execution of *twist* prints 'no'. If it prints 'no', then *WhatTwistPrints* returns 'no' according to its specification, and so we see from the body of *twist* that execution of *twist* prints 'yes'. This is a contradiction (inconsistency). Therefore the body of function *WhatTwistPrints* cannot have been written according to its specification; *WhatTwistPrints* is incomputable.

The body of function *WhatTwistPrints* is one of *WhatTwistPrints*:= 'yes' or *WhatTwistPrints*:= 'no' or *WhatTwistPrints*:= 'not applicable', so we cannot call *WhatTwistPrints* an incomputable function. But we can rule out all three possibilities, so the specification of *WhatTwistPrints* is inconsistent. No matter how simple and clear the specification may seem to be, it refers to itself (indirectly, by referring to *twist*, which calls *WhatTwistPrints*) in a self-contradictory manner. That's exactly what the *halts* specification does: it refers to itself (indirectly by saying that *halts* applies to all procedures including *diag*, which calls *halts*) in a self-contradictory manner.

The following example is similar to the previous example.

function *WhatStraightPrints*: **string**;
{return 'yes' if *straight* is a Pascal procedure whose execution prints 'yes';}
{return 'no' if *straight* is a Pascal procedure whose execution does not print 'yes';}
{return 'not applicable' if *straight* is not a Pascal procedure}

procedure *straight*;
{if *WhatStraightPrints* = 'yes' then print 'yes' ; otherwise print 'no'}
begin
    if *WhatStraightPrints* = 'yes' **then** *print* ('yes') **else** *print* ('no')
end

To advocates of the Program Answer, *straight* is not a Pascal procedure because the body of *WhatStraightPrints* has not been written. Therefore, *WhatStraightPrints* should return 'not applicable', and its body is easily written: *WhatStraightPrints*:= 'not applicable'. As soon as it is written, it is wrong. Advocates of the Specification Answer do not have that problem, but they have a different problem: it is equally correct for *WhatStraightPrints* to return 'yes' or to return 'no'.

The halting function *halts* has a similar dilemma when applied to

procedure *what* (*s*: **string**); {execution terminates if and only if *halts* (*s*, *s*) = 'yes'}
begin
    if *halts* (*s*, *s*) **not**= 'yes' **then** *what* (*s*)
end

The specification of *halts* may sound all right, but we are forced by the examples to admit that the specification is not as it sounds. In at least one instance (*diag*), the *halts* specification is overdetermined (inconsistent), and in at least one instance (*what*), the *halts* specification is underdetermined.

7 Limited Halting

It is inconsistent to ask for a Pascal function to compute the halting status of all Pascal procedures. But we can ask for a Pascal function to compute the halting status of some Pascal procedures. For example, a function to compute the halting status of just the two procedures

procedure *stop* (*s*: **string**); **begin end**
procedure *go* (*s*: **string**); **begin** *go* (*s*) **end**

is easy. Perhaps we can ask for a Pascal function to compute the halting status of all Pascal procedures that do not refer to this halting function, neither directly nor indirectly. Here is its header, specification, and a start on its implementation.

function *halts1* (*p*, *i*: **string**): **string**;
{return 'yes' if *p* represents a Pascal procedure with one string input parameter}
{   that does not refer to *halts1* (neither directly nor indirectly)}
{   and whose execution terminates when given input *i*;}
{return 'no' if *p* represents a Pascal procedure with one string input parameter}
{   that does not refer to *halts1* (neither directly nor indirectly)}
{   and whose execution does not terminate when given input *i*;}
{return 'maybe' if *p* represents a Pascal procedure with one string input}
{   parameter that refers to *halts1* (either directly or indirectly);}
{return 'not applicable' if *p* does not represent a Pascal procedure}
{   with one string input parameter}
begin
  if (*p* does not represent a Pascal procedure with one string input parameter)
  then *halts1*:= 'not applicable'
  else if (*p* refers to *halts* directly or indirectly)
     then *halts1*:= 'maybe'
     else (return halting status of *p*, either 'yes' or 'no')
end

The first case checks whether *p* represents a (valid) procedure exactly as a Pascal compiler does. The middle case looks like a transitive closure algorithm, but it is problematic because, theoretically, there can be an infinite chain of calls. Thus we may be able to compute halting for this limited set of procedures, but not determine whether a procedure is in this limited set. The last case may not be easy, but at least it is free of the reason it has been called incomputable, that it cannot cope with

procedure *diag1* (*s*: **string**); {execution terminates if and only if *halts1* (*s*, *s*)$\neq$'yes'}
begin
  if *halts1* (*s*, *s*) = 'yes' **then** *diag1* (*s*)
end

Procedure *diag1* refers to *halts1* by calling it, so *halts1* ('*diag1*', '*diag1*') = 'maybe', and execution of *diag1* ('*diag1*') is terminating.

Calling is one kind of referring, but not the only kind. In the specification of *halts1*, the name *halts1* appears, and also in the body. These are self-references, whether or not *halts1* calls itself. We exempt *halts1* from having to determine the halting status of procedures containing any form of reference to *halts1*; the result is 'maybe'. We might try to circumvent the limitation by writing another function *halts2* that is identical to *halts1*, but renamed (including in the specification, the return statements, and any recursive calls).

function *halts2* (*p*, *i*: **string**): **string**;
{return 'yes' if *p* represents a Pascal procedure with one string input parameter}
{   that does not refer to *halts2* (neither directly nor indirectly)}
{   and whose execution terminates when given input *i*;}
{return 'no' if *p* represents a Pascal procedure with one string input parameter}
{   that does not refer to *halts2* (neither directly nor indirectly)}

{   and whose execution does not terminate when given input *i*;}
{return 'maybe' if *p* represents a Pascal procedure with one string input}
{   parameter that refers to *halts2* (either directly or indirectly);}
{return 'not applicable' if *p* does not represent a Pascal procedure}
{   with one string input parameter}
begin
   if (*p* does not represent a Pascal procedure with one string input parameter)
   then *halts2*:= 'not applicable'
   else if (*p* refers to *halts2* directly or indirectly)
      then *halts2*:= 'maybe'
      else (return halting status of *p*, either 'yes' or 'no')
end

Of course, *halts2* has its own nemesis:

procedure *diag2* (*s*: **string**); {execution terminates if and only if *halts2* (*s*, *s*)≠'yes'}
begin
   if *halts2* (*s*, *s*) = 'yes' **then** *diag2* (*s*)
end

The point is that *halts2* can determine halting for procedures that *halts1* cannot, and *halts1* can determine halting for procedures that *halts2* cannot. For example,

halts1 ('*diag1*', '*diag1*') = 'maybe' because *diag1* calls *halts1*
halts2 ('*diag1*', '*diag1*') = 'yes' because execution of *diag1* ('*diag1*') terminates
halts2 ('*diag2*', '*diag2*') = 'maybe' because *diag2* calls *halts2*
halts1 ('*diag2*', '*diag2*') = 'yes' because execution of *diag2* ('*diag2*') terminates

But there are procedures that refer to both *halts1* and *halts2*, for which both *halts1* and *halts2* say 'maybe'. The most interesting point is this: even though *halts1* and *halts2* are identical except for renaming, they produce different results when given the same input, according to their specifications.

8   Unlimited Halting

In Pascal, as originally defined, identifiers cannot contain underscores. I now define a new programming language, Pascal_, which is identical to Pascal except that identifiers can contain underscores. Pascal_ is a larger language than Pascal, but no more powerful: they are both Turing-Machine-equivalent. In this new language, perhaps we can write a function named *halts_* that determines the halting status of all Pascal procedures. Pascal procedures are syntactically prevented from referring to *halts_*, so the problem of determining whether a Pascal procedure refers to *halts_* disappears, along with the 'maybe' option.

function *halts_* (*p*, *i*: **string**): **string**;
{return 'yes' if *p* represents a Pascal procedure with one string input parameter}
{   whose execution terminates when given input *i* ;}
{return 'no' if *p* represents a Pascal procedure with one string input parameter}
{   whose execution does not terminate when given input *i* ;}
{return 'not applicable' if *p* does not represent a Pascal procedure}
{   with one string input parameter}
begin
   if (*p* does not represent a Pascal procedure with one string input parameter)
   then *halts_*:= 'not applicable'
   else (return halting status of *p* , either 'yes' or 'no')
end

If it is possible to write a Pascal function to compute the halting status of all Pascal procedures that do not refer to this function, then by writing in another language we can compute the halting status of all Pascal procedures.

There is an argument that, at first sight, seems to refute the possibility of computing the halting status of all Pascal procedures just by programming in another language. Suppose that in writing *halts_* we do not use any underscores in any other identifiers, and we do not use the identifier *halts*. Then we can easily obtain a Pascal function *halts* just by deleting the underscore from the *halts_* identifier. We thus obtain a Pascal function with the same functionality: *halts* (*p*, *i*) = *halts_* (*p*, *i*) for all *p* and *i*. But there cannot be a Pascal function that computes the halting status of all Pascal procedures. Therefore, the argument concludes, there cannot be a Pascal_ function to do so either.

As compelling as the previous paragraph may seem, it is wrong. Even though *halts_* fulfills the specification, telling the halting status of all Pascal procedures, and *halts* is obtained from *halts_* by renaming, *halts* does not fulfill the specification. The next two sections explain why.

9   How Do We Translate?

If I say "My name is Eric Hehner." I am telling the truth. If Margaret Jackson says exactly the same words, she is lying. When I say it, there is a self-reference; when Margaret Jackson says it, there is no self-reference. The truth of that sentence depends on who says it.

Here is a Pascal_ procedure that prints its own name.

procedure *A_*; {this procedure prints its own name}
begin *print* ('*A_*') **end**

How do we translate this procedure to Pascal? There are two answers, and here is the Program Answer.

procedure *A*; {this procedure prints its own name}
begin *print* *('A_')* **end**

Ignoring the specification, which is just a comment, the Program Answer is a procedure that performs the same action(s). The original and the translation have the same output, but clearly this translation does not preserve the intention. The Pascal_ procedure *A_* meets its specification; the Pascal translation *A* does not.

The Specification Answer is

procedure *A*; {this procedure prints its own name}
begin *print* *('A')* **end**

This translation preserves the intention, meets the same specification, but it does not have the same output. Translating from *halts_* to *halts* has the same problem. We cannot preserve the intention because the specification at the head of *halts_*, which is perfectly reasonable for a Pascal_ function, becomes inconsistent when placed at the head of a Pascal function. If we just use the same Pascal_ procedure but delete the underscores, we obtain a Pascal procedure that no longer satisfies the specification.

There is another argument that, at first sight, also seems to refute the possibility of computing the halting status of all Pascal procedures just by programming in another language. In Pascal, we can write an interpreter for Pascal_ programs. So if we could write a halting function *halts_* in Pascal_ for all of Pascal, we could feed the text of *halts_* to this interpreter, and thus obtain a Pascal function to compute halting for all Pascal procedures. But there cannot be a Pascal function that computes the halting status of all Pascal procedures. Therefore, the argument concludes, there cannot be a Pascal_ function to do so either.

The reason this argument fails is the same as the reason the previous argument fails. The interpreter interpreting *halts_* is just like the translation of *halts_* into Pascal by deleting underscores. The interpreter interpreting *halts_* can be called by another Pascal program; *halts_* cannot be called by a Pascal program. That fact materially affects their behavior. Pascal_ program *halts_* can be applied to a Pascal procedure *d* that calls the interpreter interpreting *halts_* applied to *d*, and it will produce the right answer. But the interpreter interpreting *halts_* applied to *d* calls the interpreter interpreting *halts_* applied to *d*, and execution will not terminate.

10 Barber

A town named Russellville consists of some men (only men). Some of the men shave themselves; the others do not shave themselves. A barber for Russellville is a person who shaves all and only those men in Russellville who do not shave themselves. There is a barber for Russellville; his name is Bertrand_ and he lives just outside the town, in the Greater Russellville Area, known as Russellville_. Without any difficulty, he satisfies the specification of barber for Russellville.

One of the men in Russellville, whose name is Bertrand, decided that there is no need to bring in a barber from outside town. Bertrand decided that he could do the job. He would shave those men whom Bertrand_ shaves, and not shave those men whom Bertrand_ does not shave. If Bertrand_ is fulfilling the role of barber, then by doing exactly the same actions as Bertrand_ (translation by the Program Answer), Bertrand reasoned that he would fulfill the role of barber. But Bertrand is wrong; those same actions will not fulfill the role of barber when Bertrand performs them. To be a barber for Russellville, Bertrand has to shave himself if and only if he does not shave himself. A specification that is perfectly consistent and possible for someone outside town becomes inconsistent and impossible when it has to be performed by someone in town.

And so it is with the halting specification, and for the same reason. For Bertrand_, the barber specification has no self-reference; for Bertrand, the barber specification has a self-reference. For *halts_*, the halting specification has no self-reference; for *halts*, the halting specification has a self-reference (indirectly through *diag* and other procedures that call *halts*).

11 Conclusion

The question "What is a procedure?" has at least two defensible answers, which I have called the "Program Answer" and the "Specification Answer." The Program Answer says that the meaning of a procedure (or any other unit of program) is its body; the Specification Answer says that the meaning of a procedure is its specification. These two answers have quite different consequences throughout computer science.

To find the meaning of a procedure that contains calls to other procedures, the Program Answer requires the bodies of those other procedures; and if they contain calls, then also the bodies of those procedures; and so on, transitively. For that reason, the Program Answer does not scale up; large software must be analyzed as a whole.

The Specification Answer gives the meaning of a procedure directly, without looking at its body. But this answer raises a different question: does the body satisfy the specification? If the body contains calls to other procedures, only the specifications of those other procedures are used as the meanings of the calls. There is no transitive closure. So the Specification Answer does scale up.

The Program Answer can be used to verify whether some software has a certain property, giving the answer "yes" or "no." The Specification Answer can do more: if there is an error, it isolates the error to a specific procedure.

The meaning of loops and the methods for verifying loops have the same two answers as procedures. The Program Answer uses least-fixed-points as the meaning of loops, but they are difficult to find, difficult to use in verification, and useless for program construction. The Specification Answer says that the meaning of a loop is a specification, and verification is a single unrolling. The Specification Answer enables programming by refinement, without invariants.

For translation between languages, the Program Answer says that behavior should be preserved, and the Specification Answer says that intention should be preserved. Surprisingly, the two answers give different results. Preserving behavior may not preserve intention. A specification that is consistent and satisfiable in one language may be inconsistent and unsatisfiable in another.

In the halting problem, the Program Answer requires the computability assumption; *halts* must have a body to be a function with a meaning, and for *diag* to be a procedure whose execution can be determined. But the assumption that *halts* has a body does not give us the body, so we still have no meaning for *halts*, and cannot reason about the execution of *diag*. The Specification Answer says that we know the meaning of *halts* from its specification, and we can reason about the execution of *diag*. We don't need the computability assumption, and we reach the conclusion that the specification of *halts* is inconsistent.

The standard proofs that halting is incomputable prove only that it is inconsistent to ask for a halting function for a Turing-Machine-equivalent language in which that same halting function is callable. By weakening the specification a little, reducing the domain from "all procedures" to "all procedures that do not refer to the halting function," we obtain a specification that may be both consistent and computable. Equivalently, we may be able to compute the halting status of all procedures in a Turing-Machine-equivalent language by writing a halting function in another Turing-Machine-equivalent language, assuming that the procedures of the first language cannot refer to the halting function written in the second language. In any case, we do not yet have a proof that it is impossible.

I hope that the Specification Answer will become the standard for software engineering.

References

1. Hehner, E.C.R.: A Practical Theory of Programming, 1st edn. Springer (1993); current edition online at www.cs.utoronto.ca/~hehner/aPToP, 2016
2. Hehner, E.C.R.: Formal Methods of Software Design, course online at www.cs.utoronto.ca/~hehner/FMSD (2015)
3. Hehner, E.C.R.: Several Papers on the Halting Problem, online at www.cs.utoronto.ca/~hehner/halting.html (2013–2015)

The Evolution and Ecosystem of the Unified Modeling Language

Claude R. Baudoin

Abstract This short chapter is intended as a briefing on the "state of the practice" of the Unified Modeling Language (UML) and its derivatives and associated languages. It covers the evolution of UML, its near-term future, and some of the languages that have been defined as specializations of UML through a mechanism known as UML profiles. The question of whether all software can be generated through models is briefly addressed, as well as some of the occasionally enlightening comments made by UML experts.

This chapter should not be seen as a "defense of UML," only as an illustration and discussion. It is not based on original research, but on conversations with peers, especially within the context of the standards development work of the Object Management Group (OMG), which is the custodian of UML and of several related standards. Many researchers and practitioners of software engineering methods have done exhaustive work on the analysis (and the defense when they saw it necessary) of UML; some of their work is mentioned in the references and should definitely be consulted for further information.

1 Introduction

The Unified Modeling Language is now 20 years old, but it keeps evolving, which is a good thing—unless it is evolving in a bad direction, which some have argued.

In this brief assessment, written from an industrial practitioner's point of view rather than from that of a researcher or academic, we examine some aspects of this evolution, including the emergence of a family of modeling languages derived from, associated with, or inspired by UML. We will then focus on two important questions related to the pragmatics of model-based software engineering: Can UML describe a system completely enough to allow the automatic generation of the entire code? and Has UML become so complex that it fails to bridge, as originally intended, the gap between software developers and their users?

C.R. Baudoin (✉)
cébé IT & Knowledge Management, Austin, TX, USA
e-mail: cbaudoin@cebe-itkm.com

© Springer International Publishing AG 2017   37
M. Mazzara, B. Meyer (eds.), *Present and Ulterior Software Engineering*,
https://doi.org/10.1007/978-3-319-67425-4_3

2   The State and Adoption of UML

The latest version, UML 2.5 [1], was adopted by the Object Management Group in 2012.[1] In spite of an original intent to address some of the needs to simplify the constructs contained in version 2.4, the opposite occurred and the language went up from 16 diagram types to 19. Some of the significant changes made to UML over the years in order to increase its power to represent more aspects of a system are:

- The addition of "profiles" and "stereotypes," mechanisms that allow the user of the language to extend it, both semantically and graphically, so that in fact UML becomes a generic modeling language that can be customized to represent different types of models
- The incorporation of the Object Constraint Language (OCL) to capture certain semantic properties of the objects being modeled
- The addition of mechanisms to allow the execution of models—including fUML and Alf, which will be briefly described below

It is the profile mechanism, in particular, which has allowed other languages such as the System Modeling Language (SysML) to be defined as a specialization and extension of UML; this means that a UML tool that supports profiles can automatically support the creation of SysML models.

In a somewhat more controversial instance, this capability was also used to create a UML profile for BPMN—solely for the purpose of allowing software modelers to create business process models without having to switch to a separate modeling tool. This was the result of a requirement presented to the OMG's Analysis and Design Task Force by representatives of the US government.

UML profiles are widely considered, even within OMG circles, as a clumsy mechanism to extend modeling capabilities. However, attempts to replace this with something simpler or more elegant have not succeeded so far. We will come back to that point.

More recently, there have been efforts to "tighten" the specification in areas where the language allowed too much ambiguity. For example, a specification called "Precise Semantics of Composite Structures" was developed and adopted in 2015, and similar work continues in other parts of the language.

Regardless of the fact that most users only use a small fraction of the language's capabilities, UML is widely adopted. In that sense, it has certainly succeeded in ending the cacophony of object-oriented analysis and design languages that had proliferated in the years 1988–1993, and it deserves the "U" in its name. John Whittle and his colleagues at the University of Lancaster started in 2009 a deep study

---

[1]Version numbers are important in the world of UML and related specifications. The Object Management Group's open process results not only in a relatively rapid adoption process, at least compared to the more conservative process of ISO, but also in a succession of revisions every few years. It is generally important to know about, and use, the most recent version of each language.

of the practices of model-based engineering (MBE), which they are continuing to this day [2].

Bran Selic, of Simula Research Labs, also wrote in 2012 a survey of MBE in industry on behalf of the French energy agency CEA. In his study [3], Selic describes the level of adoption as well as some of the obstacles encountered. He lists the main domains (and specific company names) where UML has been widely adopted: aerospace and defense, automotive, industrial automation, office automation, telecommunications, and financial systems.

Selic gives a balanced view of UML adoption, contrasting the success stories with the obstacles it is still facing, which he categorized into three areas: cultural (resistance to change), economic (the cost of the tools), and technological (issues related to code generation, integration with other tools, functionality limitations, etc.).

3 Evolution and Related Standards

The "ecosystem" of UML—other modeling notations and standards that feed on UML and in turn give it additional relevance—includes certain extensions, profiles, and standards that stand on their own but are aimed to complement it by modeling additional aspects of a software system. The following list is not necessarily exhaustive.

3.1 fUML and Alf

The "foundational subset for executable UML models," or fUML (currently version 1.2.1, adopted in January 2016), defines a subset of the UML 2 metamodel, and the precise semantics of those constructs, so that a model within this subset can be executed [4].

A companion specification is the Action Language for fUML, or Alf, which is a textual notation for UML behaviors, providing a simpler alternative to the creation of complex UML activity diagrams to describe computations.

3.2 MARTE

The Modeling and Analysis of Real Time and Embedded systems, or MARTE, is a profile of UML aimed at supporting the design, verification, and validation activities that are specific to software for real-time and embedded systems (RTES). Version 1.1 was adopted in 2011. The French military and control systems company Thales was one of the main forces behind the development of MARTE.

3.3   UTP

The UML Testing Profile (UTP) "provides extensions to UML to support the design, visualization, specification, analysis, construction, and documentation of the artifacts involved in testing" [5]. Prior to the adoption of UTP, UML did not offer support for testing activities. The current version, UTP 1.2, was adopted in 2013. Led by Fraunhofer FOKUS, this work is also described in a book coauthored by the leading contributors to the standard [6].

3.4   SysML

The Systems Modeling Language, or SysML, is one of the most visible examples of a full modeling language developed as a UML profile. It removes some of the more complex software-centric constructs of UML, using only seven of the original UML diagrams, but adds two more in order to cover the aspects of performance analysis required in hardware/software systems: a *requirement* diagram and a *parametric* diagram.

SysML has a somewhat complex history that resulted in an open-source version, distributed by a group called SysML Partners, and an official standard from the Object Management Group, properly called "OMG SysML," of which SysML Partners was one of the key contributors and which was also supported by the International Council on Systems Engineering (INCOSE). The current version of OMG SysML is 1.4, adopted in September 2015 [7].

SysML had achieved an excellent level of adoption, and the success of the approach known as Model-Based Systems Engineering (MBSE) is rather indissolubly tied to the adoption of the language.

3.5   IFML

With the advent of mobile platforms in particular, designing the interaction between a system and its human users has become more complex. The logic of the interaction now needs to be separated from the layout of the display, because the layout may vary widely across devices based on their size, resolution, and input capabilities (touch screen, stylus, keyboard, etc.).

This led, under the leadership of a startup team that came out of the Politecnico di Milano, to the specification of the Interaction Flow Modeling Language (IFML). IFML is one of the most recently adopted OMG standards (February 2015) and is still at version 1.0 [8].

3.6 Precise Semantics of State Machines

Perhaps surprisingly, since the "state machine diagrams" introduced in UML version 2 closely follow David Harel's "statecharts" proposed in his seminal and rather formal 1987 paper [9], UML did not define the semantics of state diagrams sufficiently to allow unambiguous execution or interpretation. This should be fixed in late 2016 or early 2017 with the adoption by the OMG of the Precise Semantics of State Machines (PSSM) specification.

3.7 Metamodel Extension Facility

Starting in 2011, a discussion arose about the mechanisms used to extend and/or specialize UML to various uses, such as those described above—systems engineering, testing, real-time and embedded systems, etc. UML *profiles* started as simple tags attached to model elements but have evolved into much more complex languages. In spite of this added complexity, they have limitations. The easiest ones to explain are:

- When defining an extension of the language, one must choose one profile or another—selecting multiple profiles is either impossible or likely to generate conflicts.
- Many OMG initiatives in the last few years have asked submitters to propose both a metamodel and a UML profile, but the mapping between the two is not defined formally and there can be inconsistencies.
- Profiles limit how new notations can be defined; therefore, a common problem is that people who create a new profile may reuse an existing shape that meets their needs, regardless of the original UML semantics associated with that shape.

In the intervening 5 years, however, the proposal to define a new Metamodel Extension Facility (MEF) has not progressed much, while the number of legacy profiles that would eventually need to be migrated to a new facility is steadily increasing. It is thus unclear whether the complexity and ambiguity generated by the current metamodel extension mechanism (profiles) will be resolved, when, or how well.

4 Key Questions in Model-Driven Software Engineering

There are currently two key questions that can be heard in discussions related to model-driven approaches to software engineering:

1. Will it be possible to generate 100% of the code of an application or system from models—and how long will it take until we get there?
2. Are the modeling languages we have developed to try to reach this goal becoming too complex?

4.1 Completeness

The first question can be answered in the positive in a trivial way: a programming language is per se a model of an application or system; therefore, it is possible to model a system completely. The question therefore needs to be rephrased: will the language allow a tool to generate 100% of the code, or to interpret the model and perform all desired actions, *while staying at a high enough level of abstraction* that creating a model at that level remains substantially simpler and less error prone than writing code? This has been the promise at each successive stage of the evolution of languages: from machine language to assembly language, to third-generation procedural languages, to 4GLs (remember those?), and now to graphical modeling notations. Up to 3GLs, there was no doubt that the language could represent every programming construct, because these languages were designed bottom-up to precisely express everything a machine could do. With 4GLs, the situation got less clear: a 4GL like Structured Query Language (SQL) can represent everything you can do in terms of inserting, updating, or deleting records in a relational database, and perform certain data aggregations, but it cannot fly a plane or run a Web site. So as we move up to modeling languages such as UML, are *all* the necessary concepts represented to be able to generate a complete system?

Suppose there is a need to sort an array of 100 numbers in the middle of the program. Surely we are not going to represent this in a UML diagram. Either we are going to assume that there is a function from some library that we can call to do this, or we are going to dust off our cherished copy of Knuth's *Sorting and Searching* from a bookshelf and program the sorting routine in some lower-level language than UML. Specifying the sorting algorithm within the UML model would seem as futile as flowcharting templates became once we moved from assembly language to 3GLs, and the diamond representing a decision became no easier to read than a well-punctuated "if" statement.

Clearly, this is where the fUML subset and the Alf language aim to bridge the gap between the model and its execution. Even with those capabilities added to UML, two key questions remain:

- Is specifying all the behaviors in an UML model using the Alf language easier, faster, and less error prone than writing those in a programming language? The answer seems to be a qualified "yes," since Alf looks a lot like Java or C++ but contains a number of constructs that simplify the navigation through data structures in particular.
- Can there be any more of a dialog between a software designer and a user on the basis of a UML model with added Alf code than there would be using a traditional programming method? There the answer is probably "no," for the same reason just mentioned: it looks a lot like Java or C++.

This discussion is perhaps best summarized by Stephen Mellor, one of the pre-UML pioneers of object-oriented analysis and design, who says that when someone asks him when it will be possible to generate an entire system from a model, he answers: "in three years—but I have been giving the same answer for twenty years."

4.2 Complexity

The second question is in fact related to the first, because if today's modeling languages can't capture all aspects of a system, then they may need to have even more constructs added to them, even though some argue that they are already too complex to meet they originally intended objective of being readable by the end users of the system.

At minimum, I tend to tell my clients and users (in the enterprise IT domain) that they need to create (a) a set of use cases, (b) one or more business process models, and (c) a conceptual information model in order to provide a good initial set of functional requirements to a software development group. Note that this already requires two modeling languages, not just one: UML for the use cases and the information model, and the Business Process Modeling Language (BPMN) for process models. This is still not too bad since this approach only requires teaching them to draw two out of nineteen diagrams contained in UML 2.5. Next, the users probably want to specify how they want the application to look on screen. We used to do this using so-called wireframe diagrams, but this did not capture the interaction between the user and the system. This need is now addressed with the OMG's Interaction Flow Modeling Language (IFML). So we need at least a third modeling language. Now we're getting past the patience and competence of most normally constituted end users. In practice, the software team (not the users) will develop those models based on written documents or on user interviews. When those modelers review the models with the users, in order to make sure that the requirements are captured correctly, the users will not be able to tell if they cannot understand the modeling language. This is actually an argument in favor of rapid iterative prototyping, as recommended in any number of agile methodologies, which is more likely to encourage constructive user feedback. However, this failure to bridge the communication gap between users and software experts may lead to a system with no documented requirements or with as-specified models that do not match the as-built system because they were never touched after the prototyping work started.

Even if we assume that the dialog with the users is limited to a few very simple models and that the rest of the required set of models is written by experts, those expert modelers are themselves starting to find the complexity of UML excessive. Very few people use all 19 diagrams in the current version of UML; most users seem to limit themselves to no more than five or six. And if they have to also learn BPMN, IFML, SysML in some cases, and "tool up" to create a complete set of models— something that may require multiple tools or the more expensive tool suites in the market—then the challenge becomes significant.

In other words, we're looking for a happy medium that will be hard to reach: we would like to create models rich enough to generate all the code, but that represent the user needs in a simple enough way that the users will still understand them as easily as they would, say, an Excel spreadsheet.

5   Concluding Thoughts

UML has clearly become a well-accepted modeling language for many software and systems organizations worldwide. It is taught in university and continuing education courses, and it has allowed a modeling tool industry to flourish, in a way that the 20-odd notations that competed prior to 1995 would certainly not have allowed. Successful adaptations to other domains, such as SysML, have further solidified its position.

Yet UML suffers from increasing complexity, and few organizations use it completely. Therein lies a paradox: if UML is not used completely, there is little hope to model 100% of the behavior of a system and therefore to be able to execute the model or automatically transform it into code so that the resulting execution is complete and the software can be maintained at the model level.

Some of the quotes we gathered (through private communications) in preparation for this chapter are worth considering.

Grady Booch, the inventor of the object-oriented design method, sounds a positive note: "I still use the UML in my work, which is currently focusing on embodied cognition." More technically, Ed Willink of the Eclipse Foundation writes that by June 2016, "Eclipse QVT (Query/View/Transformation) should provide an optimized incremental code-generated QVT-Relations and QVT-Core, so that model-to-model transformation will begin to become of high quality and high performance."

On the cautionary side, Pete Rivett of Adaptive Software, a member of the OMG's Architecture Board, admits that "UML is a bit odd." And Cory Casanave of Model Driven Solutions, an equally respected member of the model-driven architecture community and longtime participant in the work of the OMG, recently started describing the core issue underlying the multiplication of metamodels and profiles as the "OMG metamuddle."

Who is right—the optimists or the pessimists? And can we engineer our way to a better state? That's what the OMG is certainly betting on, and its plea to critics and fans alike is that instead of standing on the sidelines, those interested in improving how we use models to generate better systems with speed and reliability should participate in the work of its various task forces.

References

1. Object Management Group: Unified Modeling Language™ (UML®) Version 2.5, www.omg. org/spec/UML/2.5/
2. Whittle, J., et al.: The state of practice in model-driven engineering. IEEE Softw. **31**(3), (2013)
3. Selic, B.: What will it take? A view on adoption of model-based methods in practice. J. Softw. Syst. Model. **11**(4), 513–526 (2012). Springer-Verlag
4. Object Management Group: Semantics of a Foundational Subset for Executable UML Models (fUML™) V1.2.1, www.omg.org/spec/FUML/Current
5. Object Management Group: UML Testing Profile, http://utp.omg.org/
6. Baker, P., et al.: Model-Driven Testing – Using the UML Testing Profile. Springer, Berlin (2008)
7. Object Management Group: OMG Systems Modeling Language™ (SysML®), www.omg.org/ spec/SysML/
8. Object Management Group: Interaction Flow Modeling Language™ (IFML™), www.omg.org/ spec/IFML/
9. Harel, D.: Statecharts: a visual formalism for complex systems. Sci. Comput. Program. **8**, 231–274 (1987). North-Holland, www.sciencedirect.com/science/article/pii/0167642387900359

A Theory of Networking and Its Contributions to Software Engineering

Pamela Zave

Abstract This chapter presents a compositional theory of networking as an example of a useful and realistic domain theory. First, it uses networking to illustrate all the parts of a domain theory, including a reusable domain description with intrinsic state and behavior, software interfaces and specifications, requirements, proof obligations, and theorems. Next, the theory is extended with composition of network domains, which is directly relevant to solving today's most critical networking problems. Finally, the chapter proposes ways in which the theory can contribute directly to the design and development of network software.

1 Introduction

Currently, the biggest obstacle to doing research in software engineering that translates to industrial practice is the size and complexity of real-world software systems. They are built and maintained by large, international groups of people. Research groups are small and cannot keep up.

In [18], it is argued that one of the most promising avenues of software-engineering research is the development of reusable domain models. In this context, a *domain* is the subject matter of a software system. A *domain model* is a formal description of everything relevant that is known or assumed about the domain. To make it reusable, it must be general enough to describe all real-world instances of a family of domains, for the development of a family of software systems. The model includes the *interface* to the software system, consisting of shared phenomena controlled by the domain and input to the system, as well as those controlled by the system and output to the domain.

Two additional types of description accompany a domain model: *requirements* state the properties that the domain should have when the software system is built and installed, while *specifications* state how the software system should behave at the system/domain interface. The desired relationship, among the descriptions for a

P. Zave (✉)
AT & T Labs—Research, Bedminster, NJ, USA
e-mail: pamela@research.att.com

specific development project, is that the domain model and the specification together should guarantee that the requirements are satisfied [11, 21].

A domain model is elevated to a *domain theory* when it is enhanced with theorems [20]. Theorems capture reusable knowledge about how the system can solve the problems posed by the requirements, and assist formal reasoning to show how the effects of the system outputs propagate as intended throughout the domain.

Domain theories meeting this standard of completeness are few and far between. However, based on the many successes of model-based software engineering, it seems reasonable to expect that the benefits of a domain theory that really captures the essence of a complex domain would include the following:

- A domain theory records essential concepts and facts in an abstract, comprehensible, and reusable way.
- Having a formalization of the domain is a prerequisite for the use of any logic-based tool. Logic-based tools can perform syntactic analysis, verification, constraint satisfaction, optimization, code generation, code synthesis, and automated testing.
- A domain theory can facilitate recognition of recurring patterns, design principles, and structured trade-off spaces.
- A domain theory can provide modularity and compositional reasoning.
- A reusable theory invites the development of domain-specific languages for customizing generic descriptions. These generic descriptions might cover domains, requirements, or specifications.
- Once there is a useful domain theory, it can be improved continuously with respect to coverage, theorems, and the power and efficiency of the tools that operate on it.

The scarcity of domain theories is due (at least partially) to the difficulty of working theory-building into the schedule, budget, and process of software-development projects. The purpose of this chapter is to encourage researchers to build domain theories, as the technical challenges and potential benefits equal or exceed the challenges and benefits of other approaches to research. The chapter illustrates concretely major parts of a domain theory for networking, hopefully enough to show the nature of such work. To provide some context, Sect. 2 gives a brief overview of the current networking scene.

Section 3 sketches out the major parts of a theory of a network domain. The domain description includes generic network state and generic algorithms for how messages are processed by network elements in accordance with domain state. In networking terminology, this is the *data plane*. Most network software is part of the *control plane*, which initializes and maintains the network state so that it controls the data plane properly. Section 3 also discusses some of the requirements, specifications, and theorems used to develop software for network control planes.

The domain theory is designed to be compositional, as networks today can only be described usefully as layered compositions of many networks, each potentially serving a different purpose at a different level of abstraction. Section 4 introduces composition of networks, including uses of composition, examples from cloud computing, and how the theory in Sect. 3 must be extended to cover composition of networks.

Finally, in Sect. 5, we propose a number of ways that the theory of networks can contribute to the design and development of network software. This section focuses on composition, because composition is the aspect of networking that has been the most neglected—in fact, altogether unacknowledged—in practice. The chapter concludes (Sect. 6) with lessons about research in building theories of software domains.

The domain theory in this chapter has been called the *geomorphic view of networking* [22]. It was inspired by John Day, who showed the existence of patterns that appear in network architectures at many levels for many different purposes [5]. Although the exposition in this chapter is informal, many aspects of the theory have been formalized in Alloy [10]. Its presentation is organized according to typical parts of a domain theory, as enumerated in [20]. Although this seems to be the best way to convey what a domain theory is like, it tends to obscure the reasons why this is a *good* domain theory. A much more purpose-driven explanation of the basic ideas can be found in [19].

2 Networking Today

The original Internet architecture was intended to empower users and encourage innovation [3], and it has succeeded beyond most people's wildest dreams. As a result of this success, the Internet has outgrown its original architecture and does not meet current needs in many areas. The networking community has recognized serious deficiencies concerning security, reliability, mobility, and quality of service. It is proving difficult to achieve the desired convergence of data, telephone, and broadcast networks, and difficult to balance the needs of all of the Internet's stakeholders [4, 6, 8, 14].

At the same time that external requirements have been expanding, growth and competition have intensified the need for better resource management. Network providers must use elastic resource allocation, rather than simply overbuilding their networks, as was the previous practice. These pressures have led to widespread use of cloud computing.

The original or classic Internet architecture [3] has five layers, as shown in Fig. 1. It is similar in spirit to the OSI reference model [9], which has seven fixed layers. Figure 1 would lead us to expect that a typical Internet packet would have four headers, for example, Ethernet, IP, TCP, and HTTP. Each layer requires a message header to carry out its function. Each layer is indispensable because it has a distinct and necessary function.

Because each of the changes mentioned above has made demands that the original Internet architecture cannot satisfy, today new requirements are satisfied by adding many ad hoc intermediate layers of virtual networking, as described by Spatscheck [15]. To illustrate these ad hoc layers, Fig. 2 shows the 12 headers in a

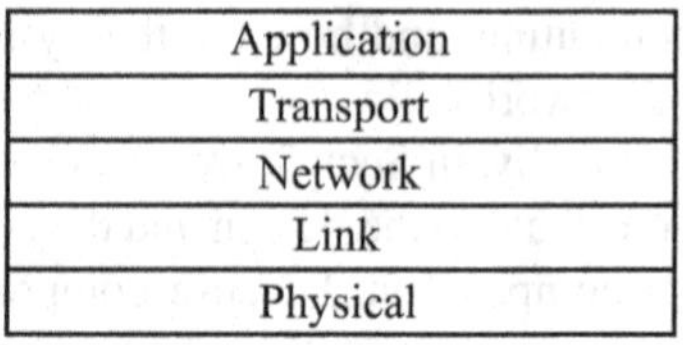

Fig. 1 The classic Internet
architecture, with exactly five
layers

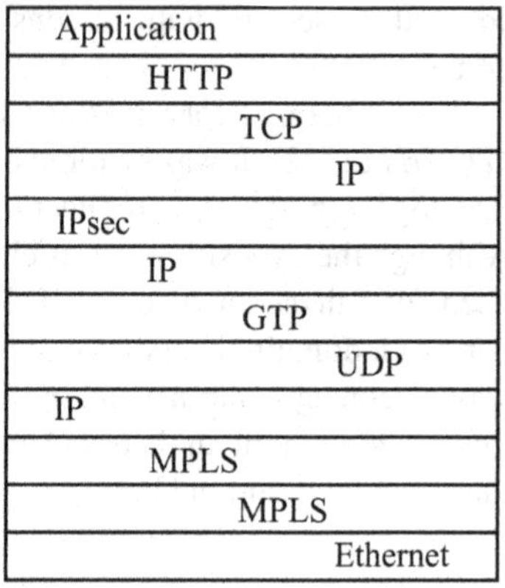

Application
Transport
Network
Link
Physical

Fig. 2 Headers in a packet in
the AT & T backbone,
suggesting the presence of
approximately seven
networks composed
hierarchically

Application			
HTTP			
	TCP		
		IP	
IPsec			
	IP		
		GTP	
			UDP
IP			
	MPLS		
		MPLS	
			Ethernet

typical packet transmitted across the AT & T backbone—obviously a lot of new
things are going on! The problem with these ad hoc layers is that each is typically
designed and understood in isolation. The overall network behavior when new layers
are run among old layers is neither understood nor predictable.

The first principle of the geomorphic view of networking is that networks as
we know them are layered compositions of modular networks. Each network-as-a-
module is a microcosm of networking, with all the basic parts and functions native to
networking. A network architecture can have as many or as few of them as needed.[1]
So the same basic network function can occur several times, at several different
levels, for several different purposes. The ultimate goal of our theory of networking
is to reason rigorously and compositionally about the properties of networks.

3 A Theory of a Network as a Software Domain

3.1 Domain Objects

A domain has objects. Figure 3 shows the most important objects in a particular
network, i.e., an instance of the domain theory.

---

[1]The name "geomorphic view" comes from the varied arrangements of layers in the earth's crust.
Layers vary in number and composition from place to place, and they can abut and overlap in
interesting ways.

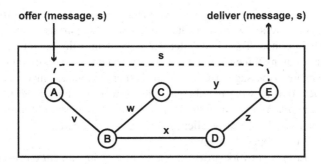

Fig. 3 In the boxed network, members are named with capital letters. Links are *solid lines*, while sessions are *dashed lines*; each link and session is named with a small letter. *Offer* is an interface operation to be invoked by a client, to give a message to the network, while *deliver* is an interface operation invoked by the network, to give a message to a client

The *members* of the network are software or hardware modules executing in computers. Each member of the network has a unique *name* drawn from the network's namespace.

Members of the network are connected by unidirectional point-to-point *links*.[2] A link is a communication channel through which its sending member can send messages to its receiving member. Physical implementations of links include wires, optical fibers, and radio channels.

In some networks, all the members are pairwise connected to each other by links. More commonly, there are fewer links, although enough to ensure that there are paths (concatenations of one or more links) connecting each pair of members in each direction. In Fig. 3, if each solid line actually represents a link in each direction, then the network members are fully connected in this way.

Now the problem is to deliver messages to their destinations over paths of links. The universal solution to this problem is:

- The name of the destination of the message is added to the message, in a data structure called the *header*.
- When a message arrives at a member, and the destination of the message is not the name of that member, the member *forwards* the message toward its destination on another link.

A *session* is like a link in being a unidirectional point-to-point communication channel. Unlike a link, it does not have an atomic implementation in the domain. Rather, a session is implemented as an identifier for a group of messages that have the same sender and receiver, are considered to be related to each other, and are treated as such by their sender and receiver.

---

[2]The theory also encompasses other kinds of link such as broadcast links. Non-point-to-point links and some other structures are omitted here for simplicity.

Unlike domains that existed before computers, networks are built for the purpose of allowing computers to communicate. To achieve this purpose, a network must have a client interface. The client interface is built into the operating system of each computer having a member of the network. When some entity on a computer wishes to transport a message to an entity on another computer, it invokes *offer* at the client interface to its network member, and the network member *sends* the message through its network. When a member *receives* a message destined for it through its network, it invokes *deliver* at its client interface, so the operating system can pass the message to the proper client entity.

More generally, a network provides one or more *communication services* to its users. The properties of a communication service are associated with sessions. For example, a network might provide the service of FIFO message delivery. This does not mean that *all* messages are delivered in the order in which they are sent, an unobservable and unimplementable global property. Rather, it means that all the messages of a particular session are delivered in the order in which they are sent. This is why the client interface in Fig. 3 shows that each message is offered and delivered within the context of a particular session.

3.2   Domain State and Behavior

A network has state, most of which is distributed over its members so that the members have quick access to what they need. Each member has known behavior, standardized across the network, that performs network functions as controlled by its state. As mentioned in Sect. 1, the known behavior is called the *data plane* because it performs all the operations on the data (messages) transmitted through the network. The software that maintains the network state is called the *control plane* because the network state controls the data plane. Most software development for network domains is development of the control plane (see Sect. 3.3).

Not surprisingly, each member has state recording all the sessions and links of which it is an endpoint. This state includes the names of the members at the far ends of these communication channels.

Network functions require that each message sent through the network has a *header*, minimally containing the source name, destination name, and identifier of the session in which it is sent.

To implement forwarding as described in Sect. 3.1, the state of a network must include *routes*, which tell the members where to forward messages so that they reach their destinations. The routes used by a member are typically formalized as a relation or table with three columns of types *header, link, link*. If a tuple *(msgHead, inLink, outLink)* is in the *routes* relation at a member, then a message with header *msgHead* received by the member on its link *inLink* must be forwarded by sending it on *outLink*. For example, consider how to get messages from *A* to *E* in Fig. 3. Simplifying headers to destination names only, *routes* of *B* may contain the tuple *(E, v, x)* and *routes* of *D* may contain the tuple *(E, x, z)*, or *B* may have *(E, v, w)* while *C* has *(E, w, y)*.

The known behavior of a network is conventionally described in two parts: a *forwarding protocol* and one or more *session protocols*. The forwarding protocol is executed by each member. Its behavior always includes at least the following aspects:

- There is a set of conventions about how digital messages are represented on the links.
- Members send messages produced by the session protocol. When members receive messages, they pass them to the session protocol.
- When a member M sends a message with header h, it finds a tuple $(P_h, self, k)$ in its *routes* relation, where P_h is a pattern that matches H, and *self* is a distinguished pseudo-link. M sends the message on outgoing link k.
- When a member M receives a message with header h on link $k1$, provided that the destination name in the header is not M, it finds a tuple $(P_h, k1, k2)$ and forwards the message on link $k2$.
- When a member M receives a message with header destination M, the message is passed to the session protocol.

A forwarding protocol can be extended to enhance security and monitor traffic, among other network functions.

The exact behavior of a session protocol depends on the communication services that it is supposed to provide. At a minimum, it does the following:

- It accepts an offered message, encapsulates it in a larger message containing the header, and passes it to the forwarding protocol.
- It gets a message received by the forwarding protocol, decapsulates it by stripping off the header, and delivers it to the operating system of its computer.

Session protocols can also offer much more. For example, consider the best-known session protocol, which is TCP.

As we shall see in Sect. 3.3, every single part of a network is dynamic. When links are changing or failing and whatever algorithm maintains the routing state is not keeping up, some messages will inevitably be lost. Despite the unreliability of forwarding, TCP provides the communication service of a reliable, FIFO, duplicate-free byte stream. TCP actions are performed by the implementations of the session protocol in each of the two members at the session endpoints. These members achieve their goals through acknowledgments, detection of lost messages, retransmission, and reconstruction of a properly ordered byte stream.

To return to the comparison between Figs. 1 and 2, if layers are viewed as having distinct and indispensable functions as in Fig. 1, then an IP header goes with the Network layer and a TCP header goes with the Transport layer. If a layer is a microcosm of networking, on the other hand, each layered network contains both a forwarding protocol (such as IP) and a session protocol (such as TCP). Allowing for the facts that in some networks some parts are vestigial, and that a packet alone does not tell us everything about how protocols are being used, Fig. 2 shows evidence of approximately seven networks layered on top of one another.

3.3   Software Development for Networks

Sections 3.1 and 3.2 have presented the objects, state, and known behavior of a network. Most software development for networks is development of the control plane. The control plane receives customer and service-provider requirements through APIs and real-time monitoring information from the network members. Its output is the initial configuration of the network state, followed by real-time updates throughout the life of the network. This section uses software for ordinary routing as an example of the control plane.

3.3.1   Routing Requirements

The primary purpose of ordinary routing is to make it possible for messages from any network member to reach any other network member. It must satisfy this requirement with whatever links are currently available, or at least satisfy it as well as possible. In addition, routing may be expected to satisfy other requirements such as these examples:

- For security, as an exception to general reachability, member A is not reachable from member B.
- There is a minimum bandwidth for certain traffic.
- Messages are delivered within a certain latency bound, with probability P.
- Averaged over 10-min periods, no link is more than 80% utilized.
- There are no loops in message forwarding.
- All messages in a session travel on the same path.

Routing must be dynamic because the state of a network is always changing, even when the requirements are not changing. Members and links can disappear as a result of failure or retired resources, and can appear as new or reinstated resources. The load on the network, i.e., the number and characteristics of the messages being sent, can also change radically over time.

These observations show how the domain model presented so far is incomplete. A complete domain model should include resource failures and restarts, and how they affect the domain state. It should also include the performance attributes of links, such as bandwidth and latency. Characterizations of the network load, for example, traffic or utilization measurements at specific points in the network, are also indispensable.

3.3.2   Specifications of Routing

Specifications state how the software system should behave at the system/domain interface. At this interface, routing software must receive as inputs information about the status of links and members. The software must also receive information about the current load and/or resource utilization. Once the software has computed changes to the current *routes*, it must output these changes to the domain. More specifically, every new tuple *(headerPattern, inLink, outLink)* must be installed in the member *forwarder* to which it belongs. Note that in many networks, there are specialized members called *routers* that do all the forwarding. The other members are the sources and destinations of ordinary messages and have only *self* tuples (see Sect. 3.2) for forwarding.

The exact content of a routing specification depends very much on the exact nature of the system/domain interface. In networking today, there are two major variations on this interface.

In older networks, the routing algorithm is distributed. There is a piece of the routing algorithm running in the computer of every router (see Fig. 4), and there is a local system/domain interface between the router and the local routing agent. At this interface, the router passes all its information to the routing agent. The local routing agents communicate through their own private messages, so that each has a sufficient view of its region of the network. Each agent of the routing algorithm is responsible for the forwarding state in its own router.

More recently, the concept of Software-Defined Networking (SDN) has become popular [13]. With SDN, the system/domain interface at the network routers is defined by the OpenFlow standard. OpenFlow allows a router to send informational messages and queries to a separate, centralized controller (see Fig. 5), and to receive new *routes* tuples from the centralized controller.

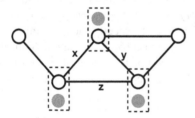

Fig. 4 A distributed routing algorithm. The *dashed boxes* are computers on which the network members are routers. The *gray dots* represent the software modules of the routing algorithm, called local routing agents. Through the routers, they communicate with each other by sending messages on links *x, y,* and *z*

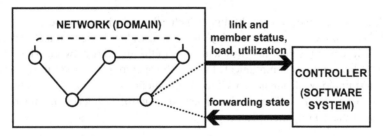

Fig. 5 A centralized routing algorithm. Each OpenFlow-enabled router communicates with a centralized software controller that implements the routing algorithm

3.3.3 Theorems About Routing

Not surprisingly, many theorems of graph theory are relevant to network routing. One use of graph theory is "network verification," in which snapshots of the *routes* tables in each router are analyzed for desirable general properties such as reachability, security blocking, and routing through middleboxes [1, 12, 17].

The most advanced theory for network routing can be found in [7] and subsequent papers. The contribution of the "metarouting" work is easiest to explain in the context of distributed routing algorithms, as in Fig. 4.

All distributed routing software uses some basic distributed algorithm based on *advertisements*. To give a trivial example based on Fig. 3, let us assume that the link labels are not letters but rather numbers representing link lengths. C advertises to all its neighbor routers that it has a path to E of length y, while D advertises to all its neighbor routers that it has a path to E of length z. Their neighbor B now knows that it has two paths to E, of lengths $w + y$ and $x + z$, respectively. B chooses whichever of these paths is shorter, and advertises to its other neighbors (not shown) that it has a path to E of the shorter length.

To generalize these basic ideas, metarouting separates the distributed advertisement algorithm (there are two important ones) from the *algebra* being used to evaluate paths. A path algebra defines a path metric, an operator to combine path metrics, and a preference ordering. In the preceding example, path lengths are combined by addition, and the shortest length is preferred. If the requirements concern minimum bandwidth of a path, on the other hand, path metrics are combined by taking their minimum, and the largest minimum bandwidth is preferred.

Supported by a theory built on these generalizations, network operators can use a domain-specific language to specify their routing requirements in terms of one or more composable algebras [16]. Tools can then check the requirements for consistency and generate a complete routing algorithm automatically. There are metarouting implementations for both distributed and centralized network control.

4 Composition of Networks

4.1 Definition of Composition

The fundamental mechanism through which all networks compose is shown in Fig. 6. When a member of an "overlay" network uses the services of an "underlay" network, its computer must also host a member of the underlay network. The overlay and underlay members communicate through the operating system of the computer. In the terminology of our network theory, the member of the overlay network is *attached* to a member of the underlay network, and the underlay member is the *location* of the overlay member.

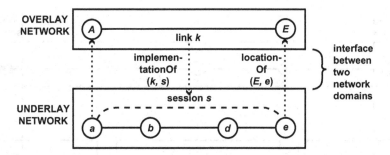

Fig. 6 Fundamental structures of network composition

As Fig. 6 shows, composition means that a session in the underlay *implements* a link in the overlay. Conversely, the overlay link *uses* the underlay session. The underlay is providing for the overlay a communication service with certain properties. These properties are guaranteed by the underlay session and can be assumed to hold for the overlay link.

In the figure, when A sends a message on virtual link k, it actually offers the message to a with session identifier s (see Fig. 3). Underlay member a encapsulates the message in the header for s in the underlay and sends it through the underlay network. When e receives the message, it decapsulates (strips off the underlay header) and delivers it to E as part of session s.

Section 3.2 stated that the minimal contents of a header are source name, destination name, and session identifier. By convention, the names are usually associated with the forwarding protocol and the identifier with the session protocol. For instance, an Internet header might be described as "TCP over IP," where "over" (referring to layers) might also be "inside" (referring to the bit string). Encapsulation due to composition is similar, so that the headers on messages in Fig. 6 could be described as "overlay header over/inside underlay header."

Figure 7 shows the geomorphic view of the classic Internet architecture. Each endpoint device (a cell phone and a Web server) hosts members of two networks, the Internet and a lower-level network with physical links. (The cellular network uses radio channels, the wide-area network uses optical fibers, and local-area links are simply wires.) At all higher levels of a graph of network composition, the links are virtual—they are implemented in software. The great benefit of the Internet is that its span is global, while each physical network has a limited span.

Note in Fig. 7 the two Internet members marked g for *gateway*. From the viewpoint of the Internet, they are merely forwarding messages from one link to another. Their significance is that each is attached to two different physical networks, so that each can forward messages from one physical network to the other. On each side of the figure, there is an Internet link between an endpoint and a gateway. Each link is implemented by a session in an "edge" or "access" network. The links between gateways, on the other hand, are implemented by sessions in a wide-area network.

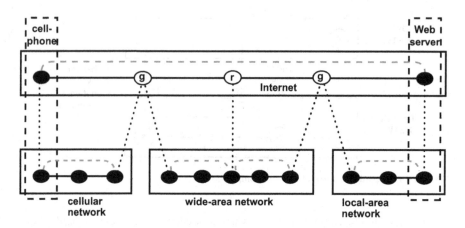

Fig. 7 Another view of the classic Internet architecture. The global Internet is composed of many local networks and acts as a bridge between adjacent networks

In Fig. 7, the Internet also has a member marked *r* for *router*. Routers are network members whose primary function is forwarding messages along desired paths; routers do not send or receive data-plane messages, but rather send and receive only through session protocols that help to implement the control plane.

The figure suggests that every cell phone served by the cellular network, when it is using what is known as "data service," has a direct virtual link to an Internet gateway. The reason for this architectural decision is to push the routing functions and forwarding needed to implement this link down to the cellular network, where the state, protocols, and control plane are specialized for cellular networks and different from what is normal for the Internet.

4.2 Domain State and Behavior

Section 3.2 explained that *sessions, links,* and *routes* are part of the state of a network domain. As shown in Fig. 6, composition of networks requires additional state that maps between members and communication channels across the network boundary. In the overlay, the required mapping is *implementationOf(k, s)*, meaning that session *s* is the implementation of link *k*. In the underlay, the required mapping is *locationOf (om, um)*, meaning that underlay member *um* is the location of overlay member *om*.

It is easiest to see the need for this extra state when links and sessions are dynamic, as they often are. In Fig. 6, imagine that there is to be a new overlay session *so* between *A* and *E*. For architectural reasons, all the real implementation work for this session is to be performed in the underlay. So there will be a one-to-one correspondence between *so* and virtual link *k* in the overlay, and a one-to-one correspondence between k and session s in the underlay. Using a generic algorithm for compositional behavior in domains, here are the steps required in A and a:

1. A initiates session to E, creating session so state.
2. A initiates link to E, creating link k state and routing state. All messages in so will be routed to k.
3. A requests implementation of k from a. a uses $locationOf$ to discover that the underlay location of E is e.
4. a initiates session to e, creating session s state. a replies to A's request with result s, and A records that $implementationOf(k, s)$.
5. A sends a session-initiation message for so, which is routed to k. Because k is implemented by s, this means offering the message to a in session s.
6. a encapsulates the session-initiation message in the s header and sends it to e. It travels by preexisting routing over static links.

When the session-initiation message arrives at e, a similar but reverse process begins, which will establish similar state at the other endpoint and enable correct delivery of messages in so.

4.3 Uses of Composition

In Sect. 4.1, we saw composition used as a way to bridge smaller networks so that they can function together as a larger network. This was the original purpose of composition in networks, but today there are many others. In this section, there are examples of three of them.

4.3.1 Encryption

Figure 8 shows a *virtual private network (VPN)* layered on top of the Internet. To its users, the VPN looks exactly like the Internet, except that all the member names are in the part of the IP address space reserved for private use. The headers on messages

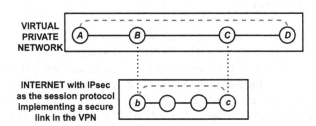

Fig. 8 Composition for the sake of security. There are two Internet-like networks, but the overlay network is private and has relatively few members

through this network are TCP over IP. This particular VPN (and many, many others like it) are composed with (and share) the Internet, using the session protocol IPsec in tunnel mode. IPsec makes the virtual link between B and C, which traverses the public Internet, secure by means of authentication and encryption. Thus, messages between B and C have headers with TCP over IP over IPsec over IP (which is part of the header stack in Fig. 2). Presumably, the links from A to B and C to D are implemented on safer private networks, which are not shown.

4.3.2 Mobility

Another important reason for composition of networks is *mobility*, which means that a network must provide a persistent name for and connectivity to a device, even though that device is changing its physical connection to the network. To visualize mobility in networking terms, imagine that the cell phone in Fig. 7 is continually moving from one cellular network or Wi-Fi network to another, depending on the strength of radio signals in its vicinity.

Mobility is a big subject, covered thoroughly in [23], which organizes a survey of real mobility mechanisms by means of the geomorphic domain model. The survey shows that there are exactly two patterns for implementing mobility in networks. One pattern simply demands updates to routing as the links through which a member can be reached change. The other pattern uses composition of two layered networks and the session protocol of the underlay. In this pattern, the session protocol of the underlay keeps overlay links alive as link endpoints change their attachments in the underlay.

There can be several instances of mobility in composed networks, at different levels and for different purposes. Do all of these implementations of mobility work together, or can they interfere with one another? Fortunately, in [24], it is proved that mobility mechanisms are indeed compositional, so that the presence of multiple implementations of mobility, in the same or interacting networks, does not interfere with each other's correct operation. This is a theorem about composed instances of our domain model and a first original contribution to the theory of networking.

4.3.3 Cloud Computing

A third example is that composition of networks is necessary for the virtualization of resources in cloud computing. Clouds often use several layers of virtualization to implement functions such as *service chaining, isolation,* and *quality-of-service (QoS) guarantees* for their tenants. At the same time, clouds must manage shared resources dynamically and effectively.

Consider the virtual link between C and D in Fig. 8. Very likely it is implemented in a cloud, where the owner of the enterprise VPN is called a *tenant*. This link in a cloud is depicted in Fig. 9. This link is implemented in the tenant's own (unshared, isolated) service network. The service network does *service chaining*, which means

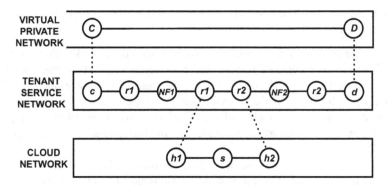

Fig. 9 Composition in a cloud. Layered networks provide special services, security, and quality-of-service guarantees, as well as simple transport

routing the tenant's messages through *network functions* such as *NF1* and *NF2*. Network functions, sometimes called "middleboxes," are network elements such as firewalls, intrusion detectors, load balancers, caches, and transcoders.

In Fig. 9, *C, c, NF1, NF2, d,* and *D* are all software running on virtual machines. *r1* and *r2* are tenant-specific routing functions running in the hypervisor of virtualized machines. Because both these functions appear twice in the path, we know that *c* and *NF1* are on virtual machines hosted in the same virtualized machine, while *d* and *NF2* are also on the same machine. Links between virtual machines and hypervisor within the same machine are physical.

The two hypervisors also have interfaces (*h1* and *h2*) to the shared cloud network, which includes other switches such as *s* within a data center. A session in the cloud network implements a link in a tenant service network. The cloud provider may have service agreements with its tenants promising them a certain quality of service, e.g., minimum bandwidth, on each tenant link. These agreements are enforced in the multiplexing of tenant-specific sessions onto the links of the cloud network. The cloud network may be a local-area network such as an Ethernet or be implemented by one in the layer below.

The boundary between the VPN and tenant service network in Fig. 9 is an important trust boundary, even though both networks are specific to a tenant. This is because members of the VPN run software that may be supplied by the tenant, while all the software below the VPN belongs to the cloud provider.

5   How the Theory Can Contribute to Network Software

Expanding the Design Space   The possibility of disciplined composition greatly expands the design space for solving networking problems. It points the way to solutions that are too unusual to be discovered or considered with ad hoc approaches. In [23], we map out the design space for solving mobility problems and, in [24], show some previously undiscovered, efficient solutions to the problem of mobile-device users temporarily connected to a Wi-Fi network that is moving, for example, on a bus.

Software Templates In a hierarchy of layered virtual networks, every network is an instance of a network domain and thus needs software to implement the behavior sketched out in Sects. 3.2 and 4.2. Our theory of networking includes a generic algorithm for domain behavior that can be specialized for each domain. This specialization would not be difficult. Much of it would consist of defining data types and header formats, a process made easy by a domain-specific language such as P4 [2].

To a lesser extent, it may be possible to derive templates for the software of control planes. Control planes deal with diverse issues, from user requirements to resource allocation, security, and fault tolerance. This makes the software more diverse, although all control planes have a common target in the data states of their networks.

Efficiency and optimization are top priorities in networking. Software templates based on the domain model are easily optimized in simple ways, such as removing vestigial structures. (For example, in any case where the mapping between two structures is one-to-one, one of them can probably be omitted.) They can also serve as the foundation for defining more sophisticated optimizations, which can then be reused at many levels for many purposes, just as the templates are.

Compositional Reasoning

In today's networks, it is extremely difficult to get vital information about the messages traveling through the network. At the highest levels, this vital information includes the persistent identities of the source and destination, the nature of the communication (e.g., Web access *versus* real-time streaming), and the set of messages that should be logically grouped. At lower levels, this information includes how resource-allocation algorithms at different levels are interacting with each other on large groups of messages. This information is often disguised and transformed by many layers of complex network functionality implemented with ad hoc tables in network elements and ad hoc tags in packet formats. There is no easy way to understand what any of these tables and tags are for.

If stakeholders cannot understand what the traffic is, then they cannot know whether requirements are being satisfied. If stakeholders cannot understand the purpose of tables and tags, then they cannot understand whether the tables and tags are being populated or used correctly.

The study of many examples has shown that, when the examples are modeled compositionally, the ad hoc tables and tags are actually instances of the network state and header information presented in this chapter (spread out over multiple composed layers). Thus, the domain theory provides a clear context and purpose for this information and many consistency constraints among them[3] that can be used for verification.

---

[3] The topic of consistency constraints is not covered in this brief overview chapter.

The other benefit of the compositional framework is that it provides traceability of messages from top to bottom layers. Preliminary experiments have shown that this traceability can be exploited to prove theorems about security. For example, we can prove compositionally that all messages in a particular high-level grouping were transmitted along a particular low-level path, where the low-level path has security mechanisms built in. Traceability is also useful for fault diagnosis. For example, when messages are not reaching their high-level destinations as expected, traceability may help locate the misconfiguration problem at a lower level.

A further goal is to reason compositionally about performance and fault tolerance. These problems appear to have many dimensions and be much more difficult, but additional structure almost always makes a hard problem somewhat easier.

6 Conclusions

In the introduction, benefits of a well-designed formal domain theory were listed. Some of them are already exemplified by the theory of networking, and we hope that future research and development will fulfill more of these aspirations.

The scarcity of domain theories is due partly to the difficulty of working theory-building into the schedule, budget, and process of software-development projects. It is also due to the fact that the skills necessary for development (especially mastery of detail) are somewhat different from the skills best suited to model-building (especially extracting simplicity from complexity). It is also due to the lack of publicity for this approach and agenda.

Researchers in software engineering are in a position to help overcome all three obstacles. We are seeing this happen more and more, as researchers tie their work on programming and verification tools to concrete problems in specific domains. Researchers only need to take the extra step, which is to generalize and improve the domain models in terms of which these problems are stated. This will expand the technical challenges to be faced, but it will also magnify the potential benefits and satisfactions of the work.

Acknowledgment This chapter is based on the results of long-term collaborations with Michael Jackson and Jennifer Rexford.

References

1. Anderson, C.J., Foster, N., Guha, A., Jeannin, J.-B., Kozen, D., Schlesinger, C., Walker, D: Netkat: semantic foundations for networks. In: Proceedings of the ACM SIGPLAN-SIGACT Symposium on Principles of Programming Languages, ACM (2014)
2. Bosshart, P., Daly, D., Gibb, G., Izzard, M., McKeown, N., Rexford, J., Schlesinger, C., Talayco, D., Vahdat, A., Varghese, G., Walker, D: P4: programming protocol-independent packet processors. ACM SIGCOMM Comput. Commun. Rev. **44**(3), 88–95 (2014)

3. Clark, D.D.: The design philosophy of the DARPA Internet protocols. In: Proceedings of SIGCOMM. ACM, Portland (1988)
4. Clark, D.D., Wroclawski, J., Sollins, K.R., Braden, R.: Tussle in cyberspace: defining tomorrow's Internet. IEEE/ACM Trans. Networking **13**(3), 462–475 (2005)
5. Day, J.: Patterns in Network Architecture: A Return to Fundamentals. Prentice Hall, Upper Saddle River (2008)
6. Feldmann, A.: Internet clean-slate design: what and why? ACM SIGCOMM Comput. Commun. Rev. **37**(3), 59–64 (2007)
7. Griffin, T.G., Sobrinho, J.L.: Metarouting. In: Proceedings of SIGCOMM. ACM, New York (2005)
8. Handley, M.: Why the Internet only just works. BT Technol. J. **24**(3), 119–129 (2006)
9. ITU: Information Technology—Open Systems Interconnection—Basic Reference Model: The basic model. ITU-T Recommendation X.200 (1994)
10. Jackson, D: Software Abstractions: Logic, Language, and Analysis. MIT Press, Cambridge (2006/2012)
11. Jackson, M., Zave, P.: Deriving specifications from requirements: an example. In: Proceedings of the 17th International Conference on Software Engineering, pp. 15–24. ACM, New York (1995)
12. Kazemian, P., Varghese, G., McKeown, N.: Header space analysis: Static checking for networks. In: Proceedings of the 9th USENIX Conference on Networked Systems Design and Implementation (2012)
13. Kreutz, D., Ramos, F.M.V., Esteves Verissimo, P., Esteve Rothenberg, C., Azoldolmolky, S., Uhlig, S.: Software-defined networking: a comprehensive survey. Proc. IEEE **103**(1), 14–76 (2015)
14. Roscoe, T.: The end of Internet architecture. In: Proceedings of the 5th Workshop on Hot Topics in Networks (2006)
15. Spatscheck, O.: Layers of success. IEEE Internet Comput. **17**(1), 3–6 (2013)
16. Taylor, P.J., Griffin, T.G.: A model of configuration languages for routing protocols. In: Proceedings of the 2nd ACM/SIGCOMM Workshop on Programmable Routers for Extensible Services of Tomorrow (PRESTO), SIGCOMM (2009)
17. Xie, G., Zhan, J., Maltz, D.A., Zhang, H., Greenberg, A., Hjalmtysson, G., Rexford, J.: On static reachability analysis of IP networks. In: Proceedings of IEEE Infocom, IEEE (2005)
18. Zave, P.: Bridging the research-industry gap: The case for domain modeling. In: Proceedings of the 37th International Conference on Software Engineering/Workshop on Software Engineering Research and Industrial Practice, IEEE (2015)
19. Zave, P.: A theory of networks: in the beginning. In: Dependable Software Systems Engineering. NATO Science for Peace and Security Series - D: Information and Communication Security, vol. 40, pp. 288–303 (2015). https://doi.org/10.3233/978-1-61499-495-4-288
20. Zave, P: Theories of everything. In: Proceedings of the 38th International Conference on Software Engineering, IEEE (2016)
21. Zave, P., Jackson, M.: Four dark corners of requirements engineering. ACM Trans. Softw. Eng. Methodol. **6**(1), 1–30 (1997)
22. Zave, P., Rexford, J.: The geomorphic view of networking: a network model and its uses. In: Proceedings of the 7th Middleware for Next Generation Internet Computing Workshop. ACM Digital Library (2012)
23. Zave, P., Rexford, J.: The design space of network mobility. In: Bonaventure, O., Haddadi, H. (eds.) Recent Advances in Networking. ACM SIGCOMM. ACM, New York (2013)
24. Zave, P., Rexford, J.: Compositional network mobility. In: Cohen, E., Rybalchenko, A. (eds.) Proceedings of the 5th Working Conference on Verified Software: Theories, Tools, and Experiments. Lecture Notes in Computer Science, vol. 8164, pp. 68–87. Springer, Cham (2014)

On Language Interfaces

Thomas Degueule, Benoit Combemale, and Jean-Marc Jézéquel

Abstract Complex systems are developed by teams of experts from multiple domains, who can be liberated from becoming programming experts through domain-specific languages (DSLs). The implementation of the different concerns of DSLs (including syntaxes and semantics) is now well established and supported by various language workbenches. However, the various services associated to a DSL (e.g., editors, model checkers, debuggers, or composition operators) are still directly based on its implementation. Moreover, while most of the services crosscut the different DSL concerns, they only require specific information on each. Consequently, this prevents the reuse of services among related DSLs and increases the complexity of service implementation. Leveraging the time-honored concept of *interface* in software engineering, we discuss the benefits of *language interfaces* in the context of software language engineering. In particular, we elaborate on particular usages that address current challenges in language development.

1 Introduction

As far back as 1972, Edsger W. Dijkstra said in his ACM Turing Lecture:

> Another lesson we should have learned from the recent past is that the development of 'richer' or 'more powerful' programming languages was a mistake in the sense that these baroque monstrosities, these conglomerations of idiosyncrasies, are really unmanageable, both mechanically and mentally.
> I see a great future for very systematic and very modest programming languages.

This quote is often cited by proponents of domain-specific languages (DSLs), which are indeed modest languages specifically designed for a single purpose.

T. Degueule
INRIA/IRISA, Rennes, France
e-mail: thomas.degueule@inria.fr

B. Combemale • J.-M. Jézéquel (✉)
IRISA, University of Rennes 1, Rennes, France
e-mail: benoit.combemale@irisa.fr; jean-marc.jezequel@irisa.fr

© Springer International Publishing AG 2017
M. Mazzara, B. Meyer (eds.), *Present and Ulterior Software Engineering*,
https://doi.org/10.1007/978-3-319-67425-4_5

Until now, however, the vision of building large systems with the help of a set of DSLs, each caring for a specific aspect of the system, did not really turn into reality. Two main reasons why it has always been hard to work with DSLs are:

1. Weaving together the various aspects of a system expressed in different DSLs is still mostly ad hoc and artisanal [20]. However, recent approaches such as the GEMOC initiative [8] have made significant progress towards that goal.
2. A DSL needs specific tool support: editors, parsers, checkers, interpreters, compilers, analyzers, refactoring tools, etc. All of this software is subject to standard software engineering issues: successive versions, simultaneous variants, and quality control (with, e.g., tests). While general-purpose languages used by millions of people can justify a high level of investment on building these supporting tools, the return on investment is more problematic for DSL used by definition by a much smaller number of people.

Regarding the second issue, the implementation of the different concerns of DSLs (including syntaxes and semantics) is now well established and supported by various language workbenches. However, the various services associated to a DSL (e.g., editors, model checkers, debuggers, or composition operators) are still directly based on its implementation. Consequently, as the implementation of a DSL evolves, all services must be updated to target the new implementation. It is also not possible to reuse services for different yet similar DSLs that target the same domain of application (e.g., two variants of state machine DSLs developed by different companies, or two versions of the same DSL). Moreover, most services require information that is scattered in the different concerns that compose a DSL, expressed in various and usually complex formalisms. Overall, the lack of abstraction mechanisms on top of DSL implementations complexifies the definition of services and hampers their reuse.

In this chapter, we reflect on the uses and benefits of interfaces in programming and software engineering (Sect. 2). We then study how the concept of interface can be adapted to software language engineering to improve the current practice of language development. Specifically, we show how the concept of *language interface* can help to address various challenges that arise from current language development practices (Sect. 3). Finally, we conclude in Sect. 4.

2   Interfaces in Programming and Software Engineering

The time-honored concept of interface has been studied since the early days of computer science in many areas of programming and software engineering. Despite variability in their exact realization, interfaces invariably rely on common fundamental concepts and provide similar benefits. Historically, the notion of interface is intrinsically linked to the need for *abstraction*, one of the fundamental concepts of computer science. As stated by Parnas et al., "an abstraction is a concept that can have more than one possible realization" and "by solving a problem in terms of the abstraction one can solve many problems at once" [30]. One can *refer* to an abstraction, leaving out the details of a concrete realization and the details that differ from one realization to another [22]. Originally, in programming, the key idea was to encapsulate the parts of a program that are more prone to change into so-called modules and to design a more stable *interface* around these change-prone parts. This concept, known as *information hiding*, eliminates hardwired dependencies between change-prone regions, thereby protecting other modules of the program from unexpected evolution [29].

As different realizations may be used in place of the same abstraction, interfaces also foster reuse: one module can substitute another one in a given context provided that they realize the same interface, as expected by a *client*. The choice of a concrete module is transparent from the point of view of the client of the interface. Because interfaces expose only a portion or an aspect of a realization, leaving out some details, the nature of an interface is highly dependent on the nature of the concrete realization it abstracts. Following the evolution of programming paradigms, authors have thus defined various kinds of interfaces for various concrete realizations: modules (*module interfaces* in Modula-2 [37]), packages (*package specifications* in Ada [19]), objects (*protocols* in Smalltalk [16]), or components in Component-Based Software Engineering (CBSE) [18], to name a few.

The expressiveness in which one can specify an interface for a given kind of realization also varies: interfaces over classes in standard Java merely consist of a set of method signatures, while languages supporting design-by-contract enable the expression of behavioral specifications, e.g., in the form of pre- and post-conditions on those signatures [26]. The expressiveness of contracts themselves ranges from purely syntactical levels to extra-functional (e.g., quality of service) levels [1]. Interfaces are also closely linked to the notion of *data type* in programming languages [4]. Types abstract over the concrete values or objects manipulated by a program along its execution. Type systems use these types to check their compatibility, reduce the possibilities of bugs, and foster reuse and genericity through polymorphism and substitutability [5].

While in programming languages the realizations hidden behind a given kind of interface are most often homogeneous, this is usually not the case in CBSE. As an illustration, component models enable communication between components written in different programming languages and deployed on heterogeneous platforms [31]. In such a case, interfaces abstract away from implementation technologies to enable interoperability between heterogeneous environments. The associated run-time model is most of the time unaware of the functional aspect of components and uses generic interfaces to manage their life cycle (e.g., deploying or reloading a component). Most component models also provide the notion of required interface as a means to make explicit the dependencies between components and to reason about how different components interact together and must be composed.

In summary, interfaces are used in many ways and vary according to the purpose they serve. While "interfaces as types" mainly target the safe reuse and substitutability of modules and objects in different contexts and focus on functional aspects, the interfaces used in CBSE allow components to be independently developed and validated, and focus on extra-functional aspects. From these observations, we explore in the next section possible applications of the concept of interfaces at the language level, to improve the current practice of software language development.

3   Language Interfaces for Software Language Engineering

"Software languages are software too" [13] and, consequently, they inherit all the complexity of software development in terms of maintenance, evolution, user experience, etc. Not only do languages require traditional software development skills, but they also require specialized knowledge for conducting the development of complex artifacts such as grammars, metamodels, interpreters, or type systems. The need for proper tools and methods in the development of software languages recently led to the emergence of the software language engineering (SLE) research field which is defined as "the application of systematic, disciplined, and measurable approaches to the development, use, deployment, and maintenance of software languages" [23]. While the notions presented in this chapter are applicable to both general-purpose and domain-specific languages (DSLs), we put particular emphasis on the specificities of DSLs, which are small languages targeted to a particular domain of application.

In the SLE community, new DSLs are usually developed using a language workbench, a "one-stop shop" for the definition of languages and their environments [34]. The notion of language workbench originates from the seminal work of Martin Fowler [14]. The main intent of language workbenches is to provide a unified environment to assist both language designers and users in, respectively, creating new DSLs and using them. Modern language workbenches typically offer a set of metalanguages that language designers use to express each of the implementation concerns of a DSL, along with tools and methods for manipulating their specifications. Examples of modern language workbenches are manifold: Xtext [12], Monticore [24], and Spoofax [21]—to name just a few.

One of the current trends in SLE is to consider more and more languages as first-class entities that can be extended, composed, and manipulated as a whole. However, to the best of our knowledge, there exists no previous work dealing with the explicitation of *language interfaces*, that is, interfaces *at the language level*, explicitly separated from language implementations, that provide the appropriate abstraction to ease the manipulation of languages as first-class entities. To motivate the need for language interfaces, we explore in this section some of the current challenges faced in SLE and highlight how they match the challenges that have been addressed with the use of interfaces in programming and software engineering.

3.1 Ingredients of a Domain-Specific Language

To clarify what language interfaces abstract over, we must first understand what languages are made of. Domain-specific languages are typically defined by their abstract syntax, concrete syntax(es), and semantics. Various approaches may be employed to specify each of those, usually using dedicated metalanguages provided by language workbenches [34]. The abstract syntax specifies the domain concepts and their relations defined by a metamodel or a grammar—the latter also defining the concrete syntax. This choice often depends on the language designer's background and culture. Examples of metalanguages for specifying the abstract syntax of a DSL include MOF [27] and SDF [17]. The semantics of a DSL can be defined using various approaches including axiomatic semantics, denotational semantics, operational semantics, and their variants [28]. Concrete syntaxes are usually specified as a mapping from the abstract syntax to textual or graphical representations, e.g., through the definition of a projectional editor [35]. DSLs usually benefit from dedicated environments that assist language users in the creation, analysis, and management of models and programs throughout their lifetime. Typically, these environments embed dedicated services such as code and documentation generators, checkers, editors, or debuggers.

Overall, the ingredients composing a language are manifold and usually complex to manipulate. Because there is no universally accepted way of implementing a language, it is difficult to directly relate languages created using different language workbenches. Moreover, the slightest variation in the syntax or semantics of a language leads to a conceptually new implementation, and all the artifacts referring to it (e.g., services) must be updated. Leveraging the concept of information hiding, the definition of explicit language interfaces on top of language implementations can help to abstract away from the change-prone implementation and switch the focus to a more stable and purpose-oriented view of languages. As we shall see in the next sections, such interfaces would ease the definition and reuse of services, the composition of languages, and the engineering of language families.

3.2 Easing the Definition and Reuse of Services

The development of services (e.g., code and documentation generators, static analyses) is an essential part of the development of software languages. Defining a new service requires to gather the appropriate information, which is often scattered in the various constituents of given language (abstract syntax, concrete syntax, semantics), in different formalisms. Naturally, the information to be extracted varies according to the *purpose* of the service. Some services, such as simple static analyses, only require access to a subset of the syntax specification of a language. More complex services may require to aggregate information from different sources. Additionally, services may be defined both at the language specification level (e.g., analysis of the completeness of a formal semantics specification) and at the instance level (e.g., dead code elimination for programs written in a particular language).

Rather than searching for the right information in the various constituents of a language, one can first design a language interface that aggregates the appropriate information in an easily manipulable form for a specific purpose. Using the appropriate interfaces eases the cognitive effort and abbreviates the definition of services. Moreover, since different languages can match the same interface, the services written on an interface can be applied to all matching languages.

One recent illustration in the programming community is the work of Brown et al., who use micro-grammars to ease the definition of static analysis tools for different programming languages [3]. Micro-grammars are partial grammars that abstract over the full-blown specification of a language using *wildcards*. Wildcards are nonterminals used to ignore parts of a language implementation. The authors show that various languages (C++, Java, JavaScript, etc.) can match the same micro-grammars and that static analysis tools written on micro-grammars are easier to develop and can be reused or adapted to new languages with little effort.

The modeling community has also shown interest in such interfaces, as illustrated by the notions of model types [32] and concepts [10]. Model types and concepts are both structural interfaces that specify a set of requirements over a metamodel—the standard way to define the abstract syntax of a language in the modeling community. A service, e.g., implemented as a model transformation, can be made generic by expressing its parameter in terms of a model type or concept, and any metamodel matching the model type or concept can benefit from this service. The duality of model types and concepts highlights the fact that there exist many ways to realize a given kind of interface. Model types are akin to subtype polymorphism, while concepts are closer to parametric polymorphism, but, overall, they are complementary and provide similar benefits. In addition, model types have also been used as unified interfaces that aggregate information from both the abstract syntax (the metamodel concepts) and the semantics (the transition steps of the operational semantics) of a language [11].

Some generic services do not even require any information on the syntax or semantics of a language. A generic debugger, for instance, only requires the ability to start, pause, or inspect the execution of a model or program [2]. This common set of operations can be captured in a generic interface, and any language implementing it can benefit from debugging facilities.

3.3 *Facing the Multiplication of DSLs*

In the last decade, the development of Model-Driven Engineering (MDE) and the advances in language workbenches have strengthened the proliferation of domain-specific languages (DSLs). MDE advocates the use of DSLs to address each concern separately in the development of complex systems with appropriate abstractions and tools [15]. As a result, the development of modern software-intensive systems often involves the use of multiple models expressed in different DSLs to capture different system aspects [8]. This trend is very similar to what was proposed by Ward in his early work on language-oriented programming [36]. Even in traditional software development, multiple languages are often used to describe different aspects of the system of interest. Java projects, for instance, typically consist of Java source files, XML files describing the structure of modules and the deployment scenarios, Gradle build files expressed in Groovy, scripts, etc.

When multiple languages are used, the need for relating "sentences" that describe the same underlying system in different languages arises. In this context, models are seldom manipulated independently: checking a given property on a system, for instance, requires to gather information that is scattered in various models written by various stakeholders in various languages. In addition, the set of languages used to describe a given system is likely to change over time. A new, more expressive language can replace an existing one. New languages may be added, merged, or split. While language workbenches support for engineering isolated languages is becoming more and more mature, there is still little support for relating concepts expressed in different DSLs together. The necessity of coordinated use of languages used in the development of a given system has recently been recognized [6, 8]. One promising approach is to leverage language interfaces to expose the appropriate information that allows to relate concepts from one language to the other [7]. The type systems of two languages, for instance, may be related through the appropriate interface that would expose their respective type definitions to allow their integration. Overall, the challenges that must be tackled are very similar to the ones that were faced a few decades ago with the use of modules in software development.

The coordinated use of DSLs engineered with different language workbenches is even more challenging. Indeed, there is no abstraction mechanism, at the language level, that allows to abstract from the concrete implementation techniques of a language workbench, e.g., a particular metalanguage for defining the abstract syntax or a particular implementation technique for the semantics. The use of interfaces and connectors has been thoroughly studied in the context of component-based software engineering to alleviate the problem of technological space compatibility. Explicitly separating the implementation of a language from its interface can help to break the barriers between language workbenches if a common agreement on technology-agnostic interfaces is found.

3.4 Enabling Language Composition

Good practices from the component-based software engineering community can also be relevant in the context of software language engineering. The idea of building reusable and independently validated language components to ease the definition of new languages has already been studied by several authors. A language component, such as a simple action language or a for-loop construct, can be defined and thoroughly validated independently and then reused as such in other languages that encompass the expression of actions or for-loops. In the same way languages are defined, the definition of such component encompasses both the definition of its abstract syntax, concrete syntax, and semantics. This leads to what is known as compositional language engineering: the ability to design new languages as assemblies of existing language components, thus lowering the development costs [24]. The actual realization of the composition may be done statically, i.e., the different modules are merged together to produce a new language specification with its associated implementation, or dynamically, i.e., the modules are kept separated but communicate to provide the composed behavior.

In this context, language interfaces serve as a support for the definition of provided and required interfaces of each component that are later used to reason about the composition of several language components and the correctness of the assembly. Interfaces are used to detect whether the constructs of different language components are in conflict, without having to dive into their intrinsic implementation. Language interfaces are also the concrete mean for several language components to communicate with each other at runtime. For instance, when two executable languages are composed together, their interpreter must also be coordinated. Language interfaces provide the appropriate information for relating together the two interpreters, for example, through a delegation pattern.

3.5   Engineering Language Families

A language family is a set of languages that share meaningful commonalities but differ on some aspects. Finite-state machine languages, for instance, are all used to model some form of computation but expose syntactic variation points (e.g., nested states, orthogonal regions) and semantic variation points (e.g., inner or outer transition priority) [9]. Altogether, these different variants form a family of finite-state machine languages. Similarly, when a language evolves, the subsequent versions form a set of variants, which raises the question of backward and forward compatibility between them. Recently, different approaches have been proposed for automating the generation of such language variants based on earlier work from the software product line engineering community [25, 33].

In the presence of a language family, language designers must be given the possibility to reuse as much as possible the environment and services (e.g., editors, generators, checkers) from one variant to the other. Naturally, the opportunities of reuse must be framed, as not all services are compatible with all variants. Language interfaces can be employed to reason about the commonalities of various language variants and the applicability of a given service or environment. Model types [32], for instance, can be used to assign a type to a language and specify the safe substitutions between different artifacts based on typing relations. The definition of those types is precisely an example of language interface. Types abstract over the details of the implementation of different variants and are used to reason about substitutability between them. In this context, language interfaces can support the definition of common abstractions that are shared by all or a subset of the members of a family, abstracting from the details that vary from one member of the family to the other.

4 Conclusion

The lack of abstraction in the manipulation of DSL implementations complexifies the definition of services (e.g., debuggers, generators, composition operators) and hampers their reuse. In this chapter, we have reflected on the use of interfaces in programming and software engineering and advocated the definition of interfaces at the language level for software language engineering. We have shown that various challenges of today's language development can be addressed through the use of language interfaces. The concept of language interface presented here is purposely abstract. We leave to future work the definition of concrete interfaces for specific purposes.

References

1. Beugnard, A., Jézéquel, J.M., Plouzeau, N., Watkins, D.: Making components contract aware. Computer **32**(7), 38–45 (1999)
2. Bousse, E., Corley, J., Combemale, B., Gray, J., Baudry, B.: Supporting efficient and advanced omniscient debugging for xdsmls. In: Proceedings of the 2015 ACM SIGPLAN International Conference on Software Language Engineering, ACM, pp. 137–148 (2015)
3. Brown, F., Nötzli, A., Engler, D.: How to build static checking systems using orders of magnitude less code. In: Proceedings of the Twenty-First International Conference on Architectural Support for Programming Languages and Operating Systems, ACM, pp. 143–157 (2016)
4. Canning, P.S., Cook, W.R., Hill, W.L., Olthoff, W.G.: Interfaces for strongly-typed object-oriented programming. In: ACM SigPlan Notices, ACM, vol. 24, pp. 457–467 (1989)
5. Cardelli. L., Wegner, P.: On understanding types, data abstraction, and polymorphism. ACM Comput. Surv. **17**(4), 471–523 (1985)
6. Cheng, B.H., Combemale, B., France, R.B., Jézéquel, J.M., Rumpe, B.: On the globalization of domain-specific languages. In: Globalizing Domain-Specific Languages, pp. 1–6. Springer, Cham (2015)
7. Clark, T., den Brand, M., Combemale, B., Rumpe, B.: Conceptual model of the globalization for domain-specific languages. In: Globalizing Domain-Specific Languages, pp. 7–20. Springer, Cham (2015)
8. Combemale, B., Deantoni, J., Baudry, B., France, R.B., Jézéquel, J.M., Gray, J.: Globalizing modeling languages. Computer **47**(6), 68–71 (2014)
9. Crane, M.L., Dingel, J.: UML vs. classical vs. Rhapsody statecharts: not all models are created equal. In: Model Driven Engineering Languages and Systems, pp. 97–112. Springer, Berlin (2005)

10. Cuadrado, J.S., Guerra, E., De Lara, J.: Generic model transformations: write once, reuse everywhere. In: Theory and Practice of Model Transformations, pp. 62–77. Springer, Berlin (2011)

11. Degueule, T., Combemale, B., Blouin, A., Barais, O., Jézéquel, J.M.: Melange: a meta-language for modular and reusable development of DSLs. In: Proceedings of the 2015 ACM SIGPLAN International Conference on Software Language Engineering, ACM, pp. 25–36 (2015)

12. Eysholdt, M., Behrens, H.: Xtext: implement your language faster than the quick and dirty way. In: Proceedings of the ACM International Conference Companion on Object Oriented Programming Systems Languages and Applications Companion, ACM, pp. 307–309 (2010)

13. Favre, J.M.: Languages evolve too! changing the software time scale. In: Eighth International Workshop on Principles of Software Evolution (IWPSE'05), IEEE, pp. 33–42 (2005)

14. Fowler, M.: Language workbenches: the killer-app for domain specific languages (2005). https://www.martinfowler.com/articles/languageWorkbench.html

15. France, R., Rumpe, B.: Model-driven development of complex software: a research roadmap. In: 2007 Future of Software Engineering, pp. 37–54. IEEE Computer Society, Los Alamitos (2007)

16. Goldberg, A., Robson, D.: Smalltalk-80: The Language and Its Implementation. Addison-Wesley, Reading (1983)

17. Heering, J., Hendriks, P.R.H., Klint, P., Rekers, J.: The syntax definition formalism SDF—reference manual. ACM SIGPLAN Not. **24**(11), 43–75 (1989)

18. Heineman, G.T., Councill, W.T.: Component-Based Software Engineering. Putting the Pieces Together, p. 5. Addison-Westley, London (2001)

19. Ichbiah, J.D., Firth, R., Hilfinger, P.N., Roubine, O., Woodger, M., Barnes, J.G., Abrial, J.R., Gailly, J.L., Heliard, J.C., Ledgard, H.F., et al.: Reference Manual for the ADA Programming Language. Castle House, Washington (1983)

20. Jézéquel, J.M.: Model driven design and aspect weaving. J. Softw. Syst. Model. **7**(2), 209–218 (2008). https://hal.inria.fr/inria-00468233

21. Kats, L.C., Visser, E.: The spoofax language workbench: rules for declarative specification of languages and IDEs, vol. 45, ACM (2010)

22. Kell, S.: In search of types. In: Proceedings of the 2014 ACM International Symposium on New Ideas, New Paradigms, and Reflections on Programming and Software, ACM, pp. 227–241 (2014)

23. Kleppe, A.: Software Language Engineering: Creating Domain-Specific Languages Using Metamodels. Pearson Education, Estados Unido (2008)

24. Krahn, H., Rumpe, B., Völkel, S.: Monticore: a framework for compositional development of domain specific languages. Int. J. Softw. Tools Technol. Trans. **12**(5), 353–372 (2010)

25. Kühn, T., Cazzola, W., Olivares, D.M.: Choosy and picky: configuration of language product lines. In: Proceedings of the 19th International Conference on Software Product Line, ACM, pp. 71–80 (2015)

26. Meyer, B.: Applying 'design by contract'. Computer **25**(10), 40–51 (1992)

27. MOF, 2.0 core final adopted specification (2004). http://www.omg.org/spec/MOF/2.0/

28. Mosses, P.D.: The varieties of programming language semantics and their uses. In: Perspectives of System Informatics, pp. 165–190. Springer, Berlin (2001)

29. Parnas, D.L.: On the criteria to be used in decomposing systems into modules. Commun. ACM **15**(12), 1053–1058 (1972)

30. Parnas, D.L., Shore, J.E., Weiss, D.: Abstract types defined as classes of variables. ACM SIGPLAN Not. **11**(SI), 149–154 (1976)

31. Siegel, J.: CORBA 3 Fundamentals and Programming, vol. 2. Wiley, New York (2000)

32. Steel, J., Jézéquel, J.M.: On model typing. SoSyM **6**(4), 401–413 (2007)

33. Vacchi, E., Cazzola, W., Pillay, S., Combemale, B.: Variability support in domain-specific language development. In: Software Language Engineering, pp. 76–95. Springer, Berlin (2013)

34. Visser, E., Wachsmuth, G., Tolmach, A., Neron, P., Vergu, V., Passalaqua, A., Konat, G.: A language designer's workbench: a one-stop-shop for implementation and verification of language designs. In: Proceedings of SPLASH, pp. 95–111 (2014)

35. Voelter, M., Kolb, B., Warmer, J.: Projecting a modular future. IEEE Softw. **32**(5) (2014)
36. Ward, M.P.: Language-oriented programming. Software-Concepts Tools **15**(4), 147–161 (1994)
37. Wirth, N.: Modula: a language for modular multiprogramming. Softw. Pract. Exp. **7**(1), 1–35 (1977)

Moldable Tools for Object-Oriented Development

Andrei Chiş, Tudor Gîrba, Juraj Kubelka, Oscar Nierstrasz,
Stefan Reichhart, and Aliaksei Syrel

Abstract Object-oriented programming aims to facilitate navigation between domain concepts and the code that addresses those domains by enabling developers to directly model those domain concepts in the code. To make informed decisions, developers then formulate detailed and domain-specific questions about their systems in terms of domain concepts and use tools to explore available information and answer those questions. Development tools however focus mainly on object-oriented idioms and do not expose or exploit domain concepts constructed on top of object-oriented programming idioms. Analysis tools are typically not tightly integrated with development tools. This has a negative effect on program comprehension, increasing the effort and the time for obtaining answers.

To improve program comprehension, we propose to better integrate domain concepts and program comprehension tools into the development environment through *moldable tools*. Moldable tools are development tools that are aware of the current development context and support inexpensive creation of domain-specific extensions. We elaborate on the idea of moldable tools and show how to apply moldable tools to support object-oriented programming. Through practical examples, we show how developers can embed domain concepts into their development tools.

1 Introduction

Software applications express domain models from the real world as executable models (i.e., programs) within the design space of a language. Program comprehension then requires developers to navigate between domain concepts and the code

A. Chiş • O. Nierstrasz (✉) • A. Syrel
Software Composition Group, University of Bern, Bern, Switzerland

T. Gîrba
feenk gmbh, Looserstrasse 14, 3084 Wabern, Switzerland

J. Kubelka
PLEIAD Laboratory, University of Chile, Santiago Chile

S. Reichhart
University of Bern, Bern, Switzerland

© Springer International Publishing AG 2017
M. Mazzara, B. Meyer (eds.), *Present and Ulterior Software Engineering*,
https://doi.org/10.1007/978-3-319-67425-4_6

that addresses those domains. In the procedural paradigm, domain concepts are spread throughout procedures and data structures, potentially making the recovery of domain concepts a tedious activity.

Object-oriented programming promised to address this problem by providing developers with better mechanisms to construct domain abstractions. Instead of using procedures and data structures, developers can model a domain in terms of objects and object interactions (i.e., message sends). Objects model domain entities and encapsulate the state of those entities together with their behavior. Despite its early promise to solve the problem of navigating between domain concepts and their implementations, developers still struggle to navigate between these worlds in object-oriented applications. Furthermore, a wide range of analyses and program comprehension tools have been proposed to aid developers in performing this navigation. Nevertheless, in spite of an ever-increasing number of program comprehension tools, these tools are still heavily underused [33]. Instead, developers mostly rely on code reading as their main technique to understand and reason about their software systems. On the one hand, code reading is highly contextual: code indicates the exact behavior of an application. On the other hand, code reading does not scale: reading one hundred thousand lines of code takes more than one man-month of work.

In previous work, we explored this aspect and argued that the lack of proper environments for developing object-oriented applications is an important factor that makes navigation between code and domain concepts an ever-present problem [26]. Two issues with current development environments that contribute to the problem are that they disconnect development and program comprehension tools and they focus on generic rather than tailored development tools.

Disconnected Comprehension Separating program comprehension and development tools creates a gap between program comprehension and development, two activities that are deeply intertwined. For example, integrated development environments (IDEs) are an essential category of tools for crafting software. They aim to support software development and evolution by providing a uniform interface for all the tools needed by programmers during the software development process (e.g., code editors, compilers, testing tools, debuggers). Nevertheless, current mainstream IDEs are centered around the code editor and promote code reading as a default way of reasoning about software. Developers can use additional program comprehension tools alongside the IDE or install them as "plug-ins"; however, with few exceptions, these new tools do not integrate with existing development tools from the IDE. This requires developers to manually bridge these two types of tools.

Generic Tools While addressing a specific task, many development tools do not make any assumptions about the actual *contexts* in which they are used. They handle in the same way different software systems, even if those systems model different domains. This means that they are unaware of application or technical domain concepts. For example, a generic object inspector handles all run-time objects in an identical manner. On the one hand, this increases its range of applicability; on the other hand, it makes it less suited to handle detailed and domain-specific questions. Generic tools force developers to refine their domain-specific questions into low-level generic ones and mentally piece together information from various sources [34]. This offers limited support for informed decision making, leading to an inefficient and error-prone effort during software development and maintenance as developers cannot directly reason in terms of domain abstractions.

Both these issues can be improved by moving from building software using generic and disconnected tools for development and program comprehension to building software using development tools tailored to specific application domains. This has the potential to reduce code reading and improve program comprehension as tailored tools can directly provide developers with domain-specific information that they would otherwise need to find during development by reading and exploring source code or using external tools. For this vision to be possible, we propose *moldable development*, an approach for crafting software in which developers continuously adapt and evolve their development tools (e.g., code editors, debuggers, run-time inspectors, search tools) to take into account their actual application domains. To support this activity, we introduced *moldable tools* [8]. A moldable tool is a development tool that is aware of the current development context and supports inexpensive creation of domain-specific extensions using a plug-in approach.

Here we extend our previous work on this topic in which we introduced the idea of moldable development [10]. We expand on the idea of moldable development and explore its applicability to the development of object-oriented applications. Our overall contributions are:

- Discussing challenges for making moldable development practical and proposing an approach to achieve this based on moldable tools
- Discussing mechanisms for designing moldable tools using object-oriented concepts
- Exemplifying the creation of moldable tools for object-oriented programming using real world examples of tools and extensions

2 Moldable Development, Moldable Tools

The key idea behind *moldable development* is that developers adapt their development tools to be aware of the domain behind the applications under development. This scenario requires both that developers are willing to extend their tools and that development tools are designed to capture domain abstractions.

2.1 Towards Moldable Development

In the context of model-driven engineering, Whittle et al. [45] observed that to improve the way they evolve their applications, many developers build their own tools or introduce major adaptations to off-the-shelf tools, even if this requires significant effort. When studying homegrown tools in a large software company, Smith et al. [36] also observed that developers take the initiative to build tools to solve problems they face, especially when their organization's culture promotes this activity. This shows that developers do build tools to help themselves in their work. Nevertheless, adapting development tools to specific domains is not a widespread activity.

To increase its adoption, we argue that moldable development has to have as its foundation development tools designed so they can inexpensively accommodate domain abstractions. As an analogy, in the past testing was perceived as difficult since writing tests was a costly activity. With the introduction of SUnit [3] and other testing frameworks, the cost of creating and managing tests decreased significantly, thus encouraging the adoption of testing as an integral activity of the software development process.

We propose to accommodate domain abstractions in development tools by designing such tools so that they:

- Support inexpensive creation of domain-specific extensions
- Enable developers to easily organize and locate suitable extensions

Both aspects are needed: even if extensions are easy to build, difficulty in finding and deciding when an extension is applicable discourages developers from embracing the activity of adapting their development tools.

2.2   Moldable Tools in a Nutshell

When looking at software development and evolution, we observe that developers use a range of widely accepted tools like code editors, compilers, debuggers, profilers, search tools, version control tools, etc. Each tool embodies a design that addresses a certain activity in the software development cycle. To support inexpensive adaptations in these tools while preserving their intended design, we proposed *moldable tools* [8]. Moldable tools enable domain-specific adaptations through development tools modeled as frameworks that support domain-specific plug-ins (i.e., extensions). To facilitate discovery of extensions, moldable tools allow extension creators to specify together with their extensions an *activation predicate* that captures the development contexts in which that extension is applicable.

By "development context," we intend both the current application domain and previous interactions with the domain. Related work on exploring how developers comprehend software showed that interactions with a domain play an important role in improving program comprehension [19, 20, 25]. For example, interaction recording tools, like Mylar [17] and DFlow [23], provide support for automatically building a context as developers interact with development tools and filtering visible information based on that context [24].

Moldable tools enable developers to "mold" domain abstractions into the tools by creating domain-specific extensions expressing those abstractions, and attaching to those extensions activation predicates that capture the development contexts in which extensions are applicable. Then, at run time, a moldable tool automatically selects extensions appropriate for the current development context. Hence, developers do not have to manually infer when an extension is applicable.

3   Designing Moldable Tools

In this section, we discuss how to design moldable tools using object-oriented concepts.

3.1   Enabling Domain-Specific Extensions

The first step towards enabling moldable tools consists in choosing how to support domain-specific extensions. To propose a solution, we start from the observation of Pawson that while objects should encapsulate all relevant behavior, in the context of business systems, many domain objects are behaviorally weak [32]: much of the functionality is contained in *"controller"* objects that sit on top of model objects, which in turn provide only basic functionality. To address this issue, Pawson proposed *naked objects* as a way to move towards behaviorally complete objects where business actions are encapsulated in the actual domain objects [29].

The same situation arises when development tools need to provide custom behavior for objects modeling different domain entities. One approach consists in designing development tools that encapsulate themselves the logic for how to handle domain-specific objects. On the one hand, this decouples the business logic from the logic used to handle objects in development tools. On the other hand, this decoupling can result in duplicated functionality between tools or the need to evolve objects and tools separately as requirements change.

Following the idea of Pawson, a second approach consists in making objects responsible for deciding how they are handled in development tools. This allows different tools to reuse the same behavior and enables a closer evolution of objects and tools. A common use for this approach is to visualize objects: in most object-oriented languages, it is the responsibility of an object to represent itself in a textual way (e.g., *toString* in Java, *printString* in Smalltalk). Development tools that need a textual representation of an object just ask that object for its representation.

Moldable tools for object-oriented programming build on the second approach and enable customization by asking objects to indicate the desired behavior (Fig. 1). Hence, objects become behaviorally complete with regard to development tools, not only to the business domain. This reduces the distance between tools and objects

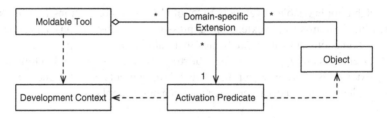

Fig. 1 Moldable tools for object-oriented programming: extensions are attached to objects; activation predicates detect applicable extensions

and encourages application developers to evolve domain-specific tools together with their objects.

3.2 Specifying Domain-Specific Extensions

The second step in applying moldable tools to object-oriented programming consists in choosing how to specify custom extensions. Researchers have explored multiple alternatives for tool building, including, but not limited to, internal DSLs, external DSLs, logical programming languages, and formal specification languages. Following the same line of reasoning as in the previous section, object-oriented programming already provides a modeling language in terms of objects. Therefore, we propose that moldable tools for object-oriented programming enable the creation of domain-specific extensions using the underlying object-oriented language of the target application. Hence, developers do not have to learn a new programming language to be able to extend their tools. Moldable tools then model domain-specific extensions as objects. Developers specify an extension by creating and configuring an object using its API (i.e., an internal DSL). This solution favors a design in which developers create custom extensions by using snippets of code to configure those extensions. Related work focusing on similar ideas indicates that this reduces the cost of creating extensions [27, 39].

3.3 Context-Aware Extensions

Domain objects provide one axis for selecting domain-specific extensions: a moldable tool selects extensions for those domain objects currently investigated in that tool. Each extension object has an activation predicate specified when the extension is created. Activation predicates can determine if the extension is applicable or not based on the state of its associated object, the state of other accessible objects from the domain model, and previous developer interactions with the domain.

For example, in many graphical frameworks, graphical widgets are organized in a tree structure. Extensions for navigating or searching through the structure of sub-widgets can have an activation predicate checking if the widget has sub-widgets. Also when navigating from a parent widget to one of its sub-widgets, an inspection tool can show a view highlighting how the sub-widget is positioned within the parent widget. This view can only be made available when navigating from a parent widget to a sub-widget and not when inspecting a sub-widget in isolation.

4 Addressing Domain-Specific Problems

To investigate the usefulness and practical applicability of moldable tools in the context of object-oriented programming, we focus on three activities performed by developers during software development and maintenance, namely: (1) reasoning about run-time objects, (2) searching for domain-specific artifacts, and (3) reasoning about run-time behavior. We selected them as they are pervasive, challenging, and time-consuming activities during software development and maintenance. For each one, we explore how relevant problems can be addressed if developers are able to adapt their development tools to their own contextual needs.[1]

4.1 Reasoning About Run-Time Objects

Since objects only exist at run time, understanding object-oriented applications entails the comprehension of run-time objects. Object inspectors are an essential category of tools that allow developers to perform this task. An object inspector provides a simple interface that allows a user to inspect all the fields of an arbitrary object and recursively dive into those fields. To better understand what software developers expect from an object inspector, we performed an exploratory investigation. We identified the need for object inspectors that support different high-level ways to visualize and explore objects, depending on both the object and the current developer need [9]. Traditional object inspectors however favor a generic view that focuses on the low-level details of the state of single objects. While universally applicable, these approaches do not take into account the varying needs of developers that could benefit from tailored views and exploration possibilities.

To address this issue, we introduced the *Moldable Inspector*. The essence of the Moldable Inspector is that it enables developers to answer high-level, domain-

---

[1]The three covered tools are developed as part of the GToolkit project. More information about the tools can be found at http://gtoolkit.org. All these tools are also part of the Pharo IDE (http://pharo. org).

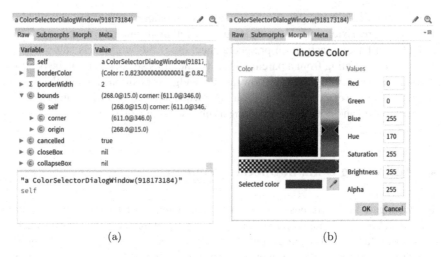

(a)   (b)

Fig. 2 Using the Moldable Inspector to explore a widget object: (**a**) The *Raw* view shows the implementation of the widget. (**b**) The *Morph* view shows the visual representation of the widget

specific questions by allowing them to adapt (i.e., mold) the whole inspection process to suit their immediate needs. To make this possible, instead of a single generic view for an object, the Moldable Inspector allows each object to represent itself using multiple domain-specific views, facilitates the creation and integration of new views, and uses the current development context to automatically find, at run time, appropriate views [9]. To validate this approach, we created until now, together with the developers of several frameworks and libraries, more than 131 custom views for 84 types of objects belonging to 15 applications, requiring, on average, 9.2 lines of code per view.

For example, depending on her task, a developer working with a widget object may need to explore both the internal structure of that object (e.g., state) and its visual representation. We can address this by attaching to a widget object two views that directly show its state (Fig. 2a) and its visual representation (Fig. 2b). Now the Moldable Inspector can show both these views when a developer interacts with a widget object (Fig. 2).

4.2 Searching for Domain-Specific Abstractions

Software systems consist of many different kinds of domain-specific and interrelated software entities. Search tools aim to support developers in rapidly identifying or locating those entities of interest. Nevertheless, our analysis of mainstream IDEs and current exploration approaches shows that they support searching through generic search tools that are not well integrated into the IDE. In particular, current IDEs decouple tools for searching through code, external data, and run-time objects. This impedes search tasks over domain-specific entities as considerable effort is wasted by developers to recover and link data and concepts relevant to their application domains. Furthermore, this limits discoverability as one has to be aware of a domain abstraction in order to know what to look for.

For example, a web server can rely on XML files to model descriptors for web services and store security roles (e.g., admin, employer, manager). In an IDE providing just generic searches, locating a server's descriptor requires developers to use a file search. Finding what web services use a given security role requires then multiple textual searches through XML files. A domain-specific search tool can enable developers to directly locate descriptor files and search through the web services that use a given security role.

To address this problem, we propose that search tools directly enable developers to discover and search through domain concepts. We have proposed the *Moldable Spotter*, a search tool that allows objects to express multiple custom searches through the data that they encapsulate [38]. Moldable Spotter further enables developers to easily create custom searches for their domain objects and automatically discover searches for domain object as they are interacting with those objects. We also show that by taking into account generic searches through code, we can provide a single entry point for embedding search support within IDEs. Based on 124 search extensions for 41 types of objects currently present in the Pharo IDE, the average cost of creating a custom search extension is, just like in the case of the Moldable Inspector, 9.2 lines of code.

4.3 *Moldable Debugger*

Debuggers are essential for reasoning about the run-time behavior of software systems. Traditional debuggers rely on generic mechanisms to introspect and interact with the running systems (i.e., stack-based operations, line breakpoints), while developers reason about and formulate domain-specific questions using concepts and abstractions from their application domains. This mismatch creates an abstraction gap between the debugging needs and the debugging support leading to an inefficient and error-prone debugging effort, as developers need to recover concrete domain concepts using generic mechanisms.

To address this abstraction gap, we have proposed the *Moldable Debugger*, a framework for developing domain-specific debuggers [7]. The Moldable Debugger is adapted to a domain by creating and combining domain-specific debugging operations with domain-specific debugging views, and adapts itself to a domain by selecting, at run time, appropriate debugging operations and views. A domain-specific debugger is attached to an object modeling the run-time stack. Hence, stack objects are allowed to express how developers interact with them. We created, on top of a template of 1500 lines of code, six custom debuggers requiring between 60 and 600 lines of code. The cost is greater than in the previous two tools as the scope of an extension is larger (i.e., it affects the entire debugger).

5   Adapting Tools to Domain Objects

To exemplify how moldable development can be applied during the development of an application to adapt moldable tools to specific domains, we present two concrete use cases. We selected two frameworks, the Opal compiler (Sect. 5.1) and PetitParser (Sect. 5.2), given that their developers or maintainers created custom extensions for moldable tools as they evolved them. These are also two mature frameworks that cover two different domains, each with its own challenges. Opal requires users to reason about and navigate between multiple representations of source code (e.g., source code, AST nodes, IR, bytecode). If an error occurs during parsing, PetitParser users need to understand how the parsing consumed the input and locate that part of the input (or the grammar) that caused the error; often the method where the error is raised is different from the method where the parser actually made an erroneous decision.

5.1   Opal Compiler

Opal[2] is a compiler infrastructure focusing on customizability that has been part of Pharo[3] since the Pharo 3 release (May 2014).[4] Initially, Opal was developed using the standard development tools of Pharo.

Developing a new compiler is a challenging activity involving multiple steps: parsing the source code into an abstract syntax tree (AST), translating the AST into an intermediate representation (IR), translating the IR into bytecode, and optimizing at the level of the AST, IR, and bytecode. Types of bugs specific to compilers and encountered during development were those related to incorrect generation of bytecode from IR and wrong mappings between source code or AST nodes and bytecode caused by compiler optimizations.[5] Debugging such bugs just by reading code or using generic debuggers and inspectors is a difficult endeavor as the information needed (i.e., the mapping between source code, AST nodes, IR, and bytecode) is highly domain specific and not present in these tools by default.

---

[2]http://www.smalltalkhub.com/#!/~Pharo/Opal.

[3]http://pharo.org.

[4]http://pharo.org/news/pharo-3.0-released.

[5]pharo.fogbugz.com/f/cases/14606,   pharo.fogbugz.com/f/cases/12887,   pharo.fogbugz.com/f/cases/13260, pharo.fogbugz.com/f/cases/15174.

To make this information explicit, we extended several development tools together with the Opal team while Opal itself was being developed.

Moldable Inspector Extensions In Pharo methods are represented as instances of the CompiledMethod class, and they hold the corresponding bytecode. Inspecting the attributes of a CompiledMethod object in a generic object inspector only gives details about the format in which bytecode is represented (header, literals, trailer) and shows the numeric code of the bytecode. For example, in Fig. 3a, we

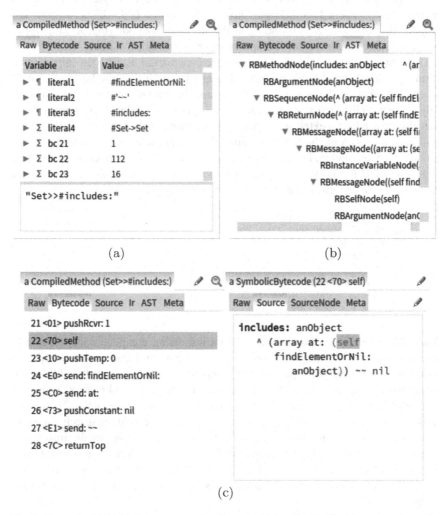

(a)   (b)

(c)

Fig. 3 Using the Moldable Inspector to visualize compiled code: (**a**) The *Raw* view shows the implementation of the object. (**b**) The *AST* view shows the AST from which the code was compiled. (**c**) The mapping between bytecode and source code can be explored by selecting bytecodes in the *Bytecode* view

can see that the inspected method has 4 literals, and the second bytecode stored at index 22 has the code 112. This provides no insight into what the actual bytecode does, the source code of the method, the AST, the IR, or the mapping between these representations. To address these issues, we gradually attached several custom views to CompiledMethod and SymbolicBytecode objects: a human-friendly representation of the bytecode (Fig. 3c, left side), the source code of the method, the AST (Fig. 3b), and the IR. Using the bytecode view, the developer can see that the bytecode at index 22 corresponds to pushing self[6] onto the top of the stack. To show the mapping between bytecode and source code, whenever a bytecode is selected a new view is opened to the right showing the source code of the method and highlighting the code corresponding to the selected bytecode (Fig. 3c); this relies on the ability of the inspector to display two or more objects at once.

Extensions to the Moldable Inspector are constructed using code snippets that return graphical objects. We provide an internal domain-specific language (i.e., a fluent API) that can be used to directly instantiate several types of basic graphical objects such as list, tree, table, text, and code; any other graphical object from Pharo can also be used in an extension. Extensions are then attached to objects by defining within their classes methods that construct those extensions and marking them with a predefined annotation. For example, lines 1–8 show the code for creating the AST view displayed in Fig. 3b. Using this approach, development tools can ask objects for their graphical representations.

```
1      gtInspectorASTIn: aComposite
2      <gtInspectorPresentationOrder: 35>
3      aComposite tree
4        rootsExpanded;
5        title: 'AST';
6        display: [ :aMethod | aMethod ast ];
7        children: [ :aNode | aNode children ];
8          format: [ :aNode | aNode gtPrintString ]
```

Moldable Spotter Extensions Apart from inspecting compiled code, especially when compiling long methods, common tasks consist in locating certain types of bytecode instructions (e.g., pop, return), message sends (e.g., send: printString), or accesses to literal values (pushLit: Object). A generic tool to search through source code or object state does not provide this type of functionality. To support these tasks, we attached to CompiledMethod objects a custom search (lines 9–15) through the human-friendly representation of bytecode previously introduced. Creating extensions for Moldable Spotter follows the same principle as in the case of the Moldable Inspector; only a different API and annotation are used. As a result, development tools can also ask objects which domain-specific searches they support.

---

[6]self represents the object that received the current message; this in Java.

```
9   spotterForBytecodesFor: aStep
10    <spotterOrder: 15>
11    aStep listProcessor
12      title: 'Bytecode';
13      allCandidates: [ self symbolicBytecodes ];
14      itemName: #printString;
15      filter: GTFilterSubstrings
```

This extension supports all the aforementioned searches as well as others, such as looking for when a constant is pushed to the stack (Fig. 4a) or finding all instructions that access temporary variables (local variables and method parameters; Fig. 4b). After finding a bytecode, the developer can open it in the inspector or directly spawn the view showing the mapping to source code in the search tool (Fig. 4c).

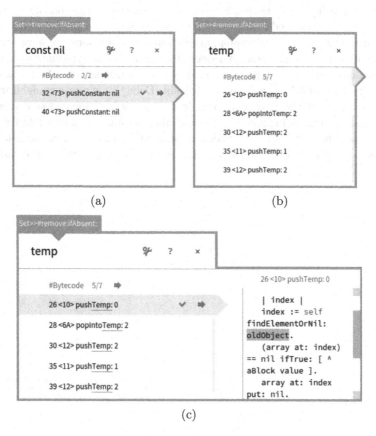

Fig. 4 Searching through bytecode using Moldable Spotter: (**a**) searching for accesses to nil; (**b**) searching for instructions accessing temporary variables; (**c**) when selecting a bytecode, the mapping with the source code is shown

Moldable Debugger Extensions One cannot easily use source-level debuggers to reason about bytecode. Debugging actions in these debuggers normally skip over multiple bytecode instructions. For example, stepping into a message send with multiple parameters skips over all *push* instructions that place the required parameters on the stack. The same issue arises when developing compiler plugins that alter the default bytecode generated for given instructions (e.g., slots can generate custom bytecode for reading and writing object attributes [42]).

As a use case illustrating this problem, consider a class that uses a boolean slot. A boolean slot occupies a single bit of a (hidden) integer slot that is shared by all classes of a single hierarchy. If multiple classes within the same hierarchy introduce boolean slots, they will be efficiently mapped to this shared integer slot. This is however transparent to users who can use the attribute normally (in the method from Fig. 5a isHorizontal is defined as a boolean slot). Although transparency is useful when using slots, when debugging the actual slot objects, one needs access to the bytecode generated by the slot. This is not available in a generic debugger.

To facilitate bytecode debugging, in this and other situations, we developed an extension to the Pharo debugger that gives direct access to the bytecode and supports stepping through the execution of a program one bytecode instruction at a time. Creating a custom debugger from the Moldable Debugger is not as straightforward as in the case of the previous two tools. In the current implementation, extensions are created by subclassing predefined classes for customizing the user interface and logic of the debugger. For this extension, we needed to create a custom user interface by subclassing DebuggingView and a custom debugging action by creating a

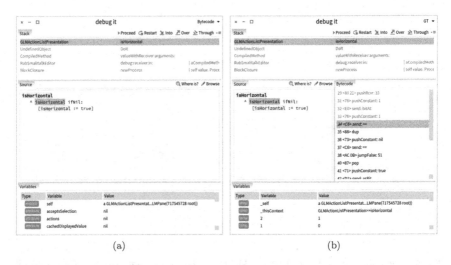

(a)   (b)

Fig. 5 Debugging a boolean slot: (**a**) Developers cannot use a generic debugger to access the bytecode generated by the boolean slot. (**b**) An extension to the debugger shows the bytecode of the current method and supports stepping at the bytecode level; this gives direct access to bytecode generated by the boolean slot

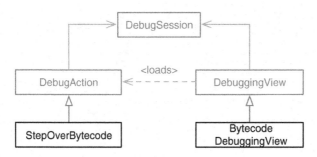

Fig. 6 The structure of a custom extension for debugging bytecode. The extension provides a custom user interface and a debugging action for stepping over bytecode instructions. DebugSession provides basic functionality for supporting debugging and does not need to be extended

subclass of DebugAction (Fig. 6). The total cost of this extension is 200 lines of code. The same debugging scenario is shown in Fig. 5b using this extension. Now the developer can see and interact with the actual bytecode generated by the boolean slot.

5.2   PetitParser

PetitParser is a framework for creating parsers, written in Pharo, that makes it easy to dynamically reuse, compose, transform, and extend grammars [30]. A parser is created by specifying a set of grammar productions in one or more dedicated classes. To specify a grammar production, a developer needs to (1) create a method that constructs and returns a parser object for that part of the grammar and (2) define in the same class an attribute having the same name as the method.

PetitParser is a framework meant to be used by many developers, other than just its creators, to specify parsers. As the specification of a parser consists of classes and methods, parsers can be developed only using generic development tools, like code editors and debuggers. This raises some problems: the specification of the parser is used to instantiate at run time a *tree* of primitive parsers (e.g., choice, sequence, negation); this tree is then used to parse the input. Developers debugging a parser need to manually link primitive parsers to the grammar production that generated them. Adding, renaming, and removing productions require working with both a method and an attribute having the same name.

To ease the creation of parsers, the PetitParser developers initially built a custom code editor that allowed the creators of a parser to just work in terms of grammar productions instead of attributes and methods. This only covers part of the problem. To further improve the development and debugging of parsers, we created, together

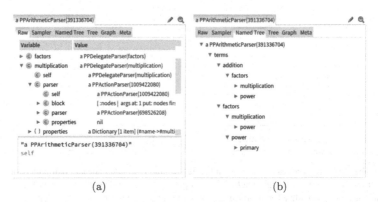

(a)   (b)

Fig. 7 Using Moldable Inspector to visualize a parser object: (**a**) The *Raw* view shows how the parser is implemented. (**b**) The *Named tree* view shows only the structure of the grammar using a tree view

with the current maintainers of PetitParser, extensions for several other development tools. These development tools were built after the release of PetitParser, during its maintenance cycles.

Moldable Inspector Extensions As previously mentioned, actual parsers are instantiated as objects. Viewing these objects using a generic object inspector only shows how they are implemented and gives no immediate insight into the structure of the parser. For example, in Fig. 7a, showing the attributes of a parser for arithmetic expressions, the structure of the underlying grammar is not clearly evident from the inspected objects. To provide this information directly in the inspector, we attached to parser objects views that show the tree structure of the grammar using other representations. Figure 7b contains a view showing the structure of the grammar using a tree list.

Moldable Spotter Extensions Parser classes can contain also other methods and attributes apart from those used to model grammar productions. When using a method or attribute search to look for a production, these extra methods and attributes can return unrelated results. To avoid this, we extended the search infrastructure from Pharo by attaching to classes representing parsers, searches that work at the level of grammar productions (lines 16–27). As this search should only be applicable to classes modeling parsers, an activation predicate checks this explicitly (lines 26–27). Attaching this search to an object requires an environment to also model code entities (e.g., methods, classes, annotations) as objects. Figure 8 illustrates a scenario in which a developer searches in a parser for Java code for productions that contain the word "hex."

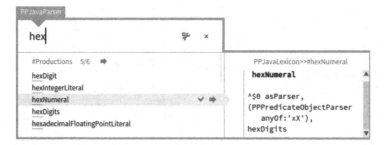

Fig. 8 Using Moldable Spotter to search for productions containing the word "hex" in a parser for Java code

```
16    spotterForProductionsFor: aStep
17    <spotterOrder: 10>
18    aStep listProcessor
19      title: 'Productions';
20      allCandidates: [ :aParserClass |
21        aParserClass productionMethods ];
22      candidatesLimit: 5;
23      itemName: [:aProduction | aProduction selector];
24      filter: GTFilterRegex;
25      itemFilterName: [:aProduction| aProduction selector];
26      when: [ :aParserClass |
27        aParserClass inheritsFrom: PPCompositeParser ];
```

Moldable Debugger Extensions Debugging a parser using a generic debugger also poses challenges. On the one hand, generic debuggers only provide debugging actions and breakpoints at the level of source code instructions (e.g., step over instruction). On the other hand, they neither display the source code of grammar productions nor do they provide easy access to the input being parsed. This is evident in Fig. 9a, which shows a debugger opened on a PetitParser parser for Java code: the stack trace shows only parseOn: methods belonging to primitive parsers; to determine how much parsing has advanced, one needs to use the inspector to locate the input stream and the current position in the stream and then manually determine the character corresponding to that position in the stream.

To overcome these issues, other tools for working with parser generators provide dedicated domain-specific debuggers (e.g., ANTLR Studio, an IDE for the ANTLR [1]). In the case of PetitParser, we developed a custom extension for the debugger (Fig. 9b). First, this extension offers debugging operations at the level of the input (e.g., setting a breakpoint when a certain part of the input is parsed) and of the grammar (e.g., setting a breakpoint when a grammar production is exercised). Second, it provides a dedicated user interface for the debugger that highlights the grammar productions in the stack, shows information about a selected grammar production (e.g., source code, visual representation), shows the input being parsed, and highlights how much parsing has advanced in the input stream. Third, this

Fig. 9 Debugging a parser: (**a**) A generic debugger has no knowledge about parsing and cannot provide information and debugging actions related to the parser grammar or the input stream. (**b**) An extension for the Moldable Debugger showing parsing related information and providing debugging actions at the level of the grammar and the input stream

extension is applicable only when the run-time stack contains a call to a parser object. Creating this extension followed the same approach as for Opal. We further reused several custom extensions already provided by PetitParser, like a graph view showing the structure of a grammar production (Fig. 9b), and functions for computing the first and follow sets for a grammar production. In the end, this debugger required 600 lines of code (excluding the aforementioned extensions). It required more code than for the Opal debugger mainly because it provides more custom debugging actions.

6   Discussion

In this section, we discuss the applicability of moldable tools for other application domains and IDEs and emphasize future challenges.

6.1   Applicability

Section 5 presented two examples showing how to improve reasoning about applications by extending development tools. The chosen examples cover a compiler and a parser. We also applied moldable development to other types of applications from various domains: Glamour [6] (a framework for creating data browsers based on ideas from reactive programming), FileSystem [5] (a library for interacting with file systems), MessageTally (a library for profiling code), Metacello [5] (a package management system), etc. Developers of other libraries related to Pharo also started to create and provide extensions, especially for the Moldable Inspector and Moldable Spotter, as part of their releases. Examples of such libraries include Zinc,[7] a framework to deal with the HTTP networking protocol, and Roassal [2], an engine for scripting visualizations.

Section 5 also shows that by adapting development tools, comprehension can be improved from multiple perspectives: in the case of Opal, improving tools helps the developers of Opal to better reason about their system and fix bugs faster; in the case of PetitParser, improving tools does not directly help the developers of PetitParser itself but rather developers that use it to create and evolve parsers.

For the two examples presented here, as well as in other situations, as discussed in Sect. 3.1, developers do build tools to help them in their activities. Nevertheless, in many cases, these tools are being built and used outside of the main development environment. Through moldable development, we aim to encourage developers to adapt development tools to their application domains.

6.2 Moldable Tools in Other Languages

Currently, we are using Pharo as an environment for exploring tool building; however, there is no conceptual limitation that ties moldable development and moldable tools to Pharo. Indeed, Pharo offers expressive introspection capabilities that simplify the creation of tools like debuggers and inspectors. Nevertheless, we anticipate no technical limitations that would make it difficult to provide moldable tools for other programming languages and IDEs. Mainstream IDEs, like Eclipse or IntelliJ, provide multiple customization possibilities (e.g., plug-ins, extensions and extension points, perspectives) that can be leveraged to support moldable tools.

One key requirement for moldable tools is that the application entities that the tools are to become aware of must be modeled as run-time entities. Such entities include not only domain objects but also other software entities such as packages, classes, methods, annotations, files, source code, bug reports, documentation, examples, repositories, configurations, etc. Custom extensions can then be uniformly attached to domain objects, source code entities, and external resources. Pharo provides direct support for this requirement as all code entities are modeled as objects. Modern IDEs also provide an object-oriented model for representing code and project-related data (e.g., JDT in Eclipse). Hence, we do not view this aspect as a limitation in porting moldable tools to other IDEs.

---

[7]http://zn.stfx.eu.

6.3 Future Challenges

Until now we have explored moldable development and moldable tools by investigating how to incorporate domain concepts into several development tools. Nevertheless, these development tools do not live in isolation but are integrated in an IDE. IDEs contain many other tools that need to interact and work together. As more tools offer the possibility to create extensions, these extensions will need to be synchronized. This raises the need for a *moldable environment* that can adapt tools to domains in a uniform and consistent way.

Moldable development is based on developers evolving moldable tools during the software development process. Hence, as the application evolves, changes in the application can lead to changes in the created tools. This requires a more thorough methodology to keep domain-specific extensions synchronized with the actual applications.

7 Related Work

There exists a large body of research that investigates tool building with the aim of improving program comprehension. In this section, we restrict our focus to approaches that target development tools. We classify and discuss related work in this area based on how development tools are created.

7.1 Automatic Generation of Tools

Early examples of adapting development tools consisted in generating projectional editors based on language specifications (e.g., ALOE [22], The Synthesizer Generator [31]). They were followed by more complex development environments targeting a wider range of language specifications. The Gandalf project, for example, extends ALOE with support for version control with the goal of *"permitting environment designers to generate families of software development environments semiautomatically without excessive cost"* [14]. Meta-Environment [18] generates editors and TIDE [41] generates debuggers for languages defined using ASF+SDF. LISA [15] generates a wide range of tools for visualizing program structures and animating algorithms for languages defined using attribute grammars. The Xtext[8] project from Eclipse can generate complex text editors, while MPS[9] provides dedicated projectional editors. These examples cover only a small part of solutions

---

[8]http://www.eclipse.org/Xtext/.
[9]https://www.jetbrains.com/mps/.

that generate development tools from a formal language specification. Unlike them, moldable development through moldable tools focuses on the creation of tools where a language specification is missing. The example discussed here is object-oriented programming where applications can be expressed in terms of an object model that does not require a formal specification.

Based on these solutions for building development tools, several approaches were proposed that focus on improving program comprehension by improving the language. An example is *Generic Tools, Specific Languages* [43]. This approach focuses on first creating domain-specific languages for an application and then adapting development tools to those languages. An instance of this approach is *mbeddr*,[10] an extensible set of integrated languages for embedded software development that supports tools like projectional editors [44] and debuggers [28]. Another example is *Helvetia*, an extensible system for embedding language extensions into an existing host language. Helvetia enables extensions of the syntax of the host language in a way that does not break development tools like debuggers and compilers. These approaches aim to improve program comprehension by first improving the programming language and then adapting development tools to those languages. Moldable development focuses on improving the tool rather than the language.

7.2 Manual Creation of Tools

Apart from automatic generation of development tools, a different direction consists in enabling developers to manually adapt development tools or create new ones. This direction is at the core of several live environments that blur the line between applications and IDEs. For example, within a Smalltalk-80 [13] system, there is no distinction between the application code and the code of the system (e.g., compiler, parser, IDE, development tools). Developers can access and modify the code of the IDE in the same way as they do their own application code. In Self [40], a prototype-based system, developers evolve an application by only interacting with objects. Furthermore, Self draws no system-level distinction between using an application and changing or programming it [35]. Both actions are performed by manipulating the state and behavior of objects. Nevertheless, while these environments do not directly support cheap and context-aware tooling, they provide a solid foundation for tool building.

Modern IDEs, like Eclipse, IntelliJ, or Visual Studio, enable developers to customize their functionality using plug-ins; however, developing a new plug-in is not a straightforward activity. Through moldable tools, we aim to significantly reduce this effort. Several text editors, like Emacs and Vi, also have a direct focus on extensibility. Vi is built on the idea of command composability: it provides a set of

---

[10]http://mbeddr.com/.

minimalist commands that can be composed together [16]. Emacs allows developers to cleanly add new commands [37]; unlike Vi, it targets more monolithic commands for special-purpose activities.

To support the creation of sophisticated development tools, OmniBrowser [4] relies on an explicit meta-model. To create a new development tool, developers need to specify the domain model of the tool as a graph and indicate the navigation paths through the graph. JQuery [11] supports the creation of various code browsers through a declarative language that extracts and groups code-related data. A visual approach to building development tools is proposed by Taeumel et al. [39]: developers create new tools by visually combining concise scripts that extract, transform, and display data. They show that their solution supports the creation of tools like code editors and debuggers with a low effort. Like moldable tools, these approaches also promote the creation of custom development tools to improve comprehension.

8　Conclusions

We have investigated the issue of navigating between domain concepts and their implementation in the context of object-oriented applications. We argued that one solution for improving this navigation and also reducing the reliance on code reading during program comprehension is to enable developers to evolve their development tools alongside their applications. We proposed *moldable development* as an approach for achieving this goal. Through two use cases, we showed that navigation can be improved if developers persevere in customizing their tools.

Moldable development poses a predicament as developers have to invest time and effort in customizing development tools. Nevertheless, this can make considerable economical sense, if the cost of adapting tools outweighs the effort required to reason about applications using generic and disconnected tools. To reduce the cost of creating domain-specific extensions, we proposed *moldable tools*. Moldable tools enable customization through fine-grained plug-ins, and they support developers in locating applicable plug-ins. We showed that by attaching extensions to objects and providing internal APIs for the creation of extensions, the cost can be low even when adapting complex tools.

Moldable development also raises challenges related to how to enable meaningful customizations in development tools, how to better incorporate them in the software development cycle, and how to design complete integrated development environments that support this approach, rather than just individual tools. We are actively pursuing these challenges by analyzing how developers use and extend moldable tools [21] and exploring how to better incorporate visualizations into tools [12].

Acknowledgments We gratefully acknowledge the financial support of the Swiss National Science Foundation for the project "Agile Software Analysis" (SNSF project No. 200020-162352, Jan 1, 2016—Dec 30, 2018). We also thank Claudio Corrodi for his corrections and improvements to the final draft.

References

1. ANTLR – debugging ANTLR grammars using ANTLR Studio: http://www.placidsystems.com/articles/article-debugging/usingdebugger.htm. Accessed 3 June 2016
2. Araya, V.P., Bergel, A., Cassou, D., Ducasse, S., Laval, J.: Agile visualization with Roassal. In: Deep Into Pharo, pp. 209–239. Square Bracket Associates, Bern (2013)
3. Beck, K.: Simple Smalltalk testing: with patterns. www.xprogramming.com/testfram.htm
4. Bergel, A., Ducasse, S., Putney, C., Wuyts, R.: Creating sophisticated development tools with OmniBrowser. J. Comput. Lang. Syst. Struct. **34**(2–3), 109–129 (2008)
5. Bouraqadi, N., Fabresse, L., Bergel, A., Cassou, D., Ducasse, S., Laval, J.: Sockets. In: Deep Into Pharo, p. 21. Square Bracket Associates, Bern (2013)
6. Bunge, P.: Scripting browsers with Glamour. Master's thesis, University of Bern, April 2009
7. Chiş, A., Denker, M., Gîrba, T., Nierstrasz, O.: Practical domain-specific debuggers using the moldable debugger framework. Comput. Lang. Syst. Struct. **44**(Part A), 89–113 (2015). Special issue on the 6th and 7th International Conference on Software Language Engineering (SLE 2013 and SLE 2014)
8. Chiş, A., Gîrba, T., Nierstrasz, O.: Towards moldable development tools. In: Proceedings of the 6th Workshop on Evaluation and Usability of Programming Languages and Tools, PLATEAU '15, pp. 25–26. Association for Computing Machinery, New York (2015)
9. Chiş, A., Gîrba, T., Nierstrasz, O., Syrel, A.: The moldable inspector. In: Proceedings of the 2015 ACM International Symposium on New Ideas, New Paradigms, and Reflections on Programming and Software, Onward! 2015, pp. 44–60. Association for Computing Machinery, New York (2015)
10. Chiş, A., Gîrba, T., Kubelka, J., Nierstrasz, O., Reichhart, S., Syrel, A.: Exemplifying moldable development. In: Proceedings of the 1st Edition of the Programming Experience Workshop (PX 2016), pp. 33–42 (2016)
11. De Volder, K.: JQuery: a generic code browser with a declarative configuration language. In: Proceedings of the 8th International Conference on Practical Aspects of Declarative Languages, PADL'06, pp. 88–102. Springer, Berlin/Heidelberg (2006)
12. Gîrba, T., Chiş, A.: Pervasive software visualizations. In: Proceedings of 3rd IEEE Working Conference on Software Visualization, VISSOFT'15, pp. 1–5. IEEE, Piscataway, NJ (2015)
13. Goldberg, A.: Smalltalk 80: the Interactive Programming Environment. Addison Wesley, Reading, MA (1984)
14. Habermann, A.N., Notkin, D.: Gandalf: software development environments. IEEE Trans. Softw. Eng. **12**(12), 1117–1127 (1986)
15. Henriques, P.R., Pereira, M.J.V., Mernik, M., Lenic, M., Gray, J., Wu, H.: Automatic generation of language-based tools using the LISA system. IEE Proc. Softw. **152**(2), 54–69 (2005)
16. Joy, W.: An introduction to display editing with Vi. In: UNIX User's Manual Supplementary Documents. USENIX Association, Berkeley (1980)
17. Kersten, M., Murphy, G.C.: Mylar: a degree-of-interest model for IDEs. In: AOSD '05: Proceedings of the 4th International Conference on Aspect-Oriented Software Development, pp. 159–168. ACM Press, New York (2005)
18. Klint, P.: A meta-environment for generating programming environments. ACM Trans. Softw. Eng. Methodol. (TOSEM) **2**(2), 176–201 (1993)

19. Ko, A.J., Aung, H., Myers, B.A.: Eliciting design requirements for maintenance-oriented IDEs: a detailed study of corrective and perfective maintenance tasks. In: ICSE '05: Proceedings of the 27th International Conference on Software Engineering, pp. 125–135 (2005)

20. Ko, A., Myers, B., Coblenz, M., Aung, H.: An exploratory study of how developers seek, relate, and collect relevant information during software maintenance tasks. IEEE Trans. Softw. Eng. **32**(12), 971–987 (2006)

21. Kubelka, J., Bergel, A., Chiş, A., Gîrba, T., Reichhart, S., Robbes, R., Syrel, A.: On understanding how developers use the Spotter search tool. In: Proceedings of 3rd IEEE Working Conference on Software Visualization – New Ideas and Emerging Results, VISSOFT-NIER'15, pp. 145–149. IEEE, Piscataway, NJ (2015)

22. Medina-Mora, R.I.: Syntax-directed editing: towards integrated programming environments. Ph.D. thesis, Carnegie Mellon University (1982). AAI8215892

23. Minelli, R., Mocci, A., Lanza, M.: I know what you did last summer: an investigation of how developers spend their time. In: Proceedings of the 2015 IEEE 23rd International Conference on Program Comprehension, ICPC '15, pp. 25–35. IEEE Press, Piscataway, NJ (2015)

24. Minelli, R., Mocci, A., Robbes, R., Lanza, M.: Taming the IDE with fine-grained interaction data. In: Proceedings of ICPC 2016 (24th International Conference on Program Comprehension), pp. 1–10 (2016)

25. Murphy, G.C., Kersten, M., Robillard, M.P., Čubranić, D.: The emergent structure of development tasks. In: Proceedings of the 19th European Conference on Object-Oriented Programming, ECOOP'05, pp. 33–48. Springer, Berlin/Heidelberg (2005)

26. Nierstrasz, O.: The death of object-oriented programming. In: Stevens, P., Wasowski, A. (eds.) FASE 2016. Lecture Notes in Computer Science, vol. 9633, pp. 3–10. Springer, Berlin (2016)

27. Ousterhout, J.K.: Scripting: higher level programming for the 21st century. IEEE Comput. **31**(3), 23–30 (1998)

28. Pavletic, D., Voelter, M., Raza, S., Kolb, B., Kehrer, T.: Extensible debugger framework for extensible languages. In: de la Puente, J.A., Vardanega, T. (eds.) Reliable Software Technologies – Ada–Europe 2015. Lecture Notes in Computer Science, vol. 9111, pp. 33–49. Springer, Berlin (2015)

29. Pawson, R.: Naked objects. Ph.D. thesis, Trinity College, Dublin (2004)

30. Renggli, L., Ducasse, S., Gîrba, T., Nierstrasz, O.: Practical dynamic grammars for dynamic languages. In: 4th Workshop on Dynamic Languages and Applications (DYLA 2010), Malaga, pp. 1–4, June 2010

31. Reps, T., Teitelbaum, T.: The synthesizer generator. SIGSOFT Softw. Eng. Notes **9**(3), 42–48 (1984)

32. Riel, A.: Object-Oriented Design Heuristics. Addison Wesley, Boston (1996)

33. Roehm, T., Tiarks, R., Koschke, R., Maalej, W.: How do professional developers comprehend software? In: Proceedings of the 2012 International Conference on Software Engineering, ICSE 2012, pp. 255–265. IEEE Press, Piscataway, NJ (2012)

34. Sillito, J., Murphy, G.C., De Volder, K.: Asking and answering questions during a programming change task. IEEE Trans. Softw. Eng. **34**, 434–451 (2008)

35. Smith, R.B., Maloney, J., Ungar, D.: The Self-4.0 user interface: manifesting a system-wide vision of concreteness, uniformity, and flexibility. SIGPLAN Not. **30**(10), 47–60 (1995)

36. Smith, E.K., Bird, C., Zimmermann, T.: Build it yourself! Homegrown tools in a large software company. In: Proceedings of the 37th International Conference on Software Engineering. IEEE – Institute of Electrical and Electronics Engineers, Piscataway, NJ (2015)

37. Stallman, R.M.: Emacs the extensible, customizable self-documenting display editor. ACM SIGOA Newslett. **2**(1–2), 147–156 (1981)

38. Syrel, A., Chiş, A., Gîrba, T., Kubelka, J., Nierstrasz, O., Reichhart, S.: Spotter: towards a unified search interface in IDEs. In: Proceedings of the Companion Publication of the 2015 ACM SIGPLAN Conference on Systems, Programming, and Applications: Software for Humanity, SPLASH Companion 2015, pp. 54–55. Association for Computing Machinery, New York (2015)

39. Taeumel, M., Perscheid, M., Steinert, B., Lincke, J., Hirschfeld, R.: Interleaving of modification and use in data-driven tool development. In: Proceedings of the 2014 ACM International Symposium on New Ideas, New Paradigms, and Reflections on Programming and Software, Onward! 2014, pp. 185–200. Association for Computing Machinery, New York (2014)
40. Ungar, D., Smith, R.B.: Self: the power of simplicity. In: Proceedings OOPSLA '87, ACM SIGPLAN Notices, vol. 22, pp. 227–242 (1987)
41. van den Brand, M., Cornelissen, B., Olivier, P., Vinju, J.: TIDE: a generic debugging framework — tool demonstration —. Electron. Notes Theor. Comput. Sci. **141**(4), 161–165 (2005). Proceedings of the Fifth Workshop on Language Descriptions, Tools, and Applications (LDTA 2005) Language Descriptions, Tools, and Applications 2005
42. Verwaest, T., Bruni, C., Lungu, M., Nierstrasz, O.: Flexible object layouts: enabling lightweight language extensions by intercepting slot access. In: Proceedings of the 2011 ACM International Conference on Object Oriented Programming Systems Languages and Applications, OOPSLA '11, pp. 959–972. Association for Computing Machinery, New York (2011)
43. Voelter, M.: Generic tools, specific languages. Ph.D. thesis, Delft University of Technology (2014)
44. Voelter, M., Ratiu, D., Schaetz, B., Kolb, B.: Mbeddr: an extensible C-based programming language and IDE for embedded systems. In: Proceedings of the 3rd Annual Conference on Systems, Programming, and Applications: Software for Humanity, SPLASH '12, pp. 121–140. Association for Computing Machinery, New York (2012)
45. Whittle, J., Hutchinson, J., Rouncefield, M., Burden, H., Heldal, R.: Model-driven engineering languages and systems: 16th international conference, (MODELS 2013). In: Chapter Industrial Adoption of Model-Driven Engineering: Are the Tools Really the Problem?, pp. 1–17. Springer, Berlin/Heidelberg (2013)

The Changing Face of Model-Driven Engineering

Richard F. Paige, Athanasios Zolotas, and Dimitris Kolovos

Abstract Model-Driven Engineering has been studied and applied for many years, and it has evolved to a state where it has been used successfully in a variety of substantial projects. It is now at a state of maturity where there are potentially significant challenges to future adoption. In this chapter, we outline the state of practice in Model-Driven Engineering and point to two important future research directions: support for more flexible approaches to modelling and support for legacy models and modelling technologies.

1 Introduction

Model-Driven Engineering (MDE) is the principled application of structured, machine-processable *models* to the engineering of systems [1]. Models, constructed for a particular purpose, are expressed in modelling languages which are designed first and foremost to be processable by tools. This may be contrasted with modelling languages which are designed to have a sound (consistent, complete) mathematical semantics to enable reasoning [2]. The modelling languages that are used in MDE are generally (but not exclusively) defined using *metamodels*, which capture the *abstract syntax* and certain *static semantics* constraints associated with the language [3]. Both general-purpose languages (such as UML[1] or SysML[2]) and domain-specific languages have been successfully applied in a variety of MDE projects; there is compelling evidence that many successful applications have exploited domain-specific approaches [4].

When processing models with tools, engineers carry out a variety of important tasks, ranging from constructing and editing the models, to transforming models from one language into another, to comparing models. The set of *operations* that can

---

[1] http://www.omg.org/spec/UML/.

[2] http://www.omg.org/spec/SysML/.

R.F. Paige (✉) • A. Zolotas • D. Kolovos
University of York, York, UK
e-mail: richard.paige@york.ac.uk; thanos.zolotas@york.ac.uk; dimitris.kolovos@york.ac.uk

© Springer International Publishing AG 2017   103
M. Mazzara, B. Meyer (eds.), *Present and Ulterior Software Engineering*,
https://doi.org/10.1007/978-3-319-67425-4_7

be applied to models is generally referred to as *model management*, and powerful tools exist today to implement these operations (AMMA,[3] the former components of OAW[4] [now part of the Eclipse Modeling Project], Epsilon[5]).

In principle, MDE techniques and tools can be used to automate significant parts of a typical systems engineering life cycle: models of requirements, architecture, detailed design, implementation, tests and deployment policies can be expressed, and automated model management operations can be applied to support the transition from one phase of the life cycle to another. If tools such as ATL [5], Epsilon [6] or the Eclipse Modelling Framework (EMF) [7] are used, then it is even possible to *audit* and *validate* the model management workflows, as traceability information is generated as a side effect of executing operations. However, a fully automated process for systems engineering is neither possible in general, nor desirable, in part because many of the models that are used will require configuration and optimisation by domain experts, the fully automated process may not respect such optimisations, nor may it provide efficient and effective ways to support it.

By many measures, MDE is a success: we have powerful tools for supporting model management tasks and for creating purposeful models. We have evidence that MDE can improve productivity [4, 8]. We have techniques for connecting MDE tools and techniques with non-MDE tools and techniques (bridges of technical spaces, spreadsheets, XML, etc.). We have deployed MDE in real projects: different flavours of MDE are being used on a day-to-day basis in many organisations. We also have a better idea of where the "sweet spot" for use of MDE sits—where it is most efficient, effective and productive—that is, in automating repetitive, error-prone and pattern-based activities, such as code generation, refactoring or even automating the process of building graphical editors [9].

With any relatively mature and reasonably widely deployed approach to systems engineering comes challenges. Mature or maturing approaches to systems engineering must continue to evolve to take into account changes in the discipline and application domain, e.g. new standards for modelling or validation/certification, new tools and different capabilities on the part of engineers. As well as systems engineering approaches continue to be used, or even grow in use, there must be consideration of how to maintain the artefacts that are constructed; these artefacts have significant business value.

In this chapter, we attempt to give an overview of where we currently are with the state of practice of MDE. We then discuss two key challenges facing MDE going forward: the significant entry barrier to adoption of the state-of-the-art tools and techniques that exist today, and support for legacy MDE artefacts, both those created in the early days of MDE research and those that are being created today.

---

[3]https://wiki.eclipse.org/AMMA.

[4]http://www.openarchitectureware.org/.

[5]http://www.eclipse.org/epsilon.

2   The State of MDE Practice

In this section, we attempt to synthesise some of the state of practice of MDE: we outline a generic MDE process, highlight some of the key research foci over the last 10–15 years and then attempt to argue that by many measures, research and application of MDE is a relative success story in systems and software engineering.

2.1   A Quasi-Typical MDE Process

There are many engineering approaches that make use of MDE, and they all vary depending on the problem that is being solved and the engineering objectives that must be attained. A reasonably generic outline of an MDE process is as follows:

1. *Construct or select modelling languages.* These may be general-purpose languages (such as SysML) or domain-specific languages. Use of domain-specific languages may require the development of new infrastructure—so-called *meta-models*—to support the language. A tutorial on metamodelling [10] provides an introduction to standard terminology, process and tools (particularly for researchers more familiar with grammar-based tools).
2. *Build models* and validate the models using appropriate domain- and task-specific techniques, e.g. testing, proof and checking of well-formedness constraints.
3. *Persist models*, i.e. store them in a suitable repository that permits archiving, retrieval, versioning and querying.
4. *Manage models* to enable the engineering process. That is, use automated model management techniques to support engineering tasks, e.g. transformation from architecture models to high-level design models, generation of unit tests, performance analysis and simulation.

2.2   Research Themes in MDE

The focus of much research in MDE—particularly in the 2002–2009 period—was on model management (i.e. step 4 of the process above). This led to the development of a significant number of tools for model transformation (e.g. Epsilon, ATL, Eclipse QVTo), model validation (e.g. Eclipse OCL, EVL), model comparison (e.g. EMF Compare, ECL), model refactoring (e.g. Henshin, EWL) and model migration (e.g. COPE, Epsilon Flock). This focus on tools led to revisions of relevant MDE standards, particularly from the OMG, which in turn led to enhanced tool development, typically from the Eclipse community. From 2008 onwards, there was increased emphasis on applications of MDE, culminating in research on some of the success stories in MDE. More recently (e.g. starting in the 2011–2013 window), there has been substantial research on persistence frameworks for models, as the scale and scope of problems has changed, and requirements for persisting very large (more than ten million elements) models have increased.

2.3   The Success of MDE

By what measures do we judge MDE as a success? One has to be slightly careful in defining measures, because there are both academic and industrial notions of success. A typical academic measure might be in terms of the liveliness of the academic research field, e.g. the number of papers published, grants awarded, conferences or events focused on the topic. A typical industrial measure might be successful applications of MDE concepts, techniques or tools on real projects *and* with measurable improvements in productivity. Both academic and industry-focused measures for MDE paint a suggestive picture of significant activity and some significant success—but with reasons to be concerned:

- *Industry deployment.* There are now numerous successful stories of deployment of MDE in industry. The recent special issue of Science of Computer Programming[6] detailed a number of these, each describing different applications of MDE techniques and tools, from various domains (e.g. health care, web application development, critical systems). What is interesting about these different deployments is the diversity of model management—not every project exploited model-to-text or model-to-model transformation, for example—the significant benefits ascribed to modelling by itself, and the different maturity levels of the organisations involved.
- *Diversity of domain.* If diversity is an indication of a thriving industry, then MDE has to be considered a success. There have been successful deployments of MDE in many domains, including the chip industry [11], avionics systems [12], systems-of-systems/network-enabled capability [13], railway systems [14] and many more.
- *Productivity gains.* There is compelling evidence to suggest that productivity gains can be acquired across a range of different MDE activities [4, 15], in terms of promoting better understanding of problems, reuse of languages/domain models, automation of error-prone activities, etc.
- *Best practice guides.* Large organisations are developing best practice guides, describing appropriate ways and means to deploy MDE in their projects and activities. Arguably not all of these guides are as of yet mature, but they indicate an increasing maturity in terms of how organisations evaluate MDE technologies and languages and how they are managing their relationships with these technologies and language (e.g. in terms of participating in standards).

---

[6]http://www.di.univaq.it/page.php?page_id=22.

- *Successful companies.* There are a number of successful companies that provide MDE consulting and tools, including MetaCase,[7] Obeo[8] and itemis.[9] As well, there are successful practitioners who provide consulting on a commercial basis. There is a market for such expertise, and it does sell.
- *Education and training.* For a long time, there were few textbooks and courses that focused on MDE. Predominantly, there were textbooks that taught use of UML and how it could be applied in object-oriented design—or there were guides to Model-Driven Architecture [16]. Today, there are excellent books [17–19] and courses (both continuing professional development and part of undergraduate or postgraduate degrees[10]) that teach the foundations and practice of MDE.
- *Events and publications.* There are numerous academic and industry-focused events related to modelling (MoDELS, ECMFA, ICMT, EclipseCon to name but a few) that, if measured in terms of attendance, are thriving. There are academic journals that publish significant papers on modelling and MDE (*Software and Systems Modelling, IEEE Transactions on Software Engineering, Formal Aspects of Computing*).

These are all positive indicators; MDE as a research discipline is arguably healthy. As a research and development activity, it also seemingly thrives. But there are at least two significant challenges that may hinder future success, which we now briefly discuss.

3 Lowering the Entry Barrier to MDE with Flexible Modelling

Adopting MDE, modelling and metamodelling can be painful: it requires training, familiarity with the use of complicated tools (such as Eclipse and EMF) and practice. In particular, it requires the ability to translate detailed knowledge of domain concepts into the idioms of Model-Driven Engineering.

This is exemplified by metamodelling: the key concepts appearing in a meta-model are generally produced via domain analysis. For example, when building a language for supporting technical conference registrations, the domain of interest is conference management, and we might expect to identify key domain concepts such as registration types, fees, sessions chosen by registrants, etc. To start the process of constructing a metamodel, these domain concepts must be expressed or translated into MDE idioms, e.g. Ecore constructs such as EClass. While we may well expect a

---

[7]http://www.metacase.com.

[8]http://www.obeo.fr/.

[9]http://www.itemis.com/.

[10]For example, http://www.cs.york.ac.uk/postgraduate/modules/mode.html.

domain expert to successfully identify domain concepts, it may be difficult for them to adapt these concepts to a platform-specific technology and express them in the form of a metamodel.

The issue of translating domain concepts into platform-specific concepts arises in other forms in MDE: besides metamodelling, there is also the issue of model management, i.e. expressing *what* you want to do with models in terms of platform-specific model management idioms. This requires translating/expressing problem-specific concepts into platform-specific model management idioms, e.g. ATL programs.

More generally, this is an example of a classic problem in translational research: how can we lower the entry barrier to the adoption of MDE? Arguably, the technology platforms that have been accepted by the MDE research community—largely based on Eclipse—have a significant impact on adoption. There is evidence that some of these tools can be challenging to adopt [20].

In a nutshell, the conventional MDE/metamodelling process may be understandable for MDE experts, but this is not always the case with domain experts [21] who are more familiar with tools like simple drawing editors [22]. However, the involvement of domain experts is important in the definition of high-quality and well-defined MDE languages that cover all the essential aspects of a domain [21, 23–25].

3.1 Flexible Modelling

To address these issues, flexible modelling approaches have been proposed (e.g. [21, 26–28]). Such approaches are based on sketching tools and do not require the definition of a metamodel during the initial phases of language engineering. Such approaches can and have been extended to support *engineering* as well—so-called flexible MDE. In flexible MDE, sketches are semi-formal artefacts that, under certain conditions (related to consistency, which we elaborate in the following sections), can be automatically processed by tools.

More specifically, flexible MDE starts with the definition of example models [21, 29, 30]. These example models help language engineers to better understand the concepts of any envisioned language and can be used to infer *prototype metamodels* manually or (semi-)automatically. These prototypes can be used in the definition of a final metamodel. In this fashion, a richer understanding of the domain can be developed *incrementally*, while concrete insights (e.g. type information) pertaining to the envisioned metamodel are discovered. The sketching tools used allow the quick definition of example models, sacrificing the formality that MDE editors offer. In particular, drawing tools do not require MDE-specific expertise.

Flexible modelling attempts at providing a trade-off between rigour and formality (offered by MDE editors, which will enforce syntactic and static semantics rules defined by a metamodel and any corresponding well-formedness constraints) and flexibility (offered by drawing tools, which do not enforce syntactic and static semantics rules). Some problems may benefit from greater rigour (and hence a metamodel-based approach), whereas others may benefit from flexible MDE. It may be that for organisations in the early stages of adoption of MDE, the value of a flexible MDE approach exceeds that of a rigorous MDE approach.

Even though flexible MDE approaches can offer appealing ways to supporting the adoption of MDE, there are two key challenges associated with their development and use:

1. Dealing with the various types of errors that flexible modelling tools permit
2. Transitioning from flexible models to more traditional (and rigorous) MDE approaches

Our recent work has been attempting to address these two points. We now briefly outline how we have been doing this.

3.2 Flexible MDE Based on Muddles

Since sketching tools cannot enforce syntactic and semantic correctness rules, flexible models are prone to various types of errors [31]:

1. *User errors:* elements that should share the same type have different types assigned to them by mistake. For example, we might create a sketch that makes use of ellipses, but we use ellipses to represent two different things.
2. *Evolution:* the type that we may want to assign to a drawing element may need to change over time, but the sketch may not be updated. For example, we might use a triangle at the start of a modelling process to represent a conference registration, but later use it to represent a form of payment. Without a metamodel, we cannot catch this.
3. *Inconsistencies due to collaboration:* when multiple people collaborate to create the sketch, multiple diagrammatic elements representing the same concept can be used. This is related to the previous point, but this class of error arises due to collaborative editing.
4. *Omissions:* elements can be left untyped, especially when models become large as it becomes possible to overlook some of the elements. For example, I may create a sketch using triangles, squares and circles, but I may never use the squares to represent a concept of value and may ignore squares in any model management program.

Ideally, we would like to have mechanisms for automatically identifying all of these types of errors, while also supporting the transition from flexible MDE to standard (formal) MDE, i.e. inferring a metamodel from a set of flexible models.

Computing Conference

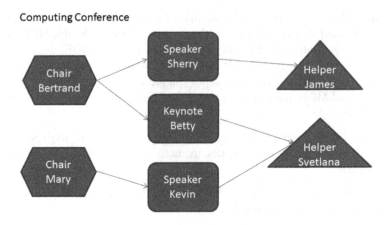

Fig. 1 An example conference diagram

In our work, we use the Muddles approach [26] for sketching example models. The Muddles approach makes use of GraphML-compliant tools such as yEd[11] for sketching. More particularly, the domain engineer can use simple drawing editors to express example models of an envisioned language. The produced drawing, called a *muddle*, can be consumed by model management tools, like the Epsilon platform [32], to support MDE activities (e.g. queries, transformations) enabling the language engineer to experiment with the models, gain better understanding and decide if they are fit for purpose.

An example of such a muddle is shown in Fig. 1.

In this example, the intention of the language engineer is the creation of a simple language for designing conference programs. The process starts with the definition of example models of this envisioned DSL by the domain experts. The language engineer can then annotate types and typing information (e.g. properties) for each node. This drawing can be then consumed by model management programs that can be written in parallel to check if it fulfils the needs of the engineer. This process may expose more features of the language. In contrast to related work [21], shapes and other graphical characteristics of each node are not bound to types. For example, in the drawing of Fig. 1, elements of type "Keynote" are expressed using rounded rectangles, the same shape that is used to define elements of type "Speaker". Moreover, elements of the same type can be expressed using different shapes; for instance, two different elements of type "Speaker" can be expressed using the rounded rectangle for one of them and a circle for the second. By doing so, the domain expert is not constrained in any sense and can express herself freely.

Types and type-related information for each element are defined using custom GraphML properties;[12] example properties include the role in a source of an edge,

---

[11]http://www.yworks.com/en/products_yed_about.html.

[12]http://yed.yworks.com/support/manual/properties.html/.

the type of an element, properties of nodes and edges (e.g. the name Betty), etc. More details on these properties can be found elsewhere [26].

Model management programs use this type-related information to access and manipulate elements of the diagram. For example, if the rounded rectangle element (typed as *Speaker*) has a String attribute named *name* assigned to it, then the following Epsilon Object Language (EOL) [33] script returns the names of all the elements of Type *Speaker*. As such, muddles can be programmatically processed like other models, without having to transform them to a more rigorous format (e.g. Ecore).

```
1 var speakers = Speaker. all () ;
2 for (s in Speaker) {
3   ("Speaker: " + s .name). println () ;
4 }
```

Listing 1 EOL commands executed on the drawing

Interestingly, the above EOL program would also be valid for an Ecore model possessing an EClass `Speaker`; this is an artefact of Epsilon's connectivity layer, which we discuss briefly in the next section.

Muddles can be used as lightweight models [26] and manipulated programmatically, using, for example, Epsilon. But if we want to transition from muddles to more rigorous models and attempt to address some of the errors identified earlier, we need ways by which we can *infer* metamodels and identify errors in the process.

3.3 Inference Approach

An overview of our approach to model typing inference is shown in Fig. 2; this is based on results introduced elsewhere [31].

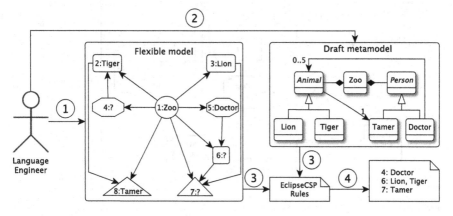

Fig. 2 An overview of the proposed approach

A language engineer constructs a flexible model using a GraphML-compliant drawing tool. The engineer annotates the model with as much type information as they see fit; after this, some elements will have known types, while others will have no type. This annotated muddle is then analysed to extract characteristics of interest, and these characteristics are passed to the CART algorithm, which performs type inference. Type inference takes an annotated (typed) muddle and attempts to match unannotated elements with those that are annotated. To support this via the CART algorithm, we first specify a set of characteristics that describe attributes of each element. Each characteristic is known as a *feature*; the set of characteristics for each element is a *feature signature*. At the end of the signature, the type of the element (if known) is also attached. In this approach, we used a set of five features, namely, the number of attributes an element has, the number of different types of incoming and outgoing references, and the number of different types of parents [31]. These features were selected because the intention was to base the similarity measurement and prediction on structural and semantic characteristics of the models; these features measure these characteristics.

We implemented an automated process of generating feature signatures from muddles (using Epsilon) and running CART against test and training sets. We then needed to evaluate this process. The overall experimental process is shown in Fig. 3.

As there are no publically available repositories of muddles, we applied our approach to a number of publically available metamodels that were collected as part of the work presented in [34]. For each of these metamodels, we produced ten random instances using the Crepe tool [35] (step ① in Fig. 3). The values

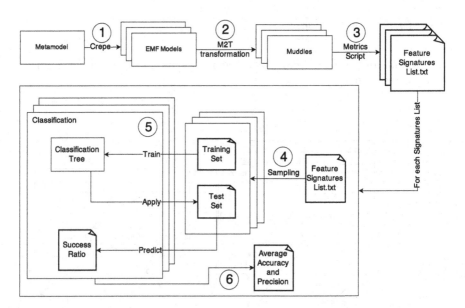

Fig. 3 The experimentation process [31]

that were assigned to the attributes of the instance models were randomly selected (the content of the attributes has no effect on the final feature signature of the element). Having generated experimental models, we transformed them to muddles and randomly erased the types of some of them in order to simulate a scenario where some node types are known while others are not. For that purpose, a Model-to-Text transformation was implemented that transforms instances of Ecore metamodels to GraphML files that conform to the Muddles metamodel (step ②). In step ③, we extracted the feature signature of each node using a script. We then ran a sampling procedure (step ④) to split the feature signature list into a training and a test set; the former is used to train the CART algorithm, whereas the latter is used for testing.

Full experimental details can be found in [31]; it is shown that there is a strong dependency between sampling rate and success score for classification and that there is a negative correlation between the number of types in a metamodel and the success score (i.e. when a drawing is left heavily untyped, the success score is affected by the number of different types in the drawing).

In effect, this work demonstrates that it is feasible to infer prototype metamodels from annotated example models with good accuracy. Of course, the inferred metamodel is not necessarily fit for purpose, in terms of being suitable to support model transformation, code generation, etc.—as such, it should be considered a prototype that may need to be further evolved or modified. Zolotas et al. [31] also demonstrate that the inference process is efficient on moderately sized example models. Currently, we are experimenting with different inference techniques as well as constraint solving to obtain a better understanding of where inference is effective (and ineffective).

4 Support for Legacy MDE Artefacts

A second challenge facing the continued adoption and maturation of MDE is ensuring that there is support for legacy MDE artefacts (such as models or metamodels), both today and for the foreseeable future.

While MDE has gained traction since around 2005, when the first robust model transformation and model-to-text tools became available, modelling tools have been around much longer. For example, UML 1.0 was published in 1997 and thereafter UML-compliant models started to be created around the same time. The standard persistence mechanism for UML, XMI, was first published in 2000 and has since undergone numerous changes. The first version of the Eclipse Modelling Framework (EMF) was published in 2002, and hence Ecore-compliant models started to be created from that date. Models created using these legacy technologies exist to this day, and the business value they embody needs to remain accessible: that is, we need to continue to be able to load these models and manage them. Though it may be possible to accomplish this using legacy tools (e.g. legacy versions of Rational Rose or EMF), we must question the efficacy of this when we also want to use modern state-of-the-art MDE tools, such as Epsilon or ATL, at the same time, and possibly even on the same models.

There is a broader issue here. The MDE community has, for better or for worse, agreed on a de facto standard for modelling and supporting model management: EMF. There are very good reasons for doing this: it is an open standard, reliable implementations exist, it is relatively straightforward to use in defining a variety of modelling languages, and there is good training material and documentation (there are also limitations with EMF; some of them, in the context of models at runtime, are discussed in [36]). But industry has *not* standardised on EMF—they use a wide variety of technologies for modelling, and some of it does not conform to the usual notions of modelling technology: they may not have explicit metamodels. Such technologies include schema-less XML, spreadsheets, GraphML (as discussed in the previous section), HTML, JSON, CSV, models stored in CDO repositories, Artisan, EA, petal files, etc. A technology like spreadsheets is one of the most widely used modelling approaches in the world.

The question is, how can we support legacy technologies for modelling, including those like UML or older versions of EMF, where there is an *explicit* metamodel, as well as those without explicit metamodels?

There seem to be at least two approaches to address this:

1. Build translators/transformations from each legacy technology (e.g. XMI 1.0, Excel spreadsheets) to modern MDE technology (e.g. Ecore). Migrate legacy models to the new technology and thereafter work with the migrated models. One issue with this approach is the loss of information that may arise in the translation. In some cases, there will be no loss because the languages involved are semantically equivalent, but information in the form of concrete syntax (e.g. layout) may still be discarded. Another issue is that the resulting model may be less efficient to manipulate using the state-of-the-art tools. Consider a spreadsheet and a query thereupon: this query is likely to be highly optimised by the spreadsheet's native query engine. If we translate the spreadsheet to an EMF model, the query will then likely be expressed in a different format (e.g. OCL) that will not benefit from the native optimisations of spreadsheets.

2. Provide mechanisms for state-of-the-art modelling tools to load, save and manipulate models in their native format. In this way, the original models can be maintained for as long as is needed, while state-of-the-art tools can be used to manipulate them.

While it may be inevitable that migration (in the form of a transformation) from a legacy format to a modern format for modelling should take place, there is significant value in supporting the second option above. This is what we have been pursuing in the Epsilon project. The particular approach we have been taking is the *driver* approach (based on the Driver design pattern). This is illustrated in Fig. 4, which shows the Epsilon Model Connectivity layer that implements the Driver pattern.

The idea with the connectivity layer is one of separation of concerns. Epsilon provides a family of task-specific model management languages (e.g. ETL for

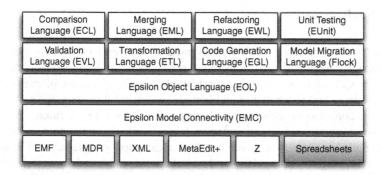

Fig. 4 The Epsilon Architecture

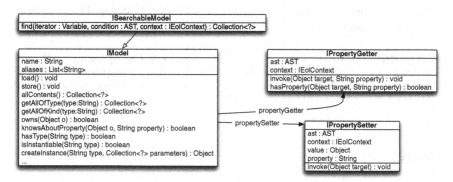

Fig. 5 Epsilon Model Connectivity interfaces

model transformation, EOL for general-purpose model management), but these are independent of the technology used for representing models. This characteristic is provided via the connectivity layer (EMC in Fig. 4). Different drivers are provided for different modelling technologies, e.g. EMF and spreadsheets. When an Epsilon program is configured, it is bound to specific modelling technologies, and hence appropriate drivers are loaded. Then, when an Epsilon instruction requires access to a model, the connectivity layer redirects that instruction to the technology-specific features provided (e.g. accessors, creators, mutators).

In this way, support for a new modelling technology (e.g. a particular dialect of Rational Rose's petal file format) requires implementing a new driver. In practice, this means implementing a set of interfaces in the connectivity layer; Fig. 5 illustrates the interfaces that are provided in EMC. In effect, this API defines a set of basic queries and mutators on model persistence formats.

Providing support for legacy models and legacy MDE projects requires more than just the ability to manage legacy models: there needs to be continued support for other artefacts (e.g. documentation, tutorials, bug reports, tests). Migration and digital curation of these artefacts is another subject in its own right.

5 Conclusions

Model-Driven Engineering is, by many measures, a research success story, but the research community needs to be concerned about both front-end and back-end issues: how do we lower the rather considerable entry barrier to use of state-of-the-art MDE tools and technologies and how do we ensure that the models in which we invest considerable effort in developing remain of use in the future. We have described ongoing work in addressing these questions. One issue going forward is the difficulty in encouraging research in these areas: supporting legacy and adoption are worthy subjects, particularly if researchers are interested in ensuring their research has impact and in supporting industrial collaborations and collaborators. But such work often does not appear to have the explicit novelty that is required to publish in leading conferences, particularly in software engineering. This is an issue that many disciplines, not just MDE, will have to face.

Acknowledgements We gratefully acknowledge the support of the UK Engineering and Physical Sciences Research Council, via the LSCITS initiative, as well as the support of the European Commission via the MONDO and OSSMETER projects. Finally, we acknowledge the support of Innovate UK via the SECT-AIR project.

References

1. Schmidt, D.C.: Guest editor's introduction: model-driven engineering. IEEE Comput. **39**(2), 25–31 (2006)
2. Woodcock, J., Larsen, P.G., Bicarregui, J., Fitzgerald, J.S.: Formal methods: practice and experience. ACM Comput. Surv. **41**(4), 19 (2009)
3. Paige, R.F., Kolovos, D.S., Polack, F.A.C.: A tutorial on metamodelling for grammar researchers. Sci. Comput. Program. **96**, 396–416 (2014)
4. Hutchinson, J., Whittle, J., Rouncefield, M., Kristoffersen, S.: Empirical assessment of MDE in industry. In: Proceedings – International Conference on Software Engineering, pp. 471–480 (2011)
5. Jouault, F., Allilaire, F., Bézivin, J., Kurtev, I., Valduriez, P.: ATL: a QVT-like transformation language. In: OOPSLA Companion, pp. 719–720 (2006)
6. Epsilon: http://www.eclipse.org/epsilon/ (2014)
7. Eclipse modeling framework project (EMF): website. http://www.eclipse.org/modeling/emf/
8. di Ruscio, D., Paige, R.F., Pierantonio, A.: Guest editorial to the special issue on success stories in model driven engineering. Sci. Comput. Program. **89**, 69–70 (2014)
9. Kolovos, D.S., Rose, L.M., bin Abid, S., Paige, R.F., Polack, F.A.C., Botterweck, G.: Taming EMF and GMF using model transformation. In: MoDELS (1), pp. 211–225 (2010)
10. Paige, R.F., Kolovos, D.S., Polack, F.A.C.: A tutorial on metamodelling for grammar researchers. Sci. Comput. Program. **96**, 396–416 (2014)
11. Baker, P., Loh, S., Weil, F.: Model-driven engineering in a large industrial context – motorola case study. In: MoDELS, pp. 476–491 (2005)
12. Gray, J.G., Zhang, J., Lin, Y., Roychoudhury, S., Wu, H., Sudarsan, R., Gokhale, A.S., Neema, S., Shi, F., Bapty, T.: Model-driven program transformation of a large avionics framework. In: GPCE, pp. 361–378 (2004)

13. Clowes, D., Kolovos, D.S., Holmes, C., Rose, L.M., Paige, R.F., Johnson, J., Dawson, R., Probets, S.G.: A reflective approach to model-driven web engineering. In: ECMFA, pp. 62–73 (2010)
14. dos Santos, O.M., Woodcock, J., Paige, R.F.: Using model transformation to generate graphical counter-examples for the formal analysis of xUML models. In: ICECCS, pp. 117–126 (2011)
15. Mohagheghi, P., Gilani, W., Stefanescu, A., Fernández, M.A., Nordmoen, B., Fritzsche, M.: Where does model-driven engineering help? experiences from three industrial cases. Softw. Syst. Model. **12**(3), 619–639 (2013)
16. Kleppe, A., Warmer, J., Bast, W.: MDA Explained. Addison-Wesley, Boston (2003)
17. Stahl, T., Völter, M., Bettin, J., Haase, A., Helsen, S.: Model-Driven Software Development: Technology, Engineering, Management. Wiley, Hoboken (2006)
18. Brambilla, M., Cabot, J., Wimmer, M.: Model-Driven Software Engineering in Practice. Synthesis Lectures on Software Engineering. Morgan and Claypool Publishers, San Rafael (2012)
19. Voelter, M., Benz, S., Dietrich, C., Engelmann, B., Helander, M., Kats, L.C.L., Visser, E., Wachsmuth, G.: DSL Engineering – Designing, Implementing and Using Domain-Specific Languages. dslbook.org (2013)
20. The Eclipse Foundation: Eclipse community survey report (2013)
21. López-Fernández, J.J., Cuadrado, J.S., Guerra, E., de Lara, J.: Example-driven meta-model development. Softw. Syst. Model. **14**(4), 1323–1347 (2015)
22. Ossher, H., Bellamy, R., Simmonds, I., Amid, D., Anaby-Tavor, A., Callery, M., Desmond, M., de Vries, J., Fisher, A., Krasikov, S.: Flexible modeling tools for pre-requirements analysis: conceptual architecture and research challenges. ACM SIGPLAN Not. **45**(10), 848–864 (2010)
23. Izquierdo, J.L.C., Cabot, J.: Enabling the collaborative definition of DSMLs. In: Advanced Information Systems Engineering, pp. 272–287. Springer, Berlin (2013)
24. Izquierdo, J.L.C., Cabot, J.: Community-driven language development. In: 2012 ICSE Workshop on Modeling in Software Engineering (MISE), pp. 29–35. IEEE, Piscataway, NJ (2012)
25. Völter, M., Benz, S., Dietrich, C., Engelmann, B., Helander, M., Kats, L.C.L., Visser, E., Wachsmuth, G.: DSL engineering – designing, implementing and using domain-specific languages. dslbook.org (2013)
26. Kolovos, D.S., Matragkas, N., Rodríguez, H.H., Paige, R.F.: Programmatic muddle management. In: XM 2013–Extreme Modeling Workshop, p. 2 (2013)
27. Gabrysiak, G., Giese, H., Lüders, A., Seibel, A.: How can metamodels be used flexibly. In: Proceedings of ICSE 2011 Workshop on Flexible Modeling Tools, Waikiki/Honolulu, vol. 22 (2011)
28. Wüest, D., Seyff, N., Glinz, M.: Flexisketch: a mobile sketching tool for software modeling. In: Mobile Computing, Applications, and Services, pp. 225–244. Springer, Berlin (2013)
29. Bak, K., Zayan, D., Czarnecki, K., Antkiewicz, M., Diskin, Z., Wasowski, A., Rayside, D.: Example-driven modeling: model = abstractions + examples. In: Notkin, D., Cheng, B.H.C., Pohl, K. (eds.) 35th International Conference on Software Engineering, ICSE '13, San Francisco, CA, 18–26 May 2013, pp. 1273–1276. IEEE/ACM, Piscataway, NJ (2013)
30. Sánchez-Cuadrado, J., De Lara, J., Guerra, E.: Bottom-Up Meta-Modelling: An Interactive Approach. Springer, Berlin (2012)
31. Zolotas, A., Matragkas, N., Devlin, S., Kolovos, D.S., Paige, R.F.: Type inference in flexible model-driven engineering. In: Taentzer, G., Bordeleau, F. (eds.) Modelling Foundations and Applications. Lecture Notes in Computer Science, vol. 9153, pp. 75–91. Springer, Berlin (2015)
32. Paige, R.F., Kolovos, D.S., Rose, L.M., Drivalos, N., Polack, F.A.C.: The design of a conceptual framework and technical infrastructure for model management language engineering. In: 2009 14th IEEE International Conference on Engineering of Complex Computer Systems, pp. 162–171. IEEE, Piscataway, NJ (2009)
33. Kolovos, D.S., Paige, R.F., Polack, F.A.C.: The epsilon object language (EOL). In: Model Driven Architecture–Foundations and Applications, pp. 128–142. Springer, Berlin (2006)

34. Williams, J.R., Zolotas, A., Matragkas, N.D., Rose, L.M., Kolovos, D.S., Paige, R.F., Polack, F.A.C.: What do metamodels really look like? EESSMOD@ MoDELS **1078**, 55–60 (2013)
35. Williams, J.R., Paige, R.F., Kolovos, D.S., Polack, F.A.C.: Search-based model driven engineering. Technical report, Technical Report YCS-2012-475, Department of Computer Science, University of York (2012)
36. Fouquet, F., Nain, G., Morin, B., Daubert, E., Barais, O., Plouzeau, N., Jézéquel, J.-M.: An eclipse modelling framework alternative to meet the models@runtime requirements. In: Proceedings Model Driven Engineering Languages and Systems – 15th International Conference, MODELS 2012, Innsbruck, 30 Sept–5 Oct 2012, pp. 87–101 (2012)

Borealis Bounded Model Checker: The Coming of Age Story

Marat Akhin, Mikhail Belyaev, and Vladimir Itsykson

Abstract Our research group has been developing a bounded model checker called Borealis for almost 4 years now, and it has been mostly a research prototype with all that it entails. A lot of different ideas have been tested in Borealis, and this chapter draws a bottom line for most of them. We believe this chapter would be of interest to other researchers as a brief introduction to the topic of bounded model checking, and to us as a cornerstone on which to build our future work on making Borealis into a tool.

1 Introduction

Development of any program analysis tool is a very interesting journey, as it compels one to delve into many different areas, starting from logic and formal semantics to language design and compiler construction. But it is also a very difficult journey with a lot of [undecidable] problems you need to solve to make your tool work.

This chapter is the *summa experitur* of our journey in the development of a bounded model checking tool nicknamed Borealis.[1,2] We talk about the problems most often encountered in bounded model checking and how we decided to tackle them in Borealis. We also attempt to explain the reasonings about our decisions, to share not only the *results* but also the *process*. In a sense, this chapter is our personal cornerstone in Borealis' development, which summarizes what has already been done and records our plans for the future.

The rest of the chapter is organized as follows. Section 2 introduces the basics of bounded model checking in general and its implementation in Borealis. Our takes on the problems of loop and interprocedural analyses are described in Sects. 3 and

---

[1] https://bitbucket.org/vorpal-research/borealis.

[2] https://hub.docker.com/r/vorpal/borealis-standalone/.

M. Akhin (✉) · M. Belyaev · V. Itsykson
Peter the Great St. Petersburg Polytechnic University, Saint Petersburg, Russia
e-mail: akhin@kspt.icc.spbstu.ru; belyaev@kspt.icc.spbstu.ru; vlad@icc.spbstu.ru

© Springer International Publishing AG 2017
M. Mazzara, B. Meyer (eds.), *Present and Ulterior Software Engineering*,
https://doi.org/10.1007/978-3-319-67425-4_8

4, respectively. In Sect. 5 we present our approach to the precision/recall problem, which is based on a semi-symbolic program execution. We talk about the practical evaluation of Borealis in Sect. 6; Sect. 7 wraps up with some discussion of our future work.

2   The Basics of Borealis Bounded Model Checker

As simple and trivial as it may seem to a more experienced reader, we still believe we should begin our chronicles of Borealis' research and development from the very basics. Therefore, in this section we outline the inner workings of Borealis, both to set a context for our work and to make a solid foundation for the rest of this chapter.

The first step in developing any bounded model checking (BMC) tool for a given programming language is to decide what "M" stands for, i.e., which program model you are going to use. In principle, one has three possible options to choose from:

1. OSS compilers (e.g., GCC or Clang)
2. Proprietary compilers (e.g., EDG)
3. Custom-made parsers/compilers

While the last option looks very attractive, as handcrafted tools can be tailor-fit to do exactly what is needed, creating even a parser (let alone a fully functional compiler) for a language as complex as C++ is no small feat. Paying for a proprietary compiler framework is also not an option, if we are talking about small-scale R & D. Therefore, one is left with using OSS compilers to develop her BMC tools.

There are a lot of tools for a lot of programming languages. We targeted C and chose to go with LLVM framework,[3] as it has some unique advantages compared to other alternatives. First, it was created with program analysis in mind right from the start. LLVM intermediate representation (IR) is a highly regular, typed language in static single assignment (SSA) form which makes developing analyses easy. Second, it provides a large number of analyses and optimizations, ranging from alias analyses to loop unrollings, out of the box, allowing one to focus on their problem domain and not on reimplementing collateral facilities. Third, it is designed for extensibility and composability, making it very easy to build tools with it.

As more and more software projects are switching to Clang/LLVM as their main toolchain, using LLVM for program analysis has an additional advantage of being *compiler aware*—tools built on LLVM platform are analyzing the code exactly as it is seen by the actual compiler, leaving almost no space for possible misinterpretations between the compiler and the analyzer (which are easily possible with C/C++). Of course, one might argue that the LLVM framework itself might work with the code erroneously, e.g., w.r.t. undefined behavior [30, 33], which would

---

[3]http://llvm.org/.

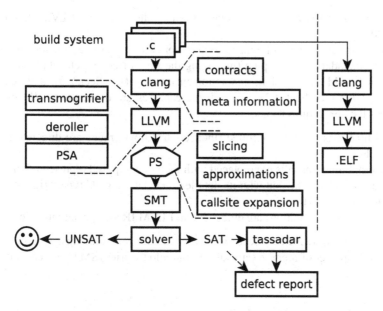

Fig. 1 High-level scheme of Borealis bounded model checker

lead to analysis tools also interpreting the code in the wrong way, but this problem lies outside the scope of this chapter.

The high-level scheme of Borealis is shown in Fig. 1. Ad initium, let us explain the main Borealis components in more detail.

2.1 Low-Level Virtual Machine Infrastructure

Borealis is built upon the standard foundation of almost every LLVM-based tool: LLVM passes. A single pass is a function that takes some LLVM IR module, either analyzes or transforms it, and returns the resulting LLVM IR module. This allows one to easily combine several passes in a processing pipeline according to her task.

As with any BMC tool, Borealis requires the code to be fully unrolled,[4] i.e., no loops are to be present in the resulting LLVM IR. To support this, we implemented a `loop-deroll` pass which is a more aggressive version of the standard LLVM `loop-unroll` pass. It also implements a novel loop unrolling technique called *loop backstabbing* which is covered in more detail in Sect. 3.2. This pass, together with a number of built-in LLVM passes (e.g., *aggressive dead code elimination*

---

[4]That is, bounded.

or *promote memory to register*), is used to make the program's LLVM IR suitable for BMC.

There are a number of other auxiliary passes that are responsible for such tasks as metadata bookkeeping (managing the flow of code metadata from Clang through LLVM to Borealis), annotation processing (see Sect. 2.3), and function decomposing (see Sect. 4.2). After all these passes are done, the LLVM module follows the next requirements:

- All functions are fully unrolled (their control flow graphs are directed acyclic graphs).
- External function calls are replaced with their decomposed representation.
- Every variable is tagged with its detailed metadata (e.g., C type, original name, source code location).
- Source-level annotations are embedded in LLVM IR via special intrinsics.

This resulting LLVM IR needs to be checked for possible bugs. To do that, we employ the power of modern satisfiability modulo theories (SMT) solvers [7].

2.2 Satisfiability Modulo Theories

The idea behind utilizing SMT for BMC is a very simple one—transform the unrolled program to an SMT formula and check if it is satisfiable w.r.t. some safeness condition [12]. If the condition is violated (formula is satisfiable), the original program contains a possible bug, otherwise it is correct. Checking is done using one of the available SMT solvers, e.g., Z3 [23] or MathSAT [14].

To make supporting different solvers easier, Borealis adds another level of indirection in the form of intermediate *predicate state* API (PS API). A simplified PS definition is shown in Fig. 2; a PS for a given LLVM IR instruction corresponds to an SMT formula equivalent to all the possible program states at that LLVM IR instruction. Instructions is mapped to *predicates*, which operate on *terms* (our equivalent of LLVM IR values). Predicate states are easily composable, retain only the information needed for LLVM-to-SMT translation, and can be efficiently (de)serialized (a feature required for incremental-style analyses).

To do the actual PS-to-SMT translation, one needs to define the transformation rules, and this is where everything gets interesting. Most terms and predicates are self-explanatory: `TernaryTerm` selects one of the two values depending on the third, `GepTerm` corresponds to LLVM `GetElementPtr` instruction, etc.; program values are represented as SMT bit vectors of their respective size. However, there are some terms which work with memory, and memory cannot be easily encoded in SMT.

We decided to use the approach similar to LLBMC [28], where memory is represented as a theoretical array with read (`LoadTerm`) and write (`StorePredicate`) operations [13]. This allows for much flexibility of if

⟨*PredicateState*⟩ ::= **PredicateStateChain** head:⟨*PredicateState*⟩ tail:⟨*PredicateState*⟩
   | **PredicateStateChoice** choices:⟨*ListOfPredicateStates*⟩
   | **BasicPredicateState** data:⟨*ListOfPredicates*⟩

⟨*Predicate*⟩ ::= **AllocaPredicate** lhv:⟨*Term*⟩ numElems:⟨*Term*⟩ origNumElems:⟨*Term*⟩
   | **DefaultSwitchCasePredicate** cond:⟨*Term*⟩ cases:⟨*ListOfTerms*⟩
   | **EqualityPredicate** lhv:⟨*Term*⟩ rhv:⟨*Term*⟩
   | **GlobalsPredicate** globals:⟨*ListOfTerms*⟩
   | **InequalityPredicate** lhv:⟨*Term*⟩ rhv:⟨*Term*⟩
   | **MallocPredicate** lhv:⟨*Term*⟩ numElems:⟨*Term*⟩ origNumElems:⟨*Term*⟩
   | **SeqDataPredicate** base:⟨*Term*⟩ data:⟨*ListOfTerms*⟩
   | **SeqDataZeroPredicate** base:⟨*Term*⟩ size:*UInt32*
   | **StorePredicate** ptr:⟨*Term*⟩ value:⟨*Term*⟩
   | **WriteBoundPredicate** ptr:⟨*Term*⟩ boundValue:⟨*Term*⟩
   | **WritePropertyPredicate** propName:⟨*Term*⟩ ptr:⟨*Term*⟩ propValue:⟨*Term*⟩

⟨*Term*⟩ ::= **ArgumentTerm** idx:*UInt32* kind:⟨*ArgumentKind*⟩
   | **ArgumentCountTerm**
   | **AxiomTerm** term:⟨*Term*⟩ axiom:⟨*Term*⟩
   | **BinaryTerm** op:⟨*BinaryOp*⟩ lhv:⟨*Term*⟩ rhv:⟨*Term*⟩
   | **BoundTerm** term:⟨*Term*⟩
   | **CastTerm** term:⟨*Term*⟩ signExtend:*Bool*
   | **CmpTerm** op:⟨*CmpOp*⟩ lhv:⟨*Term*⟩ rhv:⟨*Term*⟩
   | **ConstTerm**
   | **FreeVarTerm**
   | **GepTerm** base:⟨*Term*⟩ shifts:⟨*ListOfTerms*⟩ triviallyInbounds:*Bool*
   | **LoadTerm** ptr:⟨*Term*⟩
   | **ReadPropertyTerm** propName:⟨*Term*⟩ ptr:⟨*Term*⟩
   | **ReturnPtrTerm** funcName:*String*
   | **ReturnValueTerm** funcName:*String*
   | **SignTerm** value:⟨*Term*⟩
   | **TernaryTerm** cond:⟨*Term*⟩ tru:⟨*Term*⟩ fls:⟨*Term*⟩
   | **UnaryTerm** op:⟨*UnaryOp*⟩ value:⟨*Term*⟩
   | **ValueTerm** global:*Bool*
   | **VarArgumentTerm** index:*UInt32*
   | ...

⟨*ListOfPredicateStates*⟩ ::= ⟨*PredicateState*⟩ ⟨*ListOfPredicateStates*⟩ | ⟨*empty*⟩

⟨*ListOfPredicates*⟩ ::= ⟨*Predicate*⟩ ⟨*ListOfPredicates*⟩ | ⟨*empty*⟩

⟨*ListOfTerms*⟩ ::= ⟨*Term*⟩ ⟨*ListOfTerms*⟩ | ⟨*empty*⟩

⟨*ArgumentKind*⟩ ::= **ANY** | **STRING**

⟨*CmpOp*⟩ ::= **EQ** | **NEQ** | **GT** | ...

⟨*BinaryOp*⟩ ::= **ADD** | **SUB** | **MUL** | ...

⟨*UnaryOp*⟩ ::= **NEG** | **NOT** | **BINARY_NOT**

Fig. 2 Predicate state definition

and how we interpret bit-wise operations—we can use byte- or element-level memory representation or any combination in between. After tests we decided to use element-level representation (every program value is mapped to a single memory element) by default, as it is efficient and precise enough for most practical BMC purposes [2].

Besides the main memory, which represents the program heap, Borealis uses auxiliary *property* memories. These named memories store additional values linked to program values, e.g., every heap-allocated pointer has its bound stored in ⟨*bounds*⟩ memory. This allows us to save any kind of relevant information without the need to change Borealis' internals. For example, if one needs to work with resources and resource states, these can be stored in ⟨*resources*⟩ memory and checked for bugs when needed.

The main alternative to array-based memory modeling in SMT is predicate abstraction [21, 24]. In case of predicate abstraction, memory operations are lifted to special predicate variables, which capture only the most important slices of the memory model. If these slices happen to be inadequate for a given bug, they may be refined using, for example, counterexample-guided abstraction refinement (CEGAR [17]).

2.3   Bug Detection

After predicate state corresponding to a given program fragment is converted to an SMT formula, it needs to be checked for correctness. We employ the traditional approach to checking if condition Q always holds for formula B by asking if $B \land \neg Q$ is satisfiable. If it is unsatisfiable, $B \land Q$ is always true and the program is correct; if it is satisfiable, the program contains a bug and the resulting SMT model summarizes the fault-inducing counterexample.

Borealis has a built-in support for the following bug types:

- Null-pointer dereferences
- Buffer overflows
- Uses of undefined values
- Code assert violations
- Function contract violations

The safety conditions for these bugs are pretty straightforward, so we leave them outside the scope of this chapter.

To specify custom safety conditions (i.e., function pre- and post-conditions), Borealis uses two flavors of annotations. The first one, called ♮ACSL,[5] is heavily inspired by ANSI/ISO C Specification Language (ACSL) [8]; the specifications are given as annotations in source code comments [2] which allow to describe

---

[5]Read as "natural-ACSL".

function pre- (@requires) and post-conditions (@ensures), arbitrary assumptions (@assume), and custom checks (@assert). The other one is more in line with SV-COMP-styled checks [11], when conditions are embedded in the source code via calls to special intrinsic functions. While the latter mode is enough for many practical purposes (and is a de facto standard in software verification), the former allows for much extensibility and expressibility of complex safety conditions.

Now that we are done with the basics, we can go on. Specifically, we are going to talk about our takes on two major problems in software verification: analysis of loops and interprocedural analysis.

3 Program Loop Analysis

As we already mentioned in Sect. 2, bounded model checking expects the code to be fully unrolled in order to be converted to an SMT formula (as BMC is, by definition, "bounded"). Unfortunately, this problem is undecidable in general, as it requires one to solve the halting problem. In the following sections we describe different approaches, which can be used to implement this unrolling, and the motivation behind the hybrid approach we use in our tool.

3.1 The Unroll-and-Bound Technique

The easiest (and most common) way of dealing with program loops is unrolling each loop in the program by a constant unrolling factor. This technique is implemented in most bounded model checkers [4, 18, 19, 28] due to its simplicity, but is unsound in general. Additionally, some classes of software bugs (namely, buffer overflows) usually do not trigger on the first iterations of the loop, meaning that this technique performs poorly on these bugs.

The classic approach to constant loop unrolling is as follows: First, some heuristic-based method is used to find out whether a loop has a constant iteration count. If it does, the loop is fully unrolled up to the last iteration, and the analysis is sound by construction. If it does not, the loop is unrolled to some arbitrary constant value, and the analysis attempts to prove the program correct. It is easy to show that the value of this constant is insignificant in general (as long as it is greater than one); as for any possible constant value N sufficient to analyze any given program, a new program can be crafted requiring an unroll factor of at least $(N + 1)$.

The original BMC paper [12] describes an approach that aims to solve this problem by unrolling the original program up to a point where further unrollings do not change the analysis results. This approach does minify the unsoundness of the constant loop unrolling in general, but requires re-running the analysis with a different unrolling factor for every loop, thus introducing a multiplicative increase in execution time.

3.2 Loop Backstabbing

The unroll-and-bound technique described previously is a very simple and universal, but generally unsound, way of dealing with loops, as every iteration is different if we take the time-centric view. However, a large number of loops in typical C programs are pretty standard in their form and function (despite not having a constant unroll factor) [25]. There are techniques for reasoning about values in these kinds of loops as a single abstract entity rather than a sequence of values in time. An example of such technique is *chains of recurrences* (CR) abstraction [6, 32], which we will now describe in more detail.

3.2.1 Chains of Recurrences

A chains of recurrences (CR) expression is a special kind of symbolic expression that has the following form:

$$\Phi = \{\phi_0, \odot_0, \phi_1, \odot_1, \ldots, \phi_{k-1}, \odot_k, \phi_k\}_i$$

which is a short form of

$$\Phi = \{\phi_0, \odot_0, \{\phi_1, \odot_1, \ldots, \{\phi_{k-1}, \odot_k, \phi_k\}_i \ldots\}_i\}_i$$

where each tuple

$$f_j(i) = \{\phi_j, \odot_{j+1}, f_{j+1}\}_i$$

(also called *basic recurrence* (BR)) corresponds to a recursive formula

$$f_j(i) = \begin{cases} \phi_j & \text{if } i = 0 \\ f_j(i-1) \odot_{j+1} f_{j+1}(i-1) & \text{if } i > 0 \end{cases}$$

Each operation $\odot_k$ may be either $+$ (sum recurrence) or $*$ (product recurrence). In principle, BRs can be extended to handle other operations, but they are either too complex to operate on (e.g., exponents) or reducible to sum/product recurrences (e.g., subtraction and division). Each expression ϕ_k may be bound to any symbolic expression (possibly including other CR).

CR framework can, in general, represent a wide range of recurrently defined expressions with a seed (starting value), e.g., different kinds of loop variants such as loop-dependent expressions or induction variables. Of course, some loop variants cannot be represented as CR, most notably, values which are based on several other values from previous iterations.

After being constructed, CR may be "unrolled" to an arbitrary iteration k, where k is a symbolic expression, and the unrolled version can be converted back to the nonrecurrent form for a large subset of all possible CR, thus providing the means to symbolically evaluate an arbitrary recurrent symbolic expression at any iteration, even if the iteration number is symbolic as well. The detailed algorithm can be found in paper [32].

CR are widely employed as a code analysis technique in compilers to reason about value evolution. They improve the *scalar evolution* analysis in both LLVM [26] and GCC [10] frameworks and are the foundation of many modern code vectorization techniques.

3.2.2   Using Chains of Recurrences for Loop Analysis

If we consider a program with no side effects or memory accesses, a set of CR expressions for all inductive variables together with a set of CR-dependent expressions for all noninductive variables summarizes any given loop. On top of this, if all CR expressions can be converted back to their nonrecurrent forms, the whole loop can be turned into a universally quantified formula over the number of iterations i. Such a formula can then be used by bounded model checking as is, to represent the body of the loop.

There are, however, several problems with this approach. First, real programs do contain memory access and side effects. Second, one generally tries to avoid producing quantified formulas, as they are hard to reason about and may slow down the SMT solver due to the general undecidability of the quantifier elimination.

In order to avoid these problems, we make the following assumption. As the process of finding a safety property or contract violation (see Sect. 2) uses the formula for the whole function and makes the solver infer the values of all the variables in this formula, we assume only one iteration of a loop is needed for the analysis. That is, if a single "in-the-middle" iteration triggers the bug, the solver should be able to find this exact iteration and produce a subsequent counterexample. This assumption does not hold, however, if a violation requires something happening on two or more iterations of the same loop, but we believe this situation happens in a much smaller number of cases. Even more so, we believe the more iterations are needed to trigger a violation, the less likely this situation is in practice. Despite being without any theoretical proof, these assumptions show good results in practice [1].

Under these assumptions, we can replace a *universally* quantified formula $\forall i.\Psi(i)$, which summarizes a loop, with a set of *existentially* quantified formulae:

$$\exists (i \neq j \neq \cdots \neq k).\Psi_0(i) \wedge \Psi_1(j) \wedge \cdots \wedge \Psi_N(k)$$

It might seem we did not solve any of the problems we had before, but we actually did. These existentially quantified formulae not only represent the loop w.r.t. possible side effects but also allow to trivially skolemize the quantifiers, while producing a counterexample for a possible violation, thus reducing the formulae to the following:

$$(i \neq j \neq \cdots \neq k) \wedge \Psi_0(i) \wedge \Psi_1(j) \wedge \cdots \wedge \Psi_N(k) \text{ where } (i, j, \ldots, k) \text{ are fresh variables}$$

Another thing to consider is `continue`/`break` instructions in a loop—in the proposed CR loop representation, these instructions map to additional predicates over the induction variables $(i, j, \ldots, k)$. In order to add these predicates, we actually need to restructure the program, so that we do not introduce one-too-many iterations when doing loop unrolling.

Surprisingly enough, this technique can be easily adapted to handle infinite loops. Infinite loops happen to not have break instructions; therefore, we can just skip their addition to the resulting formulae. The rest of the approach works in the same way as for finite loops.

3.2.3   Loop Backstabbing Implementation

The actual implementation of loop backstabbing in Borealis applies CR transformation to a loop and extracts the first K (as in classic unroll-and-bound), an arbitrary iteration in the middle, and the last iteration of a loop. The biggest advantage over the classic unroll-and-bound is that these auxiliary iterations are bound by symbolic variables, and the solver may consider *any* iteration of the loop which leads to a possible bug. If the number of iterations of a particular loop is constant, and this constant is less than a certain configurable threshold, we fall back to the unroll-and-bound technique, using built-in LLVM tools. All the loops are analyzed and unrolled in the bottom-up order to avoid potential cross-loop-induction problems.

We use the built-in LLVM scalar evolution analysis, as it is a production-ready implementation easily available from within the compiler. However, while evaluating this approach, we found its CR API to be quite limited, not being able to handle exponential CR and too closely tied to the LLVM loop analysis infrastructure. In our future work we plan to explore the options of storing CR directly in the program representation and using them to also handle some cases of recursion, as well as more complex loops, which all require a full-blown stand-alone CR implementation.

We refer to this technique as *loop backstabbing*, as it tries to avoid the "start-from-the-beginning" approach of the classic unrolling (hence, "back-") and finds the exact erroneous spot of the loop execution (hence, "-stabbing"). Further details and evaluation of loop backstabbing can be found in [1].

4 Interprocedural Analysis

Another serious problem for any kind of program analysis is dealing with function calls, as any function call may have an unknown influence on the program state. There are quite a few possible ways of dealing with the problem of interprocedural analysis, and we explored most of them at some point of Borealis' research and development.

4.1 Inlining

Function inlining has always been the traditional "go-to" approach to interprocedural analysis in the BMC setting. It consists of full function body inlining at every interesting call site. While this approach fits BMC perfectly and works quite well for some programs, it has a number of downsides. The main disadvantage of inlining is that it significantly increases the state space size (in the worst case, exponentially in the depth of nested function calls), which, in turn, increases the resource requirements. It also poorly supports recursive function calls, as they require an iterative procedure similar to classic iterative loop unrolling (see Sect. 3.1).

We support this approach to interprocedural analysis by implementing a special LLVM `force-inline` pass, which, unlike the standard `inline` pass, always forces inlining. The rest of the processing pipeline is completely agnostic to the [absence of] inlining, which allows us to toggle inlining simply by enabling or disabling the `force-inline` pass.

All other approaches to interprocedural analysis reduce down to function approximation—a succinct representation of the function body that retains properties interesting to the program analysis. One option is to leave the function approximation to the user, who then provides function annotations; another is based on automatic approximation via logic inference. These options are described in more detail below.

4.2 Decomposition

The most simple way to approximate function calls (and the only way to deal with external libraries in general) is by using some function description for each external function. Annotations for functions internal to the project are provided using the already discussed ꭥACSL language (see Sect. 2.3) as structured comments in their source code. External functions need to be processed separately, as their source code cannot be easily edited. We decided to decompose every external function call into a number of basic operations over its arguments and result value, which capture its influence on the caller.

This decomposition is specified using a simple JSON-based description language. Each function description contains the ♮ACSL function contract (expressed over function parameters and result value) and its *access pattern*. The access pattern captures the information about how this function accesses memory. For each function parameter, we have an *access operation AOp*, which can have a value of Read, Write, ReadWrite, or None. For every parameter that is read from, an LLVM load instruction is generated; for parameters written to, we create store instructions. More complex access patterns can be expressed using None as an access operation and an appropriate ♮ACSL contract via @assigns and @ensures.

We use two separate mechanisms (access patterns and contract annotations) because, in many simple cases, the pattern-generated instructions can be optimized away, making the resulting code much easier to analyze; contract annotations, being separate from the code, cannot be optimized as easily.

4.3 Interpolation

Unfortunately, user-provided annotations are usually few and far between, and one has to automatically approximate a given function for the purposes of interprocedural analysis. Craig interpolation has been one of the most used approaches in BMC for quite some time now [20, 27]. It is based on the following premise: for any unsatisfiable pair of formulae (B, Q), there exists a formula I (called Craig interpolant) that satisfies the following conditions:

- $B \rightarrow I$.
- (I, Q) is unsatisfiable.
- I contains only uninterpreted symbols common to both B and Q.

Formula I can be viewed as an overapproximation of B, which means it is a function overapproximation if we take function body as B, its safeness property as Q, and our pair of formulae as $(B, \neg Q)$.

The main problem of applying Craig interpolation in practice is that an interpolant exists only for a pair of *unsatisfiable* formulae, i.e., if there is no bug in the program. If a bug is present, one might fall back to function inlining (as proposed in [31]) and skip function approximation completely. We propose another approach that tries to apply Craig interpolation to a satisfiable pair of formulae $(B, \neg Q)$ by using random model sampling [3].

The idea behind random model sampling is to strengthen the satisfiable formula $B \wedge \neg Q$ with additional premises M, such that $B \wedge \neg Q \wedge M$ becomes unsatisfiable. The outline of the random model sampling algorithm is presented in Fig. 3.

We iteratively probe possible satisfying models of $B \wedge Q$, restrict them to contain only function arguments, and retain only those that falsify the original formula. Craig interpolation is applied afterward to $B \wedge \neg Q \wedge FA$ to obtain the result.

```
if B ∧ ¬Q is UNSAT then
    Use regular Craig interpolation with B ∧ ¬Q
else
    FA = false
    repeat
        SA_i = SAT model for B ∧ Q                      ▷ excluding all previous models
        FA_i = {A ∈ SA_i|A includes a function argument}
        if B ∧ ¬Q ∧ FA_i is SAT then
            continue
        end if
        FA = FA ∨ FA_i
    until FA has enough samples
    Use regular Craig interpolation with B ∧ ¬Q ∧ FA
end if
```

Fig. 3 Random model sampling algorithm

To infer a function summary, we interpolate from function body B to its interpolant S over $\neg Q \wedge FA$. If $S \wedge \neg Q$ is unsatisfiable, we managed to extract an interesting function summary. If not, we could retry with different probes or apply another approach to interprocedural analysis. For additional details and evaluation results, see [3].

5 Improving Analysis Precision Using Semi-Symbolic Program Execution

As seen in the previous sections, before the program is analyzed, it undergoes quite a number of transformations and approximations, including (but not limited to) a simplified memory model, loop unrollings, and interprocedural approximations. All these simplifications often result in differences between the analysis results and the actual program behavior if run. In other words, the trade-off between analysis quality and performance leads to its precision and recall being less than 100%.

To be practically applicable, the analysis should have high precision, so that its results can be trusted by the users [5, 16]. To improve Borealis' precision without sacrificing performance, we augmented it via semi-symbolic program execution.

5.1 The Need to Improve Analysis Precision

There are two basic measures of analysis quality: *precision* and *recall* [15]. They are dual in that one cannot achieve 100% precision and recall at the same time— any improvement to recall tends to raise the number of false positives (lowering precision), and any change which increases precision usually lowers the number of true positives (impacting recall).

The core idea of our approach is a very simple one: if one cannot lower the false positives rate by tweaking the analysis, one could try to filter out the false positives *after* the analysis has finished, thus having no impact on recall. We do this by executing the program IR in a checked and fully analysis-aware environment; in essence, this simulates a dynamic execution of the analyzed program, which (by definition) has 100% precision.

This semi-symbolic execution must satisfy the following properties to be applicable for our purposes:

- Avoid infinite or otherwise lengthy executions.
- Minimize resource consumption.
- Mitigate as many of analysis' inaccuracies as possible.
- Capture all interesting errors.

Let us explain how we achieve these properties in practice.

5.2   Semi-Symbolic Code Execution in a Controlled Environment

If we ignore the side effects and memory accesses, executing code in SSA form is pretty straightforward. We do need to explicitly model both the call stack and the instruction pointer register, but the rest can be implemented by storing a flat `Instruction -> Value` table. As no instruction is visited twice due to loop unrolling, each value in this table is effectively immutable.

Some values (e.g., `rand()` results) should be handled in an analysis-aware way, i.e., the values during the execution should be the same as were inferred by the analysis. This should also hold for things such as initial function arguments and global variables; otherwise, the execution would not conform to the analysis results. To support this, we treat these values as unknown or *symbolic*. Unlike classic symbolic execution, however, we try to get concrete values for as much of these symbols as possible using a special *arbiter*.

Arbiter is basically a function from symbols to values, which uses external information about the code. When checking BMC counterexamples, the arbiter provides the connection between the executor and the analysis results (i.e., values from the SMT satisfying assignment). However, the arbiter is independent from the analysis and could be extended upon if needed.

A very special case of symbolic values are pointers, which are modeled using special non-null values known both to the arbiter and the memory model. Dereferencing such a value queries the arbiter instead of the memory. As of now, we do not support writing values to symbolic pointers, which presents a problem when dealing with structures passed by pointers to top-level functions. This problem can be dealt with if one reconstructs the shape graph from the SMT counterexample; it is possible, but quite complex and not yet implemented in Borealis.

As code annotations are not compiled to LLVM IR, we also need to handle them separately in the executor. The contracts are represented as special intrinsics, so when the executor encounters such an instruction, it gets the values needed for the contract interpretation either from the arbiter or the current stack frame and evaluates the contract AST; as the contracts have no side effects, this step is pretty trivial.

5.3 Memory Modeling

Modeling memory efficiently is a challenging task, which we tackle using *implicit segment trees*. A segment tree (ST) is a well-known data structure [22]; in essence, it is a balanced tree with leaves representing elements and inner nodes representing ranges, the root of the tree being the whole range, and every child node representing a range one-half of its parent's. This data structure can be used to efficiently perform a number of tasks, such as range queries with associative binary operation—changing a leaf value and recalculating the whole tree is $O(\log_2(N))$ for a range of size N.

The basic segment tree is not very efficient memory-wise, so we implemented a number of optimizations. First, the nodes of the tree are constructed lazily. Second, we reduce the height of the tree by storing a flat array of bytes at every node. Figure 4 shows these differences for our implicit segment tree.

The memory tree is structured as follows. Each node in the tree contains a tuple $\langle Q, S, F, Sz, D \rangle$. Memory status Q (Alloca, Malloc, or Unknown) defines if this node is used as a root of an allocated memory region of size Sz. Memory state S (Memset, Uninitialized, or Unknown) represents memset'ed, uninitialized, or undefined memory region, thus shortcutting reads for allocated-but-never-written-to regions. The value of F is the memset value; the value of D is the actual stored data.

For a given memory access, the address used is mapped to an index in the tree, which is then accessed in a top-down fashion, lazily creating intermediate nodes if needed. Read accesses may stop at a memset node or go to a leaf; write accesses always go to a leaf, changing the flags on nodes affected by write accordingly. Allocations do not create new nodes, as our tree is lazy, so we need to only set the corresponding memory status flags. A detailed memory access algorithm may be found in [9].

Fig. 4 Implicit segment tree

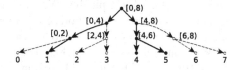

5.4   Handling External Functions

Another thing we need to execute actual C programs is to support external function calls, e.g., calls to the C standard library. Our executor uses a stub implementation of the C library and most common POSIX extensions. It does not simulate the actual side effects, but the values returned are sensible enough for most analysis purposes.

Functions directly operating with the memory are implemented on top of primitive read, write, memset, and memchr calls. memcpy is not a primitive operation at the moment and is implemented rather inefficiently, we plan to explore this problem in our future work. If one needs to provide additional external function implementations, there is no built-in support for this at the moment; however, one can use the other function approximation facilities provided by Borealis (see Sect. 4).

The executor (code named Tassadar) is implemented as a separate LLVM pass on top of Borealis' infrastructure, but is mostly independent from it. The actual execution engine is a derivative of the LLVM interpreter, with everything related to memory and contracts rewritten from scratch. For more details and evaluation, refer to [9].

6   Evaluation on Real-World Software

As mentioned before, most of small-scale evaluations for Borealis can be found in our previous papers [1–3, 9], where we focused more on if the sketched approaches actually improve anything. In this section we want to talk about our recent experiences with large-scale [attempts at] evaluation on industrial-sized projects.

There is a huge chasm between crafted programs traditionally used for software analyzer testings and real-world programs created to solve real-world problems. Our previous evaluations were done on NECLA and SV-COMP benchmarks, which have complex behavior, but are relatively small and written in a structured fashion. When you try to analyze coreutils or git or vim, your (presumably) well-tested and working bounded model checker suddenly starts to misbehave in ways you never even thought possible. Not surprisingly, when we did this with Borealis, we encountered exactly that.

First, there were crashes. A lot of them. Many of them were caused by bugs in Borealis itself, as it had never previously encountered code configurations seen in these projects. Some are attributed to incomplete or incorrect information we receive from the Clang/LLVM pipeline. Yet other ones are caused by completely missing components never needed before, e.g., Borealis works as a drop-in replacement for a compiler, but many projects also need an archiver (ar) for a successful build.

We managed to fix or work-around most of these crashes, only to run into the next problem of real-world program analysis: performance. Different parts of Borealis, starting from SMT solvers to your everyday logging facilities, suffered immense slowdowns when working with **big code**, so we had to somehow optimize Borealis. Some optimizations are easy, as one can disable logging and boost the optimization level from -O0 to -O2, getting a performance boost for free. Other optimizations are hard, making you profile your code again and again in search of fixable bottlenecks—the search only made harder by many external components with unpredictable performance.

As an example, when we started running experiments on git, it turned out 32 GBs of memory were not enough for the analysis to terminate. After aggressively optimizing for memory (and fixing a couple of logical memory leaks in the process), Borealis analyzed git successfully, after a week (sic!) of nonstop work. It was an achievement, but it was just not enough.

We started profiling the code, only to find out that parts of the system we never would have suspected were causing this slowdown. State slicing (used to prune the state of uninteresting predicates w.r.t. current safety property) was taking much too long compared even to the actual SMT procedure, because the alias analysis implementation we used was too slow. The predicate states exploded in size on git code, due to an inefficiency in our implementation which manifested only on deeply nested loops (unsurprisingly found in git). We even found some bugs in the functional programming library used extensively in Borealis.

It took us several months of trial and error, but we managed to fix these issues and reduce total git analysis time to a little over 5 h, i.e., 33× increase in performance. We still need to analyze the actual results and decide which paths we should explore next, but now it seems much more feasible than it did half a year ago.

7 Future Work

All in all, we do believe Borealis has successfully entered its adolescence but still has a long way to go. There are a lot of areas we would like to explore in the future; as of this chapter, our current work in progress includes the following:

- Using Borealis as a software repository mining tool to collect function code contracts via a combination of SMT and data mining methods
- Generating simplified function summaries based on source code heuristics
- Advancing our research on BMC-based test generation [29], e.g., improving support for complex data types
- Improving the quality of loop analysis and making the chains-of-recurrences approach work with recursion and loop-like function calls
- Designing a user-friendly function description language, which covers all aspects of [library] function behavior

Of course, we also have some long-term plans that are mainly targeted at making Borealis more of a software productivity tool than of a research prototype. When we have the resources, we would like to explore on how one might use BMC for implementing custom domain-specific analyses. We also need to continue testing

Borealis on difficult projects, so that it is stable enough to be used in continuous integration. As it is based on LLVM, we also think Borealis could be tweaked to work with other LLVM-based languages, such as C++, Rust, or Swift, and this potentially creates a plethora of interesting research questions.

8 Conclusion

In this chapter, we attempted to present all stages of research and development of our bounded model checking tool Borealis, from the basics to its evaluation on real-world programs. We discussed two of the most complicated problems in program analysis—loops and interprocedural interaction. We also presented our evaluation results on real-world programs and talked about the problems encountered and how we approached them. There are a lot of challenges ahead of us, still. Borealis needs to become more robust in terms of what code it can successfully analyze. We need to better our loop and interprocedural analyses. We also consider making Borealis into an extensible framework for domain-specific and user-defined analyses. Thankfully, all this does not seem impossible, now that we have dotted the *i*s and crossed the *t*s with this chapter.

Acknowledgements We would like to thank Bertrand Meyer for organizing the PAUSE conference and all who decided to spend their precious time reading this chapter.

References

1. Akhin, M., Belyaev, M., Itsykson, V.: Improving static analysis by loop unrolling on an arbitrary iteration. Humanit. Sci. Univ. J. **8**, 154–168 (2014)
2. Akhin, M., Belyaev, M., Itsykson, V.: Software defect detection by combining bounded model checking and approximations of functions. Autom. Control. Comput. Sci. **48**(7), 389–397 (2014)
3. Akhin, M., Kolton, S., Itsykson, V.: Random model sampling: making Craig interpolation work when it should not. Autom. Control. Comput. Sci. **49**(7), 413–419 (2015)
4. Armando, A., Mantovani, J., Platania, L.: Bounded model checking of software using SMT solvers instead of SAT solvers. Int. J. Softw. Tools Technol. Transfer **11**(1), 69–83 (2009)
5. Ayewah, N., Hovemeyer, D., Morgenthaler, J.D., Penix, J., Pugh, W.: Experiences using static analysis to find bugs. IEEE Softw. **25**, 22–29 (2008)
6. Bachmann, O., Wang, P.S., Zima, E.V.: Chains of recurrences — a method to expedite the evaluation of closed-form functions. In: ISSAC'94, pp. 242–249 (1994)
7. Barrett, C., Sebastiani, R., Seshia, S.A., Tinelli, C.: Satisfiability modulo theories. In: Handbook of Satisfiability, vol. 185, pp. 825–885. IOS Press, Amsterdam (2009)
8. Baudin, P., Filliâtre, J.C., Hubert, T., Marché, C., Monate, B., Moy, Y., Prevosto, V.: ACSL: ANSI/ISO C Specification Language. Preliminary Design, version 1.4, 2008, preliminary edn. (2008)
9. Belyaev, M., Itsykson, V.: Fast and safe concrete code execution for reinforcing static analysis and verification. Model. Anal. Inform. Sist. **22**, 763–772 (2015)

10. Berlin, D., Edelsohn, D., Pop, S.: High-level loop optimizations for GCC. In: Proceedings of the 2004 GCC Developers Summit, pp. 37–54 (2004)
11. Beyer, D.: Status report on software verification. In: TACAS'14, pp. 373–388 (2014)
12. Biere, A., Cimatti, A., Clarke, E.M., Zhu, Y.: Symbolic model checking without BDDs. In: TACAS'99, pp. 193–207 (1999)
13. Bradley, A.R., Manna, Z., Sipma, H.B.: What's decidable about arrays? In: VMCAI'06, pp. 427–442 (2006)
14. Bruttomesso, R., Cimatti, A., Franzén, A., Griggio, A., Sebastiani, R.: The MathSAT 4 SMT solver. In: CAV'08, pp. 299–303 (2008)
15. Buckland, M., Gey, F.: The relationship between recall and precision. J. Am. Soc. Inf. Sci. **45**(1), 12–19 (1994)
16. Calcagno, C., Distefano, D., Dubreil, J., et al.: Moving fast with software verification. NASA Formal Methods, pp. 3–11. Springer, Cham (2015)
17. Clarke, E., Grumberg, O., Jha, S., Lu, Y., Veith, H.: Counterexample-guided abstraction refinement for symbolic model checking. J. ACM **50**(5), 752–794 (2003)
18. Clarke, E., Kroening, D., Lerda, F.: A tool for checking ANSI-C programs. In: TACAS'04, pp. 168–176 (2004)
19. Cordeiro, L., Fischer, B., Marques-Silva, J.: SMT-based bounded model checking for embedded ANSI-C software. In: ASE'09, pp. 137–148 (2009)
20. Craig, W.: Three uses of the Herbrand-Gentzen theorem in relating model theory and proof theory. J. Symb. Log. **22**(3), 269–285 (1957)
21. Dan, A.M., Meshman, Y., Vechev, M., Yahav, E.: Predicate abstraction for relaxed memory models. Static Analysis, pp. 84–104. Springer, Berlin (2013)
22. de Berg, M., Cheong, O., van Kreveld, M., Overmars, M.: Computational Geometry: Algorithms and Applications. Springer, Berlin (2008)
23. De Moura, L., Bjørner, N.: Z3: an efficient SMT solver. In: TACAS'08, pp. 337–340 (2008)
24. Flanagan, C., Qadeer, S.: Predicate abstraction for software verification. In: POPL'02, pp. 191–202 (2002)
25. Fratantonio, Y., Machiry, A., Bianchi, A., Kruegel, C., Vigna, G.: CLAPP: characterizing loops in android applications. In: DeMobile 2015, pp. 33–34 (2015)
26. Grosser, T.C.: Enabling polyhedral optimizations in LLVM. Doctoral dissertation (2011)
27. McMillan, K.L.: Applications of Craig interpolants in model checking. In: TACAS'05, pp. 1–12 (2005)
28. Merz, F., Falke, S., Sinz, C.: LLBMC: Bounded model checking of C and C++ programs using a compiler IR. In: VSTTE'12, pp. 146–161 (2012)
29. Petrov, M., Gagarski, K., Belyaev, M., Itsykson, V.: Using a bounded model checker for test generation: how to kill two birds with one SMT solver. Autom. Control. Comput. Sci. **49**(7), 466–472 (2015)
30. Regehr, J.: A guide to undefined behavior in C and C++, part 1. http://blog.regehr.org/archives/213. Accessed 24 July 2017
31. Sery, O., Fedyukovich, G., Sharygina, N.: Interpolation-based function summaries in bounded model checking. In: HVC'11, pp. 160–175 (2012)
32. van Engelen, R.: Symbolic evaluation of chains of recurrences for loop optimization. Technical Report (2000)
33. Wang, X., Chen, H., Cheung, A., et al.: Undefined behavior: what happened to my code? In: APSYS'12, pp. 9:1–9:7 (2012)

How to Make Visual Modeling More Attractive to Software Developers

Andrey Terekhov, Timofey Bryksin, and Yurii Litvinov

Abstract The visual modeling paradigm has already been known for a number of decades, but still a vast majority of software engineers prefer traditional programming to automated code generation from visual models. This happens mostly because of the programmers' habit of creating the textual code and almost emotional attachment to it, but also because of the common prejudice toward code generation from general purpose modeling languages (especially UML) and the lack of ease of use of visual integrated development environments (IDEs). In this chapter, we address the last issue and discuss several ways to make modeling using diagrams acceptable for industrial software development. Specialized domain-specific visual languages could be used to make models clearer and more understandable. In addition, a lot of effort is required for tool developers to make tools supporting these languages less difficult to use in everyday work. We present a QReal domain-specific modeling (DSM) platform and discuss what we have done to make visual IDEs created on this platform easier and more productive to use, and the process of their creation simpler, e.g., mouse gestures recognition for rapid creation of elements and links on diagrams, or a number of special features that increase the productivity of the modeling process.

1 Introduction

Plenty of engineering psychologists believe that people perceive graphic images better than textual information. A number of authors analyze the old proverb "A picture is worth a thousand words" [1–8]. Ben Shneiderman in [9] says that the difference in preferences between flowcharts or a text is due to the difference in the style of thinking, depending on which one of the cerebral hemispheres, left or right, is leading. Individuals in whom the right hemisphere is more active (intuitive people, focused on visual information, who prefer to recognize images) may prefer flowcharts, while individuals in whom the left hemisphere is more active (focused on

A. Terekhov (✉) • T. Bryksin • Y. Litvinov
Saint Petersburg State University, Sankt-Peterburg, Russia
e-mail: a.terekhov@spbu.ru; t.bryksin@spbu.ru; y.litvinov@spbu.ru

© Springer International Publishing AG 2017
M. Mazzara, B. Meyer (eds.), *Present and Ulterior Software Engineering*,
https://doi.org/10.1007/978-3-319-67425-4_9

verbal information and inclined to deductive reasoning) enjoy reading the program code.

Later Larkin and Simon in [10] provided good analyses as to why diagrams have some advantages over propositional representations. Green and Petre in [11] stated that the main usability concerns of granularity, scalability, and screen space are closely related to the cognitive dimensions of diffuseness, viscosity, and visibility. It can help us explain developers' preferences on whether to use diagrams or not.

Visual diagram languages have been used for a long time in different fields: in telecommunications (SDL, Specification and Description Language; recommendations Z.100–Z.106 ITU [12]), in aviation and other technically complex areas (SADT, Structured Analysis and Design Technique [13]; the most famous part of SADT is IDEF0), in the descriptions of business processes (BPMN, Business Process Model and Notation [14]), and in other subject areas. Many tools were developed that support a variety of graphic models.[1]

Nevertheless, the technologies of software development based on graphical modeling did not make it into general use, with traditional textual programming in algorithmic languages remaining mainstream. For several decades now, we have been creating a tool for model-based software development at the Software Engineering Department of St. Petersburg State University, so we are interested in investigating this issue.

We realized that general-purpose languages like UML (Unified Modeling Language [15], the first version appeared in 1996) are too cumbersome [16]. It is hard to use them in real industrial practice. More than 30 years ago, Shneiderman stated in [17] that traditional block diagrams are good only at the initial stages of design, but dynamic activity diagrams of UML are very similar to block schemes. We think that the reason is very simple—UML and similar languages are too close to traditional textual languages (just the same assignments, conditions, loops, etc.).

Specialized languages, customized for narrow subject areas (DSL, Domain Specific Languages) prove to be much more convenient. They are more expressive and allow to perform automatic generation of an effective object code. Every primitive language element (icon on a screen) has rich semantics based on a chosen application area. Domain experts easily study these languages. There are several publications [18, 19] that state 3–10 times productivity boost of mobile application developers who used DSL compared to those who used traditional technologies. Our experience with DSL for programming robots [20] and for education [5, 21] shows similar results.

It is too expensive to implement graphical editors, code generators, run-time environment, debuggers, etc. for each DSL.

A better solution is to create a metatechnology that could generate all the necessary tools from a compact formal description of the desired DSL. Such tools are called DSM platforms, and visual IDEs for solving tasks in a specific domain created using such platforms are called DSM solutions. DSM platforms help

---

[1] A list of diagramming tools, URL: http://www.diagramming.org/.

developers create visual languages and appropriate tool support for them; however, it does not mean that there needs to exist an abundance of such languages. DSM solutions are still substantial pieces of technology and require language developers, domain experts, and at least several weeks to be developed. In this process, DSM platforms provide tooling support to automate language specification and creation of IDE tools by solution developers. Then such DSM solutions are used within teams or even company-wide to create software in domains that this particular solution targets.

There are several such metatools on the market [22–24], but in our opinion some are tied to a specific platform [25]; others are too large, complicated, and difficult to use [26]; while some others are expensive and little known [27], so we decided to develop our own DSM platform using our experience in this area.

Another important feature of a visual IDE is a convenient interface. We were impressed by the result of the student research work where the distance traveled by a mouse cursor was calculated. It turned out that when a user draws a complicated diagram by dragging icons from the menu bar on the main working field, the distance traveled by the cursor can reach several kilometers. From that we gained a fundamentally new understanding of the working user-space organization for our graphical software development technology.

The main contribution of this chapter is a set of usability improvements for DSM platforms that were implemented in QReal platform and are described in Sect. 4. Section 2 provides an overview of related works, Sect. 3 introduces QReal, Sect. 5 briefly describes the most successful application of QReal to date, and Sect. 6 concludes the chapter.

2 Related Works

In the 1990s (the time when CASE tools were considered as the next step in the evolution of software development tools), there were numerous papers trying to understand why CASE tools were not used as extensively as they were supposed to be. Aside from technical, economical, and administrative reasons, many researchers mentioned a serious impact of usability issues [10, 28–35].

In [32], Huang says that tools are usually technology and process centered, but not user centered. He believes that tools must adapt themselves to the level of their users: help novices (via manuals, tooltips, wizards, etc.) and give more freedom to advanced users, show different control elements to various user groups, and make different features available to them (e.g., divide complex operations into several simpler ones for novices and offer advanced techniques for more skilled users).

Jarzabek in [33] also notes that existing CASE tools are excessively formal and methodology oriented. This leads to developers spending time performing operations that the CASE tool wants them to, but not what needs to be done to solve the original business task. For example, most of the formalized modeling languages have numerous constraints on models that can be created. These strict rules describing how to use language elements not only forbid a modeler to create incorrect diagrams but also mess with his or her natural train of thought, forcing to follow the steps of a predefined process. For instance, in this case the problem could have been solved with a new graphical editor's mode that temporarily allows to create models free of syntax, semantics rules, and other constraints. It would have encouraged developers' creative thinking. The same problem is also mentioned in [29]: tools should help their users solve problems and not bring them new ones.

An easy-to-use graphical interface of modeling tools has inherent value. The research published in [30] shows that the more developers like a user interface of a CASE tool and the easier it seems to them to use its instruments, the more readily they will use it and will consider it more useful and helpful than an unattractive and inconvenient tool. Lending et al. [36] also confirm that the usability of CASE tools is a motivator that is as strong as an increase in productivity that could happen when using these tools.

In the 2000s and 2010s, CASE tools lost some attention from the industry but continued to evolve, mostly in technological aspects. The current research [37–39] shows successful cases of applications of a model-driven approach in industry, but in general its authors agree that modeling is mostly taken as a "drawing of pretty pictures": an activity that requires tiresome routine operations and interrupts the main work activity, which is coding. We believe that these operations should be automated.

3 QReal DSM Platform

QReal [40] is a DSM platform that has been developed by a research group of Software Engineering Chair of St. Petersburg State University since 2007. It was based on our previous research [41]. QReal is an open-source project, written in C++ with Qt library. Its main goals are to provide an easy-to-use cross-platform multiuser technology to create domain-specific languages, which can also serve as a base for research in visual modeling, metamodeling, visual languages, and related fields. What distinguishes QReal from other existing DSM platforms is that it is designed with a principle "one does not need to know something that he does not use." This enables even first-time users to create DSL without special training in metamodeling and visual language formalisms. It also differs from other academic DSM platforms as it provides means to create a complete DSM solution, not only visual editors or model transformation tools. There are several DSM solutions already implemented with QReal that are used in production.

QReal consists of an abstract core, which provides the functionality common to all visual languages such as generic user interface, generic visual editor, a repository with models, property and model editors, and so on, and several plug-ins, which implement all language specifics. QReal core has no code that is specific to a particular language and is designed so that it can work with a large class of graph-based visual languages. Language syntax information, such as the list of

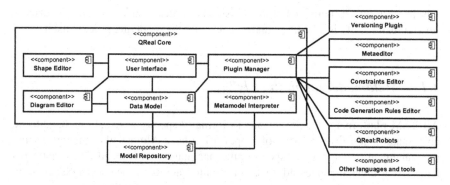

Fig. 1 QReal architecture

language elements, their properties, and shapes that could be connected by links and so on, is provided by plug-ins and is used by a generic visual editor. The core also contains utilities needed to create supporting tools such as a framework for generators creation or a graph transformation engine. High-level architecture of QReal is presented on Fig. 1.

Language syntax is specified in a XML-based textual metalanguage or using a visual metaeditor. The visual and text languages are interchangeable. A metamodel can be generated automatically to C++ code of an editor, which is then compiled to a shared library and opened in QReal as a plug-in. A metamodel can also be opened for interpretation by the core directly, without the need for generation.

Several DSM solutions were created using a QReal technology, the most notable is QReal:Robots [35] described in more detail in Sect. 5. The second DSM solution used in production is QReal:BP, a tool for business processing modeling. It is based on the BPMN modeling language and consists of a visual editor and a C#.NET code generator.

4 Usability Improvements

There are two main reasons why developers may find a visual modeling tool difficult to use: the inconvenience of the tool itself (many routine operations that are needed to be done while working, difficult to understand a user interface, tangled process of development, etc.) and the inconvenience of modeling language(s) the tool is based on. The second problem is partially solved by the DSM paradigm itself: developers create and use specialized languages that consist of well-known entities from a target domain, not abstract classes and objects. However, that raises another issue: the development of new languages and tools for them is a difficult task on its own and should be optimized too.

The following subsection describes a new metamodeling approach that allows to hide a number of implementation details from a language developer and thus makes this process less difficult for nonprofessionals. Later in this section, we discuss several features of visual editors that can simplify the modeling process itself.

4.1 "Metamodeling on the Fly"

All DSM platforms use some means to formally specify a visual language to be able to automatically generate tool support for it later. Almost all of them use some metalanguage (a language to specify other languages). Advanced DSM platforms have visual metalanguage and visual metaeditor, and the process of DSL creation consists of the development of its metamodel in a metaeditor, then automatic creation of a visual editor from the metamodel, and the automated or manual development of other tools like generators, model transformation tools, and so on.

However, for the end users this approach has one major usability drawback. To be able to create a language, even a small one, one needs to know things that may be beyond the reach of even a seasoned software engineer. Those things include working with formal syntax of a visual language, the concepts of metamodeling, understanding of metalevels (problem domain, model, metamodel, metametamodel), and so on. So, the development of a new DSL in most cases can only be done in collaboration with the authors of a selected DSM platform, who have the requisite knowledge and experience.

A QReal platform also has a visual metaeditor, but it also proposes a different approach as an alternative, called informally "metamodeling on the fly." The main idea of this approach is that a language can be specified right in the process of drawing a diagram in that language. For example, a user wants some kind of a state machine and has no adequate premade language to draw one. The user creates a new language, adds an entity named "Diagram," adds this new diagram to a model, adds an entity named "State," provides a graphical representation for it, and adds some states to the diagram. Then the user adds a link between states to the language, uses it on the diagram, and realizes that states shall have some properties like a name, and links shall have guard conditions and actions. To define them the user adds these properties to the entities of a language, and all existing instances of those entities, already drawn on a diagram, will get those properties as the default values that can be changed later. The point of this new approach is that all features commonly related to metaeditor, like adding a new element to a language or editing properties of an element, are implemented as seamless extensions of the diagram editor interface, no metaeditor is needed, and the user may not even know about the underlying metamodel and the related formalism.

This approach is aimed to help the inexperienced language developers to quickly create small visual languages without much theoretical knowledge and training in DSM platforms. It also greatly reduces the effort in the early prototyping phase of DSL creation, so it is also useful to experienced developers. For example, a prototype created with metamodeling on the fly can be opened in metaeditor for further language refining. This eliminates the cycle "make changes to a

metamodel -> recreate an editor -> try to use a language by drawing a model."
A similar methodology was proposed in Agentsheets platform [17], and its authors
proposed to create languages with the participation of an end user, when a language
developer and a user worked on the same computer, the user tries to draw a
model and the developer adds new features to a language and fixes issues right in
place (which is a form of pair programming—a widely used technique in software
development). This method is also feasible with metamodeling on the fly, but our
technology makes it possible even for the end users to develop a language entirely,
without the developers' help. It is a feasible approach because Agentsheets does
not have a metaeditor—all changes to a language are done by drawing a diagram.
In QReal, metamodeling on the fly allows to create only a prototype of a language
with many formal aspects assumed as defaults, which is good enough in many cases
and allows to keep the user interface very simple. The prototype thus created can be
refined and extended in metaeditor later, if needed.

The technology was implemented in QReal. Several small- and medium-scale
languages were created with it (ranging in complexity from a few to nearly 30
entities in a language) [42]. Some implementation issues worth noting arose in
the process. Firstly, metamodeling on the fly is only possible when a metamodel
is interpreted by the DSM platform's core, so it can be changed dynamically,
since metamodeling on the fly actually has a metamodel and changes it when a
user changes the language. Many existing DSM platforms generate the code of
an editor and load it as a plug-in; in that case such a mode will be impossible.
Secondly, an ability to change a language when editing the diagram of this language
requires implementing a concurrent model and metamodel evolution features. For
example, we may change a type of a property in a metamodel, but existing elements
already have those properties filled with some meaningful values. There are many
such situations, and also it is possible to open a project created with an earlier
version of the language, which further complicates implementation (see [24] for
details). To avoid future conflicts and enable backward compatibility, the current
implementation detects dangerous changes (e.g., when a type of a property changes
so that existing values cannot be converted to a new type) and shows a user a warning
about it. More automated ways of dealing with such problems are considered for
further research.

4.2 Mouse Gestures Recognition

The effectiveness of each tool is determined by how easy and fast it allows its users
to perform operations that this tool is created for. In modeling, some of the most
frequent operations are creation and deletion of the elements on diagrams and of
the relationships between them. In most visual modeling tools, a user should first
find an element on some kind of a palette, toolbar, or menu to create an instance,
and then click or drag-and-drop it on a diagram canvas. Despite the fact that this
kind of interaction process is pretty common, even such a basic task as creation

of an element results in a sequence of purely mechanical operations that must be repeated again and again. Needless to say that to do them a user should recall what menu, toolbar, or palette tab this particular element is located on, switching mental context from the hierarchy of models to the usage of a particular tool. It gets even worse if a tool supports a number of languages with dozens of elements in each. We believe that the task of elements creation can and should take less mechanical actions, should be more intuitive, and easy to perform.

As an alternative for the traditional element creation mechanism, mouse gestures recognition could be used. A lot of research has been made in this field.[2] A number of modeling tools allow to create elements using mouse gesture recognition (e.g., Visual Paradigm[3]), but to the best of our knowledge, there have been no attempts yet to employ this technique on domain-specific platform level (i.e., implement automated generation of mouse gesture recognizers for different visual IDEs).

In QReal, each language element is paired with a so-called ideal gesture, a recorded path of a mouse pointer that each new user's gesture will be compared to. By default, each element's ideal gesture looks similar to this element's visual representation. These default ideal gestures are set automatically when a visual editor is generated from a language metamodel. A custom ideal gesture for any element could be set using QReal's special gestures editor at any time later. While modeling users perform mouse gestures (holding the right mouse button pressed to differentiate from regular mouse movements) which are compared to ideal gestures of current language elements. If a match is found, a new element is created on a diagram (the same element that the recognized ideal gesture corresponds to).

There are no special mouse gestures for each particular association. To create a link between two elements on a diagram, one should just perform a gesture of any kind starting and ending on an existing element. A special QReal component checks what types of links are possible between these elements according to this language's metamodel and suggests choosing one of them. If there can only be one of them, it will be created automatically.

For more detailed information about the implementation of mouse gestures recognition in QReal, see [43].

4.3 Visual Editors Features

4.3.1 Linkers

In addition to mouse gestures recognition, there is another mechanism for rapid creation of relationships in QReal: the so-called linkers. Linkers are UI elements that are displayed near the elements on diagrams when users select these elements (see Fig. 2).

---

[2]Sketch recognition researchers, URL: https://en.wikipedia.org/wiki/Sketch_recognition.

[3]Visual Paradigm modeling tool, URL: https://www.visual-paradigm.com/.

Fig. 2 A selected element with a linker near it in QReal:Robots

Fig. 3 An element with embedded control widgets on a diagram (two drop-down lists and one edit line below the element icon)

Clicking on a linker and moving a mouse while holding the pressed left mouse button, one can "drag" a link out of an element. Releasing a mouse button on an existing element results in creation of a link connecting these two elements: the one the linker belongs to and the one that a mouse was released on. If a mouse is released on an empty diagram space, a special menu is shown. This menu allows to either create "dangling" links from the selected element to this position or create a new element here and connect it with the first one. Where an element can have several types of outgoing links, several linkers are displayed near it, one per each relationship type.

4.3.2 Embedded Control Widgets

Any nontrivial language elements have sets of properties (or attributes) of various types. To change these attributes, the development environments traditionally employ property editors or special modal windows that appear when an element is being clicked on. Moreover, a property editor or window is often the only way to see values of most of the properties. Switching to such a window or to a property editor multiple times is another time-consuming operation that we believe could be optimized. In QReal, we use the so-called embedded control widgets—special control elements that are placed within elements' graphical representation and are used to show and manipulate properties' values (see Fig. 3).

It is true that having many such widgets can easily make a diagram unreadable, so a language developer should find a reasonable balance between informative and compact diagrams. Using QReal's special shape editor, language developers can adjust visual representations of language elements: choose properties that will be displayed with control widgets and define the position and type of such widgets. It is also possible to specify whether a control widget will be shown always or only when an element is selected.

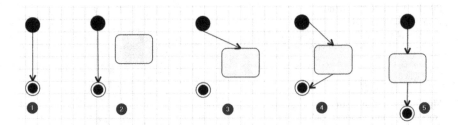

Fig. 4 Steps of inserting an element between two existing ones

4.3.3 DRAKON Language Usability Heuristics

Several usability heuristics were taken from the DRAKON[4] visual language [44]. This language was created in the 1980s–1990s with participation from the Russian Federal Space Agency and was used in the development of real-time software for Russian space shuttles. The language was created in a way to ensure good readability of created diagrams and comfort of the modeling process itself.

We describe two of these heuristics—the splittable links mechanism and creating elements in groups.

Existing diagrams often need to be extended with new elements positioned between the existing ones. For instance, this often happens in control-flow diagrams when inserting elements in the middle of a sequence of elements. It also takes a lot of mechanical operations (e.g., see Fig. 4).

To simplify this, we implemented the following: when an element is drag-and-dropped on an existing link, all steps on Fig. 4 are performed automatically, including repositioning the lowest element (and all elements that are placed lower on a diagram). The reverse action is also very helpful: when the middle element is deleted, QReal deletes one of the dangling links and connects another one to the element following the deleted one. Right now this heuristic does not work for multiple incoming and outgoing links.

Another useful feature of a visual editor is the creation of elements in logical groups. It is helpful for languages with composite elements. For example, a block diagram can have a Loop element consisting of a LoopCondition and LoopEnd element, and several other elements between them. In QReal, we added "Group" metamodel entity that allows to describe such composite elements. In a diagram editor, each group is represented by a special palette element. When such an element is drag-and-dropped on a diagram, all elements that were defined for this group in the language metamodel are created at once.

---

[4]DRAKON visual language, URL: https://en.wikipedia.org/wiki/DRAKON.

5 A Successful Application of Qreal—Qreal:Robots

The most successful application of QReal DSM platform for the creation of DSM solution to date is QReal:Robots (renamed to TRIK Studio now). QReal:Robots is a development environment for programming robots. It is now used in several Russian schools to teach fifth to seventh grade students the basics of programming; there are also organizations that use it outside Russia (teaching groups of children in England and France). QReal:Robots has a visual language consisting of about 40 elements, and a number of generators and interpreters that allow to execute diagrams on supported robotic platforms. Today we support NXT and Lego EV3 robots, TRIK robotic kit, or a simulator model included in QReal:Robots itself. Diagrams can be generated into several textual programming languages, including C, JavaScript, F#, and Pascal for autonomous execution on a robot or interpreted on a computer that controls a robot remotely using a Bluetooth, Wi-Fi, or USB interface. A simulator model and means to communicate with real robots were implemented manually, while the editor and the generators were implemented using QReal metamodeling capabilities, and it is worth noting that the editor prototype was created in just a few hours (and most of the time was spent searching images for visual language blocks).

There are numerous publications describing this case, such as [45]. Most interesting in the context of this work are our studies on the usability of QReal:Robots system that we have conducted to evaluate the impact of improvements proposed in Sects. 4.2 and 4.3. The studies [46, 47] show that QReal:Robots is well received by the users, and most of them even find it more usable than existing "handwritten" tools for robots programming. The user interface of QReal:Robots solution is presented in Fig. 5.

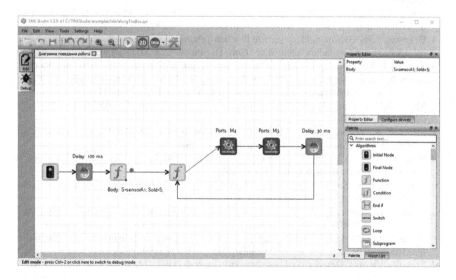

Fig. 5 QReal:Robots user interface

6   Conclusions

In this chapter, we have presented some usability improvements to a CASE system that can be implemented on the level of DSM platform, so they will be available in any DSM solution that is built with this technology. The successful implementation and adoption of QReal:Robots DSM solution described in Sect. 5 supports the point that the proposed usability improvements allow DSM platforms to generate solutions that are able to compete with custom handwritten tools.

A QReal platform also applies domain-specific modeling to itself, allowing to create DSL by using a set of specialized DSL, such as metaeditor, constraints editor, and so on. This chapter also demonstrates how the improvements presented here make the process of DSL development more effective. Our preliminary experiments [48] show that QReal allows to create a visual language and a set of tools for it several times faster than the existing state-of-the-art DSM platforms, especially in the "metamodeling-on-the-fly" mode. The more detailed comparison is the subject of future study, this chapter shows that the QReal approach is potentially effective.

We believe that with continued effort in improving the usability of CASE systems and with the future development of domain-specific modeling, visual languages will be used much more widely in the industrial programming practice.

References

1. Bishop, A.: Is a picture worth a thousand words? Math. Teach. **81**, 32–35 (1977)
2. Cleland-Huang, J.: Requirements engineering's next top model. IEEE Softw. **30**(06), 24–29 (2013)
3. DeLoache, J.S., Marzolf, D.P.: When a picture is not worth a thousand words: young children's understanding of pictures and models. Cogn. Dev. **7**, 317–329 (1992)
4. Gleitman, L.R., Gleitman, H.: A picture is worth a thousand words, but that's the problem: the role of syntax in vocabulary acquisition. Curr. Dir. Psychol. Sci. **1**(1), 31–35 (1992)
5. Koznov, D.V.: Teaching to write software engineering documents with focus on document design by means of mind maps 2012. In: Proceedings of the IASTED International Conference on Computers and Advanced Technology in Education, CATE 2012, pp. 112–118
6. Mayer, R.E., Gallini, J.K.: When is an illustration worth ten thousand words? J. Educ. Psychol. **82**(4), 718–726 (1990)
7. Miller, G.A.: The magical number seven, plus or minus two: some limits on our capacity for processing information. Psychol. Rev. **63**, 81–97 (1956)
8. Wollows, D.M.: A picture is not always worth a thousand words: pictures as distractors in reading. J. Educ. Psychol. **70**(2), 255–262 (1978)
9. Shneiderman, B.: Software Psychology. Human Factors in Computer and Information Systems. Winthrop Publishers, INC, Cambridge (1980)
10. Larkin, J.H., Simon, H.A.: Why a diagram is (sometimes) worth ten thousand words. Cogn. Sci. **11**, 65–99 (1987)
11. Green, T.R.G., Petre, M.: Usability analysis of visual programming environments: a 'cognitive dimensions' approach. J. Vis. Lang. Comput. **7**(2), 131–174 (1996)
12. Specification and Description Language specification, URL: http://www.itu.int/rec/T-REC-Z.106/en

13. Marca, D.A., McGowan, C.L.: SADT: Structured Analysis and Design Technique. McGraw-Hill, New York (1987)
14. Business Process Model and Notation specification, URL: http://www.omg.org/spec/BPMN/
15. Unified Modeling Language specification, URL: http://www.omg.org/spec/UML/
16. Petre, M.: UML in practice. In: 35th International Conference on Software Engineering (ICSE 2013), pp. 722–731. IEEE Press, Piscataway (2013)
17. Repenning, A., Sumner, T.: Agentsheets: a medium for creating domain-oriented visual languages. Computer. **28**(3), 17–25 (1995)
18. Kelly, S.: Visual domain-specific modeling: Benefits and experiences of using metaCASE tools [electronic resource]. In: Kelly, S., Tolvanen, J.P. (eds.) International Workshop on Model Engineering, at ECOOP (2000), URL: http://dsmforum.org/papers/Visual_domain-specific_modelling.pdf (online; accessed: 25 Oct 2015)
19. Tolvanen, J., Kelly, S.: Model-driven development challenges and solutions. Modelsward. **2016**, 711–719 (2016)
20. Terekhov, A.: QReal:Robots — an environment for teaching computer science and robotics in schools [electronic resource]. In: Terekhov, A., Litvinov, Y., Bryksin, T. (eds.) CEE-SECR '13 Proceedings of the 9th Central & Eastern European Software Engineering Conference in Russia. ACM, New York (2013), URL: http://dl.acm.org/citation.cfm?id=2556610.2596543 (online; accessed: 30 Nov 2015)
21. Koznov, D., Pliskin, M.: Computer-supported collaborative learning with mind-maps. Communications in Computer and Information Science 17 CCIS, pp. 478–489 (2008)
22. Ledeczi, A.: The generic modeling environment [electronic resource]. In: Ledeczi, A., Maroti, M., Bakay, A., Karsai, G., Garrett, J., et al. (eds.) Workshop on Intelligent Signal Processing (WISP'2001), Budapest, Hungary (2001)
23. Viyovic, V.: Sirius: a rapid development of DSM graphical editor. In: Viyovic, V., Maksimovic, M., Perisic, B. (eds.) IEEE 18th International Conference on Intelligent Engineering Systems INES 2014, pp. 233–238. IEEE Computer Society, Los Alamitos (2014)
24. Zhu, N., Grundy, J., Hosking, J., Liu, N., Cao, S., Mehra, A.: Pounamu: a meta-tool for exploratory domain-specific visual language tool development. J. Syst. Softw. **80**(8), 1390–1407 (2007)
25. Cook, S.: In: Cook, S., Jones, G., Kent, S., Wills, A.C. (eds.) Domain-Specific Development with Visual Studio DSL Tools, p. 576. Addison-Wesley, Crawfordsville (2007). ISBN: 978-0-321-39820-8
26. The Eclipse Foundation. Eclipse Modeling Project home page [Electronic resource], URL: http://www.eclipse.org/modeling/ (online; accessed: 12 Jan 2015)
27. Kelly, S., Tolvanen, J.-P.: Domain-Specific Modeling: Enabling Full Code Generation, p. 444. Wiley-IEEE Computer Society Press, Hoboken (2008). ISBN: 978-0-470-03666-2
28. Aaen, I.: CASE tool bootstrapping – how little strokes fell great oaks. In: Lyytinen, K., Tahvanainen, V.-P. (eds.) Next Generation CASE Tools, pp. 8–17. IOS Press, Amsterdam (1992)
29. Damm, C.H.: Creative object-oriented modelling: support for intuition, flexibility, and collaboration in CASE tools. In: Damm, C.H., Hansen, K.M., Thomsen, M., Tyrsted, M. (eds.) 14th European Conference on Object-Oriented Programming, pp. 27–43. Springer, London (2000)
30. Davis, E.D., Bagozzi, R.P., Warshaw, P.R.: Extrinsic and intrinsic motivation to use computers in the workplace. J. Appl. Soc. Psychol. **22**(14), 1111–1132 (1992)
31. Gillies, A.C.: Managing software engineering. In: Gillies, A.C., Smith, P. (eds.) Case Studies and Solutions. Chapman & Hall, London (1994)
32. Huang, R.: Making active CASE tools – toward the next generation CASE tools. ACM SIGSOFT Softw. Eng. Notes. **23**(1), 47–50 (1998)
33. Jarzabek, S., Huang, R.: The case for user-centered CASE tools. Commun. ACM **41**(8), 93–99 (1998). ACM New York
34. Ol'khovich, L.B., Koznov, D.V.: OCL-based automated validation method for UML specifications. Programmirovanie. **29**(6), 44–51 (2003)

35. Sharma, A.: Framework to define CASE tool requirements for distributed environment. ACM SIGSOFT Softw. Eng. Notes **19**(1), 86–89 (1994). ACM Press

36. Lending, D.: The use of CASE tools. In: Lending, D., Chervany, N.L. (eds.) Proceedings of the 1998 ACM SIGCPR Conference on Computer Personnel Research, pp. 49–58. ACM Press, New York (1998)

37. Hutchinson, J.: Model-driven engineering practices in industry. In: Hutchinson, J., Rouncefield, M., Whittle, J. (eds.) 33rd International Conference on Software Engineering, pp. 633–642. IEEE, New Jersey (2011)

38. Mohagheghi, P., Gilani, W., Stefanescu, A., Fernandez, M.A.: An empirical study of the state of the practice and acceptance of model-driven engineering in four industrial cases. Empir. Softw. Eng. **18**(1), 89–116 (2013). Springer US

39. Selic, B.: What will it take? A view on adoption of model-based methods in practice. Softw. Syst. Model. **11**(4), 513–526 (2012). Springer-Verlag New York

40. Kuzenkova, A., Deripaska, A., Bryksin, T., Litvinov, Y., Polyakov, V.: QReal DSM platform: an environment for creation of specific visual IDEs. In: Proceedings of 8th International Conference on Evaluation of Novel Approaches to Software Engineering (ENASE 2013), pp. 251–257. SCITEPRESS, Setúbal (2013)

41. Terekhov, A.N., Romanovskii, K.Y., Koznov, D.V., Dolgov, P.S., Ivanov, A.N.: RTST++: methodology and a CASE tool for the development of information systems and software for real-time systems. Program. Comput. Softw. **25**(5), 276–281 (1999)

42. Птахина, А.И.: Разработка метамоделирования "на лету" в системе QReal // Список-2013. In: Материалы всероссийской научной конференции по проблемам информатики. 2013г, pp. 28–36. СПб.: Изд-во ВВМ, Санкт-Петербург (2012) (in Russian)

43. Osechkina, M., Litvinov, Y., Bryksin, T.: Multistroke Mouse Gestures Recognition in QReal metaCASE Technology. In: SYRCoSE 2012: Proceedings of the 6th Spring/Summer Young Researchers' Colloquium on Software Engineering, pp. 194–200 (2012)

44. DRAKON visual language, URL: http://en.wikipedia.org/wiki/DRAKON

45. Литвинов, Ю.В.: Реализация визуальных средств программирования роботов для изучения информатики в школах. Компьютерные инструменты в образовании. (1), 36–45 (2013) (in Russian)

46. Кузенкова, А.С.: Анализ пользовательского интерфейса QReal:Robots, курсовая работа, URL: http://se.math.spbu.ru/SE/YearlyProjects/2013/YearlyProjects/2013/445/445-Kuzenkova-report.pdf (in Russian)

47. Соковикова, Н.А.: Usability в проекте QReal:Robots // Список-2012. In: Материалы всероссийской научной конференции по проблемам информатики. 25–27 апр. 2012г, pp. 66–69. СПб.: Изд-во ВВМ, Санкт-Петербург (2012) (in Russian)

48. Брыксин, Т.А.: Платформа для создания специализированных визуальных сред разработки программного обеспечения: диссертация на соискание степени кандидата технических наук, Санкт-Петербургский государственный университет, Санкт-Петербург (2016) (in Russian)

Intrinsic Redundancy for Reliability and Beyond

Alberto Goffi, Alessandra Gorla, Andrea Mattavelli, and Mauro Pezzè

Abstract Software redundancy is an essential mechanism in engineering. Different forms of redundant design are the core technology of well-established reliability and fault-tolerant mechanisms in traditional engineering as well as in software engineering. In this chapter, we discuss *intrinsic software redundancy*, a type of redundancy that is not added explicitly at design time to improve runtime reliability but is natively present in modern software system due to independent design and development decisions. We introduce the concept of intrinsic redundancy, discuss its diffusion and the reasons for its presence in modern software systems, indicate how it can be automatically identified, and present some current and future applications of such form of redundancy to produce more reliable software systems at affordable costs.

1 Introduction

Reliability, which is *the ability of a system or component to perform its required functions under stated conditions for a specified period of time* [28], is a key property of engineered products and in particular of software artifacts. Safety critical applications must meet the high reliability standards required for their field deployment, time- and business-critical applications must obey strong reliability

A. Goffi (✉)
USI Università della Svizzera italiana, Lugano, Switzerland
e-mail: alberto.goffi@usi.ch

A. Gorla
IMDEA Software Institute, Madrid, Spain
e-mail: alessandra.gorla@imdea.org

A. Mattavelli
Imperial College London, London, UK
e-mail: a.mattavelli@imperial.ac.uk

M. Pezzè
USI Università della Svizzera italiana, Lugano, Switzerland

University of Milano-Bicocca, Milan, Italy
e-mail: mauro.pezze@usi.ch

© Springer International Publishing AG 2017   153
M. Mazzara, B. Meyer (eds.), *Present and Ulterior Software Engineering*,
https://doi.org/10.1007/978-3-319-67425-4_10

requirements, and everyday and commodity products should meet less stringent but still demanding customer requirements.

Reliability exploits runtime mechanisms that prevent or mask failures by relying on some form of *redundancy*: *redundant implementation* that is based on runtime replicas of the same or similar components to temper the failure of one or more elements, *redundant design* that relies on independently designed components with the same functionality to reduce the impact of faults, and *redundant information* that replicates information to compensate for corrupted data.

In classic engineering practice, examples of redundant *implementations* are the third engine of the McDonnell Douglas DC-10 and MD-11 aircraft, added in the late 1960s to tolerate single-engine failures;[1] the Boeing 777 control system that is compiled with three different compilers and runs on three distinct processors [49]; the design of Systems-on-a-Chip (SoC), which relies on redundant Components;[2] and the Redundant Array of Independent Disks (RAID) technology that combines multiple physical disk drive components into a single logical unit [36]. An example of redundant *design* in classic engineering is the redundant design practice for building bridges to prevent localized failures from propagating to the whole bridge structure [18, 19, 32]. A well-known instance of redundant *information* is the Hadoop Distributed File System (HDFS) that improves reliability by replicating data [41].

In software engineering, redundant design is a basic principle of fault-tolerant approaches, which explicitly add redundancy to tolerate unavoidable faults [43]. Examples of redundant software design are N-version programming modules [12], rollback and recovery techniques, error-correcting codes, and recovery blocks [22, 26, 37, 38]. Redundant design relies on elements *explicitly* added to the system, which come with extra costs that limit their applicability.

In this chapter, we discuss a form of redundancy that is present in software systems independently from reliability issues and that can be exploited with negligible additional costs to improve software reliability. We refer to such form of redundancy as *intrinsic* software redundancy. Figure 1 shows a simple example of redundant methods in class `java.util.Stack`: the invocations of methods `clear()`, `removeAllElements()`, and `setSize(0)` produce the same result (an empty stack) by executing the different code fragments reported in the figure. The different albeit equivalent[3] methods derive from design choices that are independent from reliability issues, and as such we refer to them as *intrinsically redundant methods*.

Some recent studies indicate that software systems present many forms of *intrinsic* redundancy that is a form of redundancy that derives from design and implementation decisions that go beyond the explicit choice of adding redundant elements for the sake of reliability [2, 5, 6, 8–11, 17, 24, 29, 42, 44]. Intrinsic

---

[1] https://federalregister.gov/a/07-704.

[2] http://www.iso.org/iso/home/store/catalogue_tc/catalogue_detail.htm?csnumber=43464.

[3] Here and in the whole chapter, we use the term *equivalent method* to indicate methods that produce results indistinguishable from an external viewpoint, as discussed in detail in Sect. 2.

Fig. 1 Sample redundant
methods from class
java.util.Stack

```
1  public void clear() {
2      removeAllElements();
3  }

5  public synchronized void removeAllElements() {
6      modCount++;
7      // Let gc do its work
8      for (int i = 0; i < elementCount; i++)
9          elementData[i] = null;
10     elementCount = 0;
11 }

13 public synchronized void setSize(int newSize) {
14     modCount++;
15     if (newSize > elementCount) {
16         ensureCapacityHelper(newSize);
17     } else {
18         for (int i = newSize ; i < elementCount ; i++) {
19             elementData[i] = null;
20         }
21     }
22     elementCount = newSize;
23 }
```

redundancy has been successfully exploited to improve software reliability [42], build self-healing systems [2, 6, 8, 10, 44], and generate test oracles [9].

We discuss the concept of intrinsic redundancy in software systems, argue about the reasons for its presence, and provide data about the scale of the phenomenon in Sect. 2. We investigate the problem of automatically uncovering intrinsic software redundancy and present a search-based approach to automatically identify redundancy intrinsically present at the method call sequence level in Sect. 3. We illustrate how to exploit the redundancy that is intrinsically present in software systems for producing self-healing systems in Sect. 4 and for generating semantically relevant test oracles in Sect. 5. We identify challenging research problems that may be effectively addressed by exploiting intrinsic software redundancy, focusing in particular on the areas of performance optimization and security in Sect. 6.

2 Intrinsic Software Redundancy

Two *different* executions are *redundant* if they produce *indistinguishable functional results* from an external viewpoint. For example methods clear(), remove-AllElements(), and setSize(0) of class java.util.Stack in Fig. 1 execute different statements and run with different execution time, but produce the same visible functional result (an empty stack) and are thus *redundant*. Redundant executions may differ in the sequence of executed actions as in the case of

```
1 | map.setCenter(new GLatLng(37, −122),15)
2 | // is equivalent to
3 | setTimeout(``map.setCenter(new GLatLng(37, −122), 15)'', 500)

5 | map = new GMap2(document.getElementById(``map''));
6 | setTimeout(``map.setCenter(new GLatLng(37, −122), 15)'', 500);
7 | map.openInfoWindow(new GLatLng(37.4, −122), ``Hello World!'');
```

Fig. 2 Sample redundant method calls in JavaScript in the presence of multithread clients

methods `clear()`, `removeAllElements()`, and `setSize(0)`, or simply in the execution order of same shared actions, as in the case of the code of Fig. 2, where `setTimeout` does not alter the sequence of executed actions, but may result in a different order of execution with multithreaded clients.[4]

Redundancy is present in software systems at all abstraction levels, from single bits to entire software systems. The Cyclic Redundancy Check (CRC) is an example of redundancy at the bit level. Methods of the same or different classes that produce the same results, like methods `clear()`, `removeAllElements()`, and `setSize(0)`, are examples of redundancy at the method call sequence level. Libraries and services with overlapping functionality, for instance, the log4J[5] library and the standard Java class `java.util.Logging` that largely overlap, are examples of redundancy at the subsystem and system level.

In this chapter, we discuss intrinsic redundancy of software systems referring to the *method call sequence* level:

- We refer to deterministic object-oriented software systems at the method call level; the interested reader can find a generalization of the concept of intrinsic redundancy to non-deterministic systems in Mattavelli's PhD thesis [33].
- We focus on redundancy intrinsically present in the systems due to independent design or implementation decisions, and not in redundancy explicitly added at design time as a first-class design choice like in the case of N-version programming.
- We consider only externally observable functional behavior, ignoring other aspects of the executions such as differences in the internal state, data structures, execution time, and performance.

Two methods are redundant if they differ in at least one execution trace and produce indistinguishable results for all executions. Two execution traces are different if they differ in at least one event or in their order. Two methods produce indistinguishable results if their executions compute the same results and lead

---

[4]The insertion of a `setTimeout` is frequently used as workaround for issues in Google Maps.
[5]http://logging.apache.org/log4j.

to equivalent states from an external observer's viewpoint. More precisely, the executions of two methods m_1 and m_2 of a class C with inputs i_1 and i_2 that produce outputs o_1 and o_2 and reach states s_1 and s_2, respectively, are equivalent if $o_1 = o_2$ and no sequence of calls of methods of class C executed from s_1 and s_2 produces different results.

Checking for the diversity of two methods is easy, since we only need to compare the execution traces and find two different ones; checking for their equivalence is complex, since it implies demonstrating that all possible executions produce states that are indistinguishable with any interaction sequence. In Sect. 3, we present an automatic approach to infer the *likely* equivalence of method call sequences, which is based on heuristics, and as such is an imprecise albeit practical and useful approximation of equivalence.

Intrinsic redundancy may stem from many design and commercial practices, including but not limited to design for reusability, performance optimization, backward compatibility, and lack of software reuse. Reusable software systems, and in particular libraries, provide standard application programming interfaces (APIs) that emphasize flexibility over conciseness. For instance, the popular JQuery library[6] provides many alternative methods to display elements in a Web page: show(), animate(), fadeTo(), fadeIn(). Different albeit observationally equivalent functionalities are often present due to performance optimizations. For instance the GNU Standard C++ Library implements the basic stable sorting function using the insertion-sort algorithm for small inputs and merge-sort for the general case. Many libraries continue to offer legacy code to guarantee backward compatibility. For instance, the Java 8 Class Library contains dozens of deprecated classes and hundreds of deprecated methods that overlap with the functionality of newer classes and methods.[7] Time pressure and cost factors reduce the effectiveness of inter- and intra-project communications and limit the degree of reuse. Often developers are simply not aware that a functionality is already available in the system and implement the same functionality multiple times [4, 30].

Intrinsic redundancy is surprisingly widespread in many software systems. Table 1 summarizes the results of our empirical analysis of the presence of intrinsic redundancy that derives from good design for reusability practice in a set of open-source Java libraries at the intra-class method call sequence level. Table 1 indicates a large amount of redundant methods (column *Redundant methods*) within the examined classes (column *Classes*), which in turn lead to a considerable quantity of redundant methods within each class (column *Avg. per class*). Table 1 reports few summary data, interested readers can find additional details in [6, 8–11].

---

[6] http://jquery.com.

[7] http://docs.oracle.com/javase/8/docs/api/deprecated-list.html.

Table 1 Redundant method call sequences in open-source Java systems

System	Classes	Redundant methods	Avg. per class
Apache Ant	213	804	3.80
Apache Lang3	1	45	45.00
Apache Lucene	160	205	1.28
Apache Primitives	16	216	13.50
Canova	95	345	3.63
CERN Colt	27	380	14.07
Eclipse SWT	252	1494	5.93
Google Guava	116	1715	14.78
GraphStream	9	132	14.67
Oracle JDK	2	85	42.50
Joda-Time	12	135	11.25
Trove4J	54	257	4.76
Total	957	5813	6.07

3   Mining Software Redundancy

Identifying redundant method call sequences by manually inspecting the software systems is an error-prone and effort-demanding activity. This section suggests that the intrinsic redundancy of software systems can be automatically identified by an approach, *Search-Based Equivalent Synthesis (SBES)*, that automatically detects redundant method call sequences in Java classes [21, 34].

Given a target method of a Java class, *SBES* synthesizes sequences of method calls that are redundant to the target method, that is, sequences of method calls that produce results that are indistinguishable from the results of the target method while executing different actions. *SBES* approximates the equivalence of method call sequences referring to a finite set of *execution scenarios*. We refer to the method call sequences that *SBES* identifies as *likely equivalent sequences*, since they are proven equivalent to the target method for the considered finite set of execution scenarios, but may differ for other unforeseen executions.

Given a method *m* of a Java class *C*, *SBES* incrementally synthesizes candidate redundant method call sequences to *m*. For each candidate sequence, *SBES* then explores the input space of the candidate sequence, looking for inputs that produce results different from *m*. If such inputs are found, *SBES* discards the candidate sequence and proceeds with a new candidate. Otherwise, if no input that distinguishes the candidate sequence from *m* is found before a given timeout, *SBES* deems the sequence as a *likely* redundant method call sequence of *m*.

We illustrate *SBES* referring to method pop() of the java.util.Stack class. *SBES* starts with an initial scenario that consists of a set of randomly selected test cases for the target method, for instance, the simple test case test01 at lines 1–6 in Fig. 3. It then looks for a sequence of method calls that produces indistinguishable results with respect to the candidate method for the current

```
1  // Initial execution scenario
2  public void test01() {
3      Stack<Integer> s = new Stack<>();
4      s.push(1);
5      Integer result = s.pop();
6  }

8  // First candidate equivalent method call sequence:
9  // stack.remove(0) candidate equivalent to stack.pop()
10 Stack<Integer> s = new Stack<>();
11 s.push(1);
12 Integer result = s.remove(0);

14 // Counterexample
15 Stack<Integer> s = new Stack<>();
16 s.push(2);
17 s.push(1);
18 Integer result = s.pop();

20 // Second candidate equivalent method call sequence:
21 // stack.remove(stack.size() − 1) candidate equivalent to stack.pop()
22 Stack<Integer> s = new Stack<>();
23 int x0 = s.size();
24 int x1 = x0 − 1;
25 Integer result = s.remove(x1)
```

Fig. 3 Candidate method call sequences, counterexamples, and execution scenarios for method pop() of class java.util.Stack

scenario. It does so by exploiting search-based algorithms and, in particular, the genetic algorithms implemented in EvoSuite [16]. In the example, *SBES* synthesizes the candidate sequence of method calls at lines 8–12 in Fig. 3, which produces the same result of the target method pop() for the initial scenario.

SBES validates the candidate by looking for inputs that distinguish the candidate method call sequence from the target method, by exploiting again the genetic algorithms implemented in EvoSuite. In the example, *SBES* finds the counterexample shown at lines 14–18 in Fig. 3, that is, an input that differentiates the results produced by the candidate method call sequence and the target method. If *SBES* finds a counterexample, as in this case, it discards the current candidate method call sequence, adds the counterexample to the current execution scenario, and iterates, looking for a new candidate method call sequence indistinguishable from the target method for the new scenario. By incrementally adding the counterexamples to the execution scenarios, *SBES* restricts the search to a smaller set of potential candidates, thus improving the likelihood of generating method call sequences that are redundant with respect to the target method.

In the example, *SBES* synthesizes the new candidate at line 20–25 in Fig. 3. The search for inputs that differentiate the candidate method call sequence from the target method fails in identifying a counterexample with a timeout. Thus *SBES* returns the synthesized sequence as likely redundant to the target method. In the example, the synthesized sequence is indeed redundant, since it produces results that are indistinguishable from the target method for every possible input. Our experiments confirm that most sequences that *SBES* synthesizes as likely redundant

Table 2 Effectiveness of SBES

System	Class	Redundant methods	Redundant methods found by SBES	
Oracle JDK	Stack	45	32	(71%)
Graphstream	Path	5	5	(100%)
	Edge	20	20	(100%)
	SingleNode	12	12	(100%)
	MultiNode	12	12	(100%)
	Vector2	21	21	(100%)
	Vector3	22	22	(100%)
Google Guava	ArrayListMultimap	18	12	(67%)
	ConcurrentHashMultiset	16	6	(38%)
	HashBasedTable	13	2	(15%)
	HashMultimap	13	13	(100%)
	HashMultiset	19	19	(100%)
	ImmutableListMultimap	20	2	(10%)
	ImmutableMultiset	20	3	(15%)
	LinkedHashMultimap	13	12	(92%)
	LinkedHashMultiset	19	19	(100%)
	LinkedListMultimap	17	11	(65%)
	Lists	16	15	(94%)
	Maps	12	8	(67%)
	Sets	25	21	(84%)
	TreeBasedTable	17	3	(18%)
	TreeMultimap	12	8	(67%)
	TreeMultiset	34	34	(100%)
Total		421	312	(74%)

are often redundant indeed. In general, *SBES* may iterate several times before finding a likely redundant sequence. *SBES* may also fail in synthesizing a new candidate, and in this case we terminate the synthesis process and return the set of likely redundant method call sequences found.

Table 2 summarizes the experimental data reported in Goffi et al. [21] and Mattavelli et al. [34] that confirm the effectiveness of SBES in automatically identifying redundant method call sequences. The table reports the number of redundant method call sequences in the considered classes (column *Class*) as found by manually inspecting the code (column *Redundant Methods*) and the amount and percentage of automatically identified redundant method call sequences (column *Redundant Methods Found by SBES*). As reported in the table, *SBES* can find a large amount of redundant method sequences with an average of 74% and a median over 88%, and fails in identifying most of the missing redundancies for technological limitations of the current prototype implementation that does not satisfactorily deal with the subtle use of some Java constructs.

4 Runtime Failure Recovery

Intrinsic redundancy is exploited in many ways to relieve the effects of faulty code fragments at different abstraction levels, from single code statements to entire components. For instance, many approaches exploit redundancy at the service component level to overcome failures caused by either malfunctioning services or unforeseen changes in the functionality offered by the current reference implementation [2, 39, 45]. Other approaches exploit some form of intrinsic redundancy to automatically patch faulty code at the statement level, for instance, LeGoues et al. [31] and Arcuri and Yao [1] use genetic programming to automatically fix faults, while Sidiroglou-Douskos et al. make use of code fragments that are extracted from "donor" applications [42]. Automatic *runtime* code repair techniques patch the code at runtime to mitigate the effect of failures during the software execution.

In this section we illustrate the use of intrinsic software redundancy to recover from runtime failures by referring to the *Automatic Workaround Approach (AWA)*, which exploits intrinsic redundancy at the method call sequence level to automatically recover from failures at runtime [6, 8, 10]. A *workaround* substitutes a faulty code fragment with a different redundant code fragment that produces the same intended behavior while executing a different code that avoids the faulty operations. For example the redundant method call `setTimeout("map.setCenter(new GLatLng(37,-122),15)",500)` shown in Fig. 2 can be successfully exploited as a workaround for `map.setCenter(new GLatLng(37, -122),15)` to solve the now-closed issue 519 of the Google Maps API.[8]

In a nutshell, *AWA* detects a failure, rolls back to a consistent state, substitutes the faulty code fragment with a redundant code fragment, and executes the new code. The *AWA* key ingredients are as follows: (1) a *failure detection* mechanism that reveals failures at runtime, (2) a *save and restore* mechanism that rolls back the application to a consistent state after a failure, and (3) a *healing engine* that replaces the failing code fragment with a redundant fragment.

When dealing with Web applications, *AWA* focuses on JavaScript libraries and relies on the stateless nature of classic Web applications to ensure state consistency. When dealing with Java applications, *AWA* augments the core healing engine with mechanisms to detect failures, and save and restore the state. In the next paragraphs, we briefly summarize the three main *AWA* ingredients for both Web and Java applications. The interested readers can refer to [8] and [6, 10] for details on *AWA* for Java programs and Web applications, respectively. We illustrate the approach referring to *AWA* successfully exploiting the redundant method calls shown in Fig. 2 to heal the now-closed issue 519 of Google Maps API as a running example.

---

[8]https://code.google.com/p/gmaps-api-issues/.

4.1   Failure Detection

The *AWA* failure detectionv mechanism reveals failures and triggers the *AWA* healing engine at runtime. When dealing with Web applications, *AWA* takes advantage of the interactive nature of the application and relies on users who are given an intuitive way, for instance, a browser extension, both to signal undesired outputs and to validate the behavior of the application after a potential workaround is applied. When dealing with Java applications, *AWA* relies on implicit failure detectors such as runtime exceptions and violations of pre-/post-conditions and invariants. In our experiments with Web applications we provided users with a button to signal failures.

In the running example, users signal the lack of the expected pop-up window for additional information about the location on the map through a *Fix me* button that we added to Google Chrome [7].

4.2   Save and Restore

The *AWA* save and restore mechanism incrementally saves intermediate execution states to roll back to a consistent state, that is, a state before the occurrence of a failure. When dealing with Web applications, *AWA* takes advantage of the stateless nature of the client side, assuming that the JavaScript code executed on the client side implements stateless components, and simply reloads the page without worrying about possible side effects on the state of the application. When dealing with Java applications, the save and restore mechanism periodically saves the execution states, and must find a good compromise for the frequency. Saving operations should not be too frequent, to limit the overhead, and not too sporadic either, since they may also cover I/O operations that may be difficult or impossible to restore. *AWA* identifies code regions that include redundant code—and that can thus be fixed with automatic workarounds—and saves the state before executing these regions. In principle, these code regions may extend over sections of the application at any level of granularity; in practice they usually extend within a method body.

4.3   Healing Engine

The *AWA* healing engine executes a code that is redundant with respect to the code fragment likely responsible for the detected failure, aiming to restore a correct execution. In general, the *AWA* healing engine iteratively restores the state of the application to a previously saved checkpoint and executes a code fragment that is redundant with respect to the code that is a suspect responsible of the failure, until either the failure does not occur or the available redundant fragments are exhausted.

If the failure does not occur after the healing action, *AWA* successfully prevents the failure and the execution of the application proceeds as if no failure occurred. If the failure persists, *AWA* cannot prevent the failure and forwards the failure to the application. In the presence of multiple alternatives, *AWA* selects the alternative candidates by relying on heuristics based on the past success of the redundant alternatives.

When dealing with Web applications, *AWA* simply extracts the JavaScript code from the failing page, replaces the suspect code with a redundant code fragment, and displays the new page to the user, who can either continue interacting with the application or signal the persistency of a problem. In this latter case, *AWA* iterates with a new redundant code fragment.

In the running example, the failing page contains several statements with known redundant method call sequences. After two failed attempts, where *AWA* substitutes a statement in the page with a redundant one without solving the failure and triggering new user's *Fix me* requests, *AWA* substitutes statement map.setCenter(new GLatLng(37, −122), 15) with the candidate workaround shown in Fig. 2 and reloads the page successfully, healing the failure [10].

AWA assumes the availability of the set of redundant alternatives present in the target application, which can be automatically identified with the search-based approach presented in Sect. 3, and pre-processes the application off-line to enable the online healing mechanism. It analyzes the application *off-line* to locate code fragments with redundant alternatives, pre-compiles all the redundant code fragments, and instruments the application with the necessary code to select those alternative redundant fragments at runtime in response to a failure. At runtime, *AWA* saves the state of the application at the identified checkpoints and reacts to failures by executing workarounds.

The experimental data reported in [6, 8, 10] and collected on three popular Web libraries (Google Maps, JQuery, and YouTube)[9] and four Java applications (Fb2pdf, Caliper, Carrot2, and Closure compiler)[10] that use two popular Java libraries (Google Guava and JodaTime)[11] indicate that *AWA* is indeed effective: It automatically applies workarounds for 100 out of 146 known faults for the considered Web applications, and for a percentage that varies between 19% and 48% of the failure-inducing faults in the considered Java applications.

---

[9]Google Maps (http://code.google.com/apis/maps), JQuery (http://jquery.com), YouTube (http://code.google.com/apis/youtube).

[10]Caliper (https://github.com/google/caliper), Carrot2 (http://project.carrot2.org), Closure Compiler (https://github.com/google/closure-compiler), Fb2pdf (http://fb2pdf.com).

[11]Guava (https://github.com/google/guava), JodaTime (https://github.com/JodaOrg/joda-time).

5 Automated Oracles

Software testing and in particular automatic generation of test oracles is another important area where redundancy finds interesting applications. Test oracles check the results of the code execution and signal discrepancies between actual and expected behavior [3]. Their efficacy and cost play a key role in cost-effective test automation approaches. Manual test case generation produces effective oracles, but is very expensive and strongly impacts on the cost of testing. Generating useful test oracles automatically is extremely valuable, but is generally difficult and in some cases may not be practical or even possible [47].

In her seminal work, Weyuker proposes *pseudo-oracles* that exploit explicit redundancy given in the form of multiple versions of a system to check program results [47]. Doong and Frankl define the ASTOOT approach that relies on redundancy that transpires from algebraic specifications to automatically generate test inputs and oracles [15]. The metamorphic testing approach introduced by Chen et al. almost a decade later exploits a form of redundant information given as metamorphic relations to automatically generate test oracles [13].

In this section, we illustrate the role of intrinsic redundancy in automated software testing by means of *cross-checking oracles*, which exploit the intrinsic redundancy at the method call sequence level to automatically generate application specific oracles [9]. Figure 4 illustrates the cross-checking oracle approach by referring to the invocation of method `containsValue(value)` of the class `ArrayListMultimap`. Once mined the redundancy between methods (methods `map.containsValue(value)` and `map.values().contains(value)` in the example), cross-checking oracles complement each invocation of a method for which we know that there exists some redundancy (`map.containsValue(value)`) with a parallel invocation of the redundant method (`map.values().contains(value)`) followed by a comparison of the produced results and reached states (`equivalence check` in the figure). The oracle signals a problem if two redundant methods invoked in the

```
1 | void testCase() {
2 |    Map map = ArrayListMultimap.create();
3 |    map.put("Key1", 1);
4 |    map.put("Key2", 2);
5 |    ...
6 |    map.containsValue(1); ------------- map.values().contains(1);

                    ┌──────────────────────────┐
                    │    equivalence check     │
                    └──────────────────────────┘

7 |    map.containsKey("Key1");
8 |    ...
9 | }
```

Fig. 4 A visual representation of a cross-checking oracle [20]

same context either produce different results or reach states that are distinct from an external observer viewpoint.

Cross-checking oracles can be generated and executed automatically given a set of redundant code elements and provide a way of checking for faults that depend on the semantics of the program. They are automatically deployed into test suites through binary instrumentation and rely on a deep-clone mechanism to ensure a reasonable level of isolation between the executions of redundant methods, with a limited execution overhead. Cross-checking oracles implement a finite approximation of equivalence that checks the equality of both the externally visible results and the states reached after executing the redundant methods, through the concatenation of a finite sequence of method invocations.

The experimental results reported in [9] indicate that cross-checking oracles substantially improve the effectiveness of automatically generated test suites that rely on implicit oracles, and in some cases can also improve specific oracles written by the developers.

6 Beyond Functional Intrinsic Redundancy

In the previous sections, we illustrated the application of intrinsic software redundancy in the context of software reliability, and in particular for the design of mechanisms for runtime failure recovery and automated oracles, focusing on functional properties. The notion of intrinsic software redundancy can be extended to *nonfunctional* properties, and find many new applications. In this section we identify future research directions toward applications of nonfunctional software redundancy in new contexts, namely, performance optimization and security.

6.1 Performance Optimization

Redundant code fragments execute different sequences of actions that may lead to notable differences in runtime behavior and resource usage. Such differences can be exploited to alleviate performance and resource consumption problems, depending on the operative conditions. For example, mobile devices offer several connectivity options that span from mobile protocols, WiFi connectivity, Bluetooth access points, and so on. The optimal choice of connectivity depends on the operational conditions and on trade-off between performance, urgency, battery consumption, privacy, and security that cannot be predicted and efficiently wired in a design time.

Recent work has investigated the use of various forms of redundancy for improving nonfunctional properties. The GISMOE approach exploits genetic programming to generate program variants to address different nonfunctional objectives [23]. The competitive parallel execution (CPE) approach increases the overall system performance by executing multiple variants of the same program in parallel [46]. Self-adaptive containers minimize the runtime costs by monitoring the runtime performance of the application and automatically selecting the best internal data structures [27]. Misailovic et al. propose a new profiler to identify computations that can be replaced with alternative—and potentially less accurate—computations that provide better performance [35]. The applicability and effectiveness of the different approaches is bounded by the techniques used to identify and exploit redundancy and the kind of redundancy that they infer and exploit.

The redundancy intrinsically present in software systems offers new opportunities for automatically improving performance and resource consumption at runtime. The key idea is to devise a "profile" of the redundant code that captures nonfunctional differences among the alternatives, for instance, in terms of timing, memory or battery consumption, or network utilization. This *nonfunctional profile* can be updated and exploited at runtime, while efficiently monitoring the system execution, to adapt the behavior to meet, or improve, performance and resource utilization requirements.

For example, the nonfunctional differences of redundant video streaming algorithms, such as runtime performance, battery consumption, and network utilization, can be exploited to face performance problems due to unpredictable environment changes.

Figure 5 illustrates the approach with a pair of redundant *tokenize* methods, which explicitly offer different runtime performances. The two methods perform differently depending on operational conditions, like the frequency of invocations on the same or similar arrays, the dimension and the content of the arrays and so on, and coexist in the Apache Ant library to offer different design opportunities. They can be mutually exchanged based on the monitored operational profile and the discrepancies between actual and expected performance. The nonfunctional profile shall capture the various performance profiles of the two methods, identify

```
1  /**
2   * Breaks a path up into a Vector of path elements, tokenizing on File.separator.
3   * @param path Path to tokenize. Must not be null.
4   * @return a Vector of path elements from the tokenized path
5   */
6  public static Vector tokenizePath(String path) {...}

8  /**
9   * Same as tokenizePath but faster.
10  */
11 public static String[] tokenizePathAsArray(String path) {...}
```

Fig. 5 Documentation of the tokenizePath and tokenizePathAsArray methods in Apache Ant

the situations that may impact on performance differences, and in general the non-functional differences that may suggest the use of one of the two methods depending on the runtime conditions.

6.2 Security

Redundant code fragments may provide different security levels that can also be exploited to tackle security issues and overcome runtime problems. Recent work has investigated the possibility of exploiting some form of explicit redundancy to mitigate security issues. *N-variant systems* increase application security by executing different synthesized variants of the same program in parallel [14]. *Orchestra* tackles security issues by creating multiple variants of the same program based on various compiler optimizations [40]. *Replicated browsers* tackles security problems by executing different browsers in parallel [48].

Redundant code fragments offer a promising alternative to implement new security mechanisms by defining a security profile of redundant code fragments and by efficiently executing the various alternatives to identify divergences in their runtime behavior, for instance, with a multi-version execution framework [25].

Figure 6 shows an example of redundant code fragments that can be exploited to improve security. Both methods gets and scanf can be successfully exploited by attackers through buffer overflows when invoked with not well-terminated strings. Method fgets provides the same functionality of gets and scanf but prevents buffer overflows. The information about the redundancy of these three methods provides the necessary knowledge to develop mechanisms to prevent security threats.

```
1  // Reads characters from the standard input (stdin) and stores them as a C string
2  // into str until a newline character or the end–of–file is reached.
3  char * gets (char *str);

5  // Reads data from stdin and stores them according to the parameter format into
6  // the locations pointed by the additional arguments.
7  int scanf (const char *format, ...);

9  // Reads characters from stream and stores them as a C string into str until
10  // (num–1) characters have been read or either a newline or the end–of–file is
11  // reached, whichever happens first.
12  char * fgets (char *str, int num, FILE *stream);
```

Fig. 6 Documentation of the gets, fgets and scanf methods of the C standard library

7 Conclusions

Redundancy is a traditional ingredient of many mechanisms for improving reliability and fault tolerance at runtime. Classic engineering approaches rely on different forms of redundancy explicitly added at design time, and suitably exploited at runtime. Such form of redundancy may be expensive to produce, and may be relegated to systems whose reliability requirements balance the extra costs of adding redundancy explicitly, as in the case of N-version programming for safety critical applications.

Recent studies have identified a different form of redundancy that is not explicitly added at design time for improving reliability, but is present for independent design and development decisions, and that we refer to as *intrinsic software redundancy*.

In this chapter, we summarize the recent advances in the study and exploitation of intrinsic software redundancy, and we indicate promising research directions. We define intrinsic software redundancy informally, discuss the source of such kind of redundancy, and show its presence in relevant software applications. We present an approach to automatically identify intrinsic software redundancy at the method call sequence level, thus providing evidence of the limited costs of gathering information about redundant code elements at a convenient abstraction level.

We report some applications of intrinsic software redundancy to improve reliability at runtime, by proposing the automatic generation of runtime workarounds and program specific oracles. We conclude by indicating new relevant domains that can benefit from the presence of intrinsic redundancy in software systems.

Acknowledgements This work was supported in part by the Swiss National Science Foundation with projects *SHADE* (grant n. 200021-138006), *ReSpec* (grant n. 200021-146607), *WASH* (grant n. 200020-124918), and *SHADE* (grant n. 200021-138006), by the European Union FP7-PEOPLE-COFUND project *AMAROUT II* (grant n. 291803), by the Spanish Ministry of Economy project *DEDETIS*, and by the Madrid Regional Government project *N-Greens Software* (grant n. S2013/ICE-2731).

References

1. Arcuri, A., Yao, X.: A novel co-evolutionary approach to automatic software bug fixing. In: Proceedings of IEEE Congress on Evolutionary Computation, CEC'08, pp. 162–168. IEEE Computer Society, Washington (2008)
2. Baresi, L., Guinea, S., Pasquale, L.: Self-healing BPEL processes with dynamo and the JBoss rule engine. In: International Workshop on Engineering of Software Services for Pervasive Environments, ESSPE'07, pp. 11–20 (2007)
3. Barr, E.T., Harman, M., McMinn, P., Shahbaz, M., Yoo, S.: The oracle problem in software testing: a survey. IEEE Trans. Softw. Eng. **41**(5), 507–525 (2015)
4. Bauer, V., Eckhardt, J., Hauptmann, B., Klimek, M.: An exploratory study on reuse at google. In: Proceedings of the 1st International Workshop on Software Engineering Research and Industrial Practices, SER & IPs 2014, pp. 14–23. ACM, New York (2014)

5. Carzaniga, A., Gorla, A., Pezzè, M.: Fault handling with software redundancy. In: de Lemos, R., Fabre, J., Gacek, C., Gadducci, F., ter Beek, M. (eds.) Architecting Dependable Systems VI, pp. 148–171. Springer, Berlin (2009)
6. Carzaniga, A., Gorla, A., Perino, N., Pezzè, M.: Automatic workarounds for web applications. In: Proceedings of the ACM SIGSOFT International Symposium on Foundations of Software Engineering, FSE'10, pp. 237–246. ACM, New York (2010)
7. Carzaniga, A., Gorla, A., Perino, N., Pezzè, M.: RAW: runtime automatic workarounds. In: ICSE'10: Proceedings of the 32nd ACM/IEEE International Conference on Software Engineering (Tool Demo), pp. 321–322. ACM, New York (2010)
8. Carzaniga, A., Gorla, A., Mattavelli, A., Pezzè, M., Perino, N.: Automatic recovery from runtime failures. In: Proceedings of the International Conference on Software Engineering, ICSE'13, pp. 782–791. IEEE Computer Society, Washington (2013)
9. Carzaniga, A., Goffi, A., Gorla, A., Mattavelli, A., Pezzè, M.: Cross-checking oracles from intrinsic software redundancy. In: Proceedings of the International Conference on Software Engineering, ICSE'14, pp. 931–942. ACM, New York (2014)
10. Carzaniga, A., Gorla, A., Perino, N., Pezzè, M.: Automatic workarounds: exploiting the intrinsic redundancy of web applications. ACM Trans. Softw. Eng. Methodol. **24**(3), 16 (2015)
11. Carzaniga, A., Mattavelli, A., Pezzè, M.: Measuring software redundancy. In: Proceedings of the 37th International Conference on Software Engineering, ICSE'15, pp. 156–166. IEEE Computer Society, Washington (2015)
12. Chen, L., Avizienis, A.: N-version programming: a fault-tolerance approach to reliability of software operation. In: International Symposium on Fault-Tolerant Computing, FTCS'78, pp. 113–119 (1978)
13. Chen, T.Y., Cheung, S.C., Yiu, S.M.: Metamorphic testing: a new approach for generating next test cases. Tech. rep., Department of Computer Science, Hong Kong University of Science and Technology (1998)
14. Cox, B., Evans, D., Filipi, A., Rowanhill, J., Hu, W., Davidson, J., Knight, J., Nguyen-Tuong, A., Hiser, J.: N-variant systems: a secretless framework for security through diversity. In: Proceedings of the Conference on USENIX Security Symposium, SEC'06. USENIX Association, Berkeley (2006)
15. Doong, R.K., Frankl, P.G.: The ASTOOT approach to testing object-oriented programs. ACM Trans. Softw. Eng. Methodol. **3**(2), 101–130 (1994)
16. Fraser, G., Arcuri, A.: Evosuite: automatic test suite generation for object-oriented software. In: Proceedings of the European Software Engineering Conference held jointly with the ACM SIGSOFT International Symposium on Foundations of Software Engineering, ESEC/FSE'11, pp. 416–419. ACM, New York (2011)
17. Gabel, M., Su, Z.: A study of the uniqueness of source code. In: Proceedings of the ACM SIGSOFT International Symposium on Foundations of Software Engineering, FSE'10, pp. 147–156. ACM, New York (2010)
18. Ghosn, M., Moses, F.: NCHRP report 406: redundancy in highway bridge superstructures. Tech. rep., National Cooperative Highway Research Program (NCHRP), Transportation Research Board (1998). http://onlinepubs.trb.org/onlinepubs/nchrp/nchrp_rpt_406.pdf
19. Ghosn, M., Yang, J.: NCHRP report 776: bridge system safety and redundancy. Tech. rep., National Cooperative Highway Research Program (NCHRP), Transportation Research Board (2014). http://onlinepubs.trb.org/onlinepubs/nchrp/nchrp_rpt_776.pdf
20. Goffi, A.: Automatic generation of cost-effective test oracles. In: ICSE'14: Proceedings of the 36th International Conference on Software Engineering, pp. 678–681. ACM, New York (2014)
21. Goffi, A., Gorla, A., Mattavelli, A., Pezzè, M., Tonella, P.: Search-based synthesis of equivalent method sequences. In: Proceedings of the ACM SIGSOFT International Symposium on the Foundations of Software Engineering, FSE'14, pp. 366–376. ACM, New York (2014)
22. Hamming, R.W.: Error detecting and error correcting codes. Bell Syst. Tech. J. **29**(2), 147–160 (1950)

23. Harman, M., Langdon, W.B., Jia, Y., White, D.R., Arcuri, A., Clark, J.A.: The gismoe challenge: constructing the pareto program surface using genetic programming to find better programs (keynote paper). In: Proceedings of the International Conference on Automated Software Engineering, ASE'12, pp. 1–14. ACM, New York (2012)
24. Hindle, A., Barr, E.T., Su, Z., Gabel, M., Devanbu, P.: On the naturalness of software. In: Proceedings of the International Conference on Software Engineering, ICSE'12, pp. 837–847. ACM, New York (2012)
25. Hosek, P., Cadar, C.: Varan the unbelievable: an efficient n-version execution framework. In: Proceedings of the International Conference on Architectural Support for Programming Languages and Operating Systems, ASPLOS'15, pp. 339–353. ACM, New York (2015)
26. Huang, Y., Kintala, C.M.R.: Software implemented fault tolerance technologies and experience. In: Proceedings of the 23rd Annual International Symposium on Fault-Tolerant Computing, FTSC'93, pp. 2–9. IEEE Computer Society, Washington (1993)
27. Huang, W.C., Knottenbelt, W.J.: Self-adaptive containers: building resource-efficient applications with low programmer overhead. In: Proceedings of the International Symposium on Software Engineering for Adaptive and Self-Managing Systems, SEAMS'13, pp. 123–132. IEEE Computer Society, Washington (2013)
28. IEEE Recommended Practice on Software Reliability (2008)
29. Jiang, L., Su, Z.: Automatic mining of functionally equivalent code fragments via random testing. In: Proceedings of the International Symposium on Software Testing and Analysis, ISSTA'09, pp. 81–92. ACM, New York (2009)
30. Kawrykow, D., Robillard, M.P.: Improving API usage through automatic detection of redundant code. In: Proceedings of the International Conference on Automated Software Engineering, ASE'09, pp. 111–122. IEEE Computer Society, Washington (2009)
31. Le Goues, C., Nguyen, T., Forrest, S., Weimer, W.: Genprog: a generic method for automatic software repair. IEEE Trans. Softw. Eng. 38, 54–72 (2012)
32. Liu, W.D., Ghosn, M., Moses, F.: NCHRP report 458: redundancy in highway bridge substructures. Tech. rep., National Cooperative Highway Research Program (NCHRP), Transportation Research Board (2001). http://onlinepubs.trb.org/onlinepubs/nchrp/nchrp_rpt_458-a.pdf
33. Mattavelli, A.: Software redundancy: what, where, how. Ph.D. thesis, Università della Svizzera italiana (USI) (2016)
34. Mattavelli, A., Goffi, A., Gorla, A.: Synthesis of equivalent method calls in Guava. In: Proceedings of the 7th International Symposium on Search-Based Software Engineering, SSBSE'15, pp. 248–254. Springer, Berlin (2015)
35. Misailovic, S., Sidiroglou, S., Hoffmann, H., Rinard, M.: Quality of service profiling. In: Proceedings of the International Conference on Software Engineering, ICSE'10, pp. 25–34. ACM, New York (2010)
36. Patterson, D.A., Gibson, G., Katz, R.H.: A case for redundant arrays of inexpensive disks (RAID). SIGMOD Record 17(3), 109–116 (1988)
37. Randell, B.: System structure for software fault tolerance. SIGPLAN Notes 10(6), 437–449 (1975)
38. Reed, I.S., Solomon, G.: Polynomial codes over certain finite fields. J. Soc. Ind. Appl. Math. 8(2), 300–304 (1960)
39. Sadjadi, S.M., McKinley, P.K.: Using transparent shaping and Web services to support self-management of composite systems. In: Proceedings of the International Conference on Autonomic Computing, ICAC'05, pp. 76–87. IEEE Computer Society, Washington (2005)
40. Salamat, B., Jackson, T., Gal, A., Franz, M.: Orchestra: intrusion detection using parallel execution and monitoring of program variants in user-space. In: Proceedings of the ACM SIGOPS EuroSys European Conference on Computer Systems, EuroSys'09, pp. 33–46. ACM, New York (2009)
41. Shvachko, K., Kuang, H., Radia, S., Chansler, R.: The hadoop distributed file system. In: Proceedings of the 2010 IEEE Symposium on Mass Storage Systems and Technologies, MSST'10, pp. 1–10. IEEE Computer Society, Washington (2010)

42. Sidiroglou-Douskos, S., Lahtinen, E., Long, F., Rinard, M.: Automatic error elimination by horizontal code transfer across multiple applications. In: Proceedings of the Conference on Programming Language Design and Implementation, PLDI'15, pp. 43–54. ACM, New York (2015)

43. Somani, A.K., Vaidya, N.H.: Understanding fault tolerance and reliability. IEEE Comput. **30**(4), 45–50 (1997)

44. Subramanian, S., Thiran, P., Narendra, N.C., Mostefaoui, G.K., Maamar, Z.: On the enhancement of BPEL engines for self-healing composite web services. In: Proceedings of the International Symposium on Applications and the Internet, SAINT'08, pp. 33–39. IEEE Computer Society, Washington (2008)

45. Taher, Y., Benslimane, D., Fauvet, M.C., Maamar, Z.: Towards an approach for Web services substitution. In: Proceedings of the International Database Engineering and Applications Symposium, IDEAS'06, pp. 166–173. IEEE Computer Society, Washington (2006)

46. Trachsel, O., Gross, T.R.: Variant-based competitive parallel execution of sequential programs. In: Proceedings of the ACM International Conference on Computing Frontiers, CF'10, pp. 197–206. ACM, New York (2010)

47. Weyuker, E.J.: On testing non-testable programs. Comput. J. **25**(4), 465–470 (1982)

48. Xue, H., Dautenhahn, N., King, S.T.: Using replicated execution for a more secure and reliable web browser. In: Proceedings of the Annual Network and Distributed System Security Symposium, NDSS'12. The Internet Society, Reston (2012)

49. Yeh, Y.C.: Triple-triple redundant 777 primary flight computer. In: Proceedings of the IEEE Aerospace Applications Conference, vol. 1, pp. 293–307 (1996)

Sound Simulation and Co-simulation for Robotics

Ana Cavalcanti, Alvaro Miyazawa, Richard Payne, and Jim Woodcock

Abstract Software engineering for modern robot applications needs attention; current practice suffers from costly iterations of trial and error, with hardware and environment in the loop. We propose the adoption of an approach to simulation and co-simulation of robotics applications where designs and (co-)simulations are amenable to verification. In this approach, designs are composed of several (co-)models whose relationship is defined using a SysML profile. Simulation is the favoured technique for analysis in industry, and co-simulation enables the orchestrated use of a variety of simulation tools, including, for instance, reactive simulators and simulators of control laws. Here, we define the SysML profile that we propose and give it a process algebraic semantics. With that semantics, we capture the properties of the SysML model that must be satisfied by a co-simulation. Our long-term goal is to support validation and verification beyond what can be achieved with simulation.

1 Introduction

Safety is a major concern in robotics: for example, regulations for industrial robots often require them to be kept in cages, and autonomous vehicles currently cannot be certified for civil aviation. The ability to provide safety evidence can create significant opportunities. Yet, the programming techniques in use involve, on one hand, advanced robotics technology and, on the other, outdated approaches to validation and verification of software controllers (either in isolation or in the context of a specific robotic hardware platform and environment).

Figure 1 indicates, in bold, the artefacts that are currently engineered in typical developments. The other artefacts are either provided on an ad hoc basis by

A. Cavalcanti (✉) • A. Miyazawa • J. Woodcock
Department of Computer Science, University of York, York, UK
e-mail: ana.cavalcanti@york.ac.uk; alvaro.miyazawa@york.ac.uk; jim.woodcock@york.ac.uk

R. Payne
School of Computing Science, Newcastle University, Newcastle upon Tyne, UK

Present address: The Nine Software Company Limited, South Tyneside, UK
e-mail: richard.payne@newcastle.ac.uk

© Springer International Publishing AG 2017
M. Mazzara, B. Meyer (eds.), *Present and Ulterior Software Engineering*,
https://doi.org/10.1007/978-3-319-67425-4_11

Fig. 1 Robot controller
development artefacts:
current practice

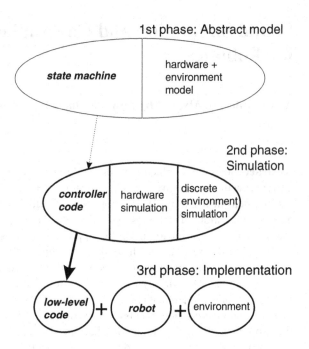

1st phase: Abstract model

state machine | hardware + environment model

2nd phase: Simulation

controller code | hardware simulation | discrete environment simulation

3rd phase: Implementation

low-level code + robot + environment

particular tools or missing. In a first development phase, a state machine is often used to define the controller. If relevant, timed and probabilistic behaviours are recorded informally. For simulation, if the tool of choice does not provide adequate hardware and environment models, they need to be adapted or developed. A main difficulty is reasoning about the effect of the environment or recording assumptions about it. Connections between the artefacts are tenuous.

We propose here extensions and restrictions to INTO-SysML [2], a SysML [30] profile for cyber-physical systems. Our goal is to support modelling of robotic applications, including facilities to specify time, probabilities, the robotic platform, and the environment. SysML is a UML-based language that is becoming a de facto standard for systems, rather than just software, modelling. The INTO-SysML profile restricts the use of SysML block and internal block diagrams to characterise a collection of potentially heterogeneous (co-)models as typically required for describing cyber-physical systems. These models may be written using a variety of notations adopting a variety of modelling paradigms. The definition of a collection of models in INTO-SysML identifies how they are described and how they are connected to each other to specify a complete cyber-physical system (CPS).

Our version of the INTO-SysML profile dictates the use of a domain-specific language for discrete modelling of robot controllers: RoboChart [28]. For continuous modelling, we use as an example Simulink [43], which is widely used in industry for simulation of control laws. We can, however, accommodate other notations for continuous modelling. To illustrate our novel SysML profile, we apply it to describe co-models for the chemical detector in [21][1] and its environment.

Tools and facilities for simulation of robotic systems range from APIs [26] to sophisticated engines [23, 34] that embed discrete hardware and environment models. The variety of tools, simulation languages, and facilities for hardware and environment modelling and simulation means that the choice is not obvious, tool-specific knowledge is required, and reuse across tools is difficult.

In the long term, we envisage the automatic generation of tool-independent simulations from models written in INTO-SysML. Typically, for the continuous models, simulation tools are available. For RoboChart, automatic generation of simulations is under development. To support overall simulation of the various heterogeneous models of components, controllers, robotic platforms, and environment, using the most adequate tool for the task, we can adopt co-simulation. This is a technique widely adopted in industry to deal with the increased complexity of cyber-physical systems via the coordinated use of heterogeneous models and tools.

An industry standard, FMI [15] (Functional Mock-up Interface), supports orchestration. It avoids the need for customised coupling of each collection of simulation tools relevant for an application. An FMI co-simulation comprises black-box slave FMUs (Functional Mock-up Units); these wrap simulation models, connected via their inputs and outputs. A master algorithm triggers and orchestrates the simulation of the FMUs. In our envisaged approach, the environment, the controllers, and sometimes the robotic platform are in different FMUs. A co-simulation evolves in steps, which are synchronisation and data exchange points. An FMI API supports the programming of the master algorithm.

An FMI-based co-simulation framework for robotic applications can help developers face the challenge of heterogeneity. Our vision is for a framework that uses automatically generated co-simulations guaranteed to preserve the properties of the co-models described using INTO-SysML.

Besides defining a version of INTO-SysML for robotics, here we also give the INTO-SysML profile a formal behavioural semantics defined using the CSP process algebra [35]. The semantics captures the properties that every realisation of the co-simulation must satisfy. It captures the behaviours of the FMI simulations that orchestrate the executions of the multi-models as specified in SysML.

The use of CSP is a front end to a semantic model that is described using Unifying Theories of Programming (UTP) [22] and can be extended to deal with continuous time and variables. With this preliminary use of CSP, we enable the use of the model checker FDR [19] for validation. Our semantics complements existing results on UTP semantics of RoboChart [28] and of FMI [9].

We present the background material to our work: SysML and the INTO-SysML profile, FMI, and RoboChart in Sect. 2. Section 3 presents our SysML profile. Section 4 presents our semantics. We consider related work in Sect. 5 and conclude in Sect. 6, discussing also our agenda for future work.

---

[1] See http://tinyurl.com/hdaws7o.

2 Preliminaries

In what follows, we present the notations used in our work.

2.1 SysML and the INTO-SysML Profile

SysML [30] is a general-purpose graphical notation for systems engineering applications, defined as an extension of a subset of UML [29]. This extension is achieved by using UML's profile mechanism, which provides a generic technique for customising UML models for particular domains and platforms. A profile is a conservative extension of UML, refining its semantics in a consistent fashion.

There are commercial and open-source SysML tools. These include IBM's Rational Rhapsody Designer,[2] Atego's Modeler,[3] and Modeliosoft's Modelio.[4] They support model-based engineering and have been used in complex systems.

Like a UML model, a SysML model can be described by a set of diagrams. A central notion in SysML is that of a block, which is a structural element that represents a general system component, describing functional, physical, or human behaviour. The SysML Block Definition Diagram (BDD) shows how blocks are assembled into architectures; it is analogous to a UML Class Diagram but is based on the more general notion of block. A BDD represents how the system is composed from its blocks using associations and other composition relations.

A SysML Internal Block Diagram (IBD) allows a designer to refine a block's structure; it is analogous to UML's Composite Structure Diagram, which shows the internal structure of a class. In an IBD, parts are assembled to define how they collaborate to realise the block's overall behaviour.

SysML includes a number of other diagrams to define state machines, flow charts, requirements, and so on. The BDD and IBD just described are the only ones relevant for our profile for description of co-simulations.

The INTO-SysML profile [2] customises SysML for architectural modelling for FMI co-simulation. It specialises blocks to represent different types of components, that is, co-models, of a CPS, constituting the building blocks of a hierarchical description of a CPS architecture. A component is a logical or conceptual unit of the system, software or a physical entity, modelled as an FMU.

The following types of components are represented in INTO-SysML using specialised blocks: `System`, `EComponent` (encapsulating component), and `POComponent` (part-of component). A `System` block is decomposed into subsystems: `EComponents`, which are further decomposed into `POComponents`. An

---

[2] See sysml.tools/review-rhapsody-developer/.

[3] See http://www.atego.com/de/products/atego-modeler/.

[4] See www.modelio.org/.

EComponent corresponds to an FMU. EComponents and POComponents may be further classified as Subsystem, a collection of inner components; Cyber, an atomic unit that inhabits the digital or logical world; or Physical, an atomic unit in the physical world. Characterising phenomena may be classified as being discrete or continuous. Decomposition of EComponents can be used to provide more information about the structure of the co-models, although that structure is hidden inside an FMU from the point of view of the FMI co-simulation.

To define the system, the components, and their relationships, INTO-SysML comprises two diagram types, Architecture Structure Diagrams (ADs) and Connection Diagrams (CDs), specialising SysML BDDs and IBDs. ADs describe a decomposition in terms of the types of system components and their relations. They emphasise multi-modelling: certain components encapsulate a model built using some modelling tool (such as VDM/RT [25], 20-sim [4], or OpenModelica [18]). CDs include AD block instances to describe the configuration of the system's components, highlighting flow and connectedness of these components.

In our examples, the multi-models are written in RoboChart (see Sect. 2.3) and Simulink [43]. The latter, developed by MathWorks, is a graphical programming environment for modelling, simulating, and analysing multi-domain dynamic systems. Its primary interface is a graphical block diagramming tool and a customisable set of block libraries. Simulink is a de facto standard for modelling and simulation of control systems in the automotive and avionics industry.

2.2 Functional Mock-Up Interface (FMI)

The Functional Mock-up Interface (FMI) [15] is an industry standard for collaborative simulation of separately developed models of CPS components: co-simulation. The key idea is that if a real product is assembled from components interacting in complex ways, each obeying physical laws (electronic, hydraulic, mechanical), then a virtual product can be created from models of those physical laws and a model of their control systems. Models in these different engineering fields are heterogeneous: they use different notations and simulation tools.

The purpose of FMI is to support this heterogeneous modelling and simulation of a CPS by using the most convenient tools to deal with the different models. FMI is used in a number of different industry sectors, including automotive, energy, aerospace, and real-time systems integration. There is a formal development process for the standard, and many tools now support FMI.

As mentioned above, an FMI co-simulation consists of FMUs, which are models encapsulated in wrappers, interconnected through inputs and outputs. FMUs are slaves: their collective simulations are orchestrated by a master algorithm. Each FMU simulation is divided into steps with barrier synchronisations for data exchange; between these steps, the FMUs are simulated independently.

A master algorithm communicates with FMUs through the FMI API, whose most important functions are those to exchange data, `fmi2Set` and `fmi2Get`, and that to command the execution of a simulation step, `fmi2DoStep`. Other functions of the FMI API support the low-level management of the FMUs: initialisation, termination, recovery of its state, and so on. They play an important role in supporting the implementation of sophisticated master algorithms. From a conceptual point of view, however, the co-simulation is characterised by the sequence of calls to `fmi2DoStep`, which define the simulation steps, and the associated values input and output using `fmi2Set` and `fmi2Get`.

The FMI standard does not specify master algorithms but restricts the use of the API functions to constrain how a master algorithm can be defined and how an FMU may respond. Formal semantics for FMI can be found in [5, 9].

2.3   RoboChart

RoboChart [28] is a diagrammatic notation tailored to the design of robotic systems. RoboChart models use Harel-style statecharts [20] but crucially also include constructs that embed concepts of robotic applications. They are used to structure models for abstraction and reuse. Moreover, distinctively, the RoboChart state machines use an action language that is both timed and probabilistic.

A RoboChart design centres around a robotic platform and its controllers. Communication between controllers can be either synchronous or asynchronous, but communication between state machines inside a controller is synchronous. The operations in a state machine may be given interface contracts using preconditions and postconditions, may be further defined by other state machines, or may come from a domain-specific API formalised separately. The formal semantics of RoboChart is mechanised in CSP [28] for model checking with FDR [19].

As a simple example, we consider a Rover robot inspired by that in [21]. It is an autonomous vehicle equipped to detect certain chemicals. It randomly traverses a designated area, sniffing its path with its onboard analysis equipment. If it detects a chemical source, it turns on a light and drops a flag as a marker.

A robotic system is specified in RoboChart by a module, where a robotic platform is connected to one or more controllers. A robotic platform is modelled by variables, events, and operations that represent built-in hardware facilities. The ChemicalDetector module for our example is shown in Fig. 2; it has a robotic platform Rover and controllers DetectAndFlagC and LightC.

The named boxes on the border of Rover declare events. The lightOn and lightOff events can be used to request that the robot built-in light is switched one way or the other. The sensor events l and r record the detection by the robot of a wall on one side or the other. Similarly, the alarm indicates the detection of a chemical source by the built-in sensor in the robot.

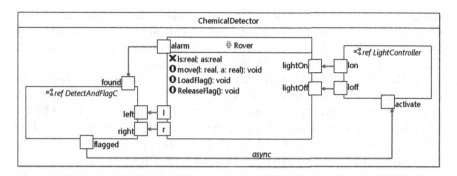

Fig. 2 RoboChart module

The variables ls and as of Rover record its linear and angular speeds. The move(l,a) operation commands the Rover to move with speeds l (linear) and a (angular); it is part of the RoboChart API. The operations LoadFlag() and ReleaseFlag(), on the other hand, are not in the RoboChart API, since they are particular to this example. They are declared but not further defined.

The two controllers DetectAndFlagC and LightC define the behaviour of Rover. DetectAndFlagC controls the events left, right, found, and flagged (see the bordered boxes), thereby interacting with Rover and LightC. These events are associated with l, r, and alarm of Rover, and activate of LightC, as indicated by the arrows, whose directions define information flow. So, when Rover finds a chemical, it sends an alarm to DetectAndFlagC. LightC uses events lon, loff, and activate to communicate with Rover and DetectAndFlagC.

RoboChart models do not provide specific facilities to specify the robot physical model and the environment. In the next section, we propose a way of considering RoboChart models in the context of a variation of the INTO-SysML profile, especially designed to deal with RoboChart co-models. In Sect. 4, we give a semantics based on the FMI API for the co-simulation specified in SysML.

3   Multi-Modelling of Robots in SysML

We propose the combined use of RoboChart with the notation of a simulation tool for continuous systems: any of Simulink, 20-sim, or OpenModelica, for instance. For illustration, we consider here control-law diagrams used in Simulink.

The goal is to support the addition of detailed models for the robotic platform and for the environment. To identify these multi-models and their relationship, we propose to adapt the INTO-SysML profile.

A RoboChart module includes exactly one robotic platform, for which it gives a very abstract account. As already said, a RoboChart robotic platform defines just the variables, events, and operations available. In many cases, the operations are left unspecified or are described just in terms of their effect on variables. In our ChemicalDetector module, for example, the operation move is specified just in terms of its effect on the variables ls and as of the robotic platform. There is no account of the actual laws of physics that control movement.

In a Simulink model, on the other hand, we can define the expected effect of the operations on the actual behaviour of the robot by capturing the laws of physics. In addition, we can also capture physical features of the environment that have a potential effect on the robot. To integrate the models, however, they need to share and expose events and variables. It is the purpose of the SysML model to depict the multi-models and their connections via events and variables.

Next, we present the extensions (Sect. 3.1) and restrictions (Sect. 3.2) to the INTO-SysML profile that we require, mainly for the specification of RoboChart and Simulink model composition. They are mostly confined to the Architecture Structure Diagrams. Some are of general interest, and some support the use of RoboChart as a co-model, in particular. In Sect. 3.3, we explain how we expect the resulting INTO-SysML profile to be used.

3.1 Extensions to INTO-SysML

The extensions are outlined in Table 1, and the restrictions later in Table 2. Both tables identify if the changes are specific to the needs of multi-models involving RoboChart diagrams or if they are more generally useful for cyber-physical systems and, therefore, could be included in the original INTO-SysML profile.

Table 1 Overview of proposed extensions to the INTO-SysML profile

#	Description	INTO-SysML/RoboCalc
E1	The components of the System block can include LComponent blocks.	Both
E2	We can have specialisations of LComponent blocks with stereotypes Environment and RoboticPlatform to group models for the environment and for the robotic platform. We can have any number of Environment blocks, but at most one block RoboticPlatform. These blocks can themselves be composed of any number of LComponent or EComponent blocks.	INTO-SysML may be extended to include an Environment block; however, RoboticPlatform should be RoboChart-specific.
E3	The type of a flow port optional.	RoboChart-specific
E4	The Platform of an EComponent is a String and can include any simulation tools. Alternatively, RoboChart and Simulink need to be admitted.	RoboChart-specific

Table 2 Overview of proposed restrictions to INTO-SysML profile

#	Description	INTO-SysML/RoboCalc
R1	There is exactly one `System` block and it cannot have flow ports.	Both
R2	An `LComponent` block has no ports.	Both
R3	In a diagram, we can have only one `EComponent` of `ComponentKind` cyber that must have `Platform` as RoboChart.	RoboChart-specific
R4	When the kind of a variable is `parameter` and when the `Direction` of a `FlowPort` with a type is `in`, its initial value must be defined.	Both
R5	Ports of a RoboChart block should be connected to the robotic platform, and not to the environment.	RoboChart-specific
R6	No use of `POComponent` is needed, if Simulink is used. If textual continuous models are adopted, these blocks can be used.	RoboChart-specific
R7	Typeless ports of a RoboChart block can be connected only to ports of type real of a Simulink block.	RoboChart-specific

Figure 3 presents the definition of the Architecture Structure Diagram for the multi-models for the chemical detection system. The block ChemicalDetector represents the RoboChart module in Fig. 2. The interface of a RoboChart module is defined by the variables and events in its robotic platform, which become ports of the SysML block that represents the module. The blocks Arena, WallSensor, MobilityHw, and ChemDHw represent Simulink models.

The first extension (E1) is about new `LComponent` blocks, which can be used to group models of the robotic platform or of the environment. They are logical blocks: they do not correspond to an actual component of the co-simulation. In our example, the `LComponent` block Rover represents the models for the robotic platform. It is composed of three `EComponent` blocks, representing Simulink models for the hardware for wall sensing, mobility, and chemical detection.

In fact, it is possible to define Rover as a `RoboticPlatform` block using the extension E2. On the other hand, we have just one `EComponent` that models one aspect of the environment, namely, the Arena where the robot moves.

Event-based communications are required in RoboChart, so we propose in E3 that ports may not carry any values. For instance, in our model, left and right are events of the robotic platform, as defined in RoboChart. As already said, they represent an indication of the presence of a wall from the sensors in the robotic platform. They carry no values; they are events declared without a type.

The INTO-SysML profile does not include operations on blocks. This is due to the fact that blocks are intended to inform FMI model descriptions. The FMI standard considers interactions to be in the form of typed data passed between

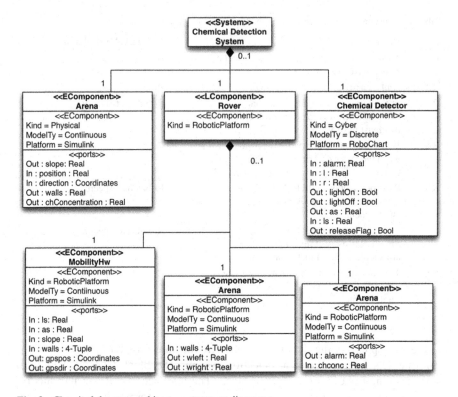

Fig. 3 Chemical detector architecture structure diagram

FMUs—this data is shared at each time step of a simulation. As such, the profile does not natively support the concepts of event-based or operation-based interactions. The new typeless ports representing RoboChart events are, therefore, handled by encoding event occurrence using real numbers 0.0 and 1.0.

Finally, the extension E4 includes extra values, namely, RoboChart and Simulink, for defining the platform of an EComponent block.

For the Connection Diagram, no changes to the INTO-SysML profile are required, except that we can have instances of LComponent blocks as well. For our example, the diagram is shown in Fig. 4.

3.2 Restrictions on INTO-SysML

As for the restrictions in Table 2, we have in R1 and R2 constraints on flow ports of System and LComponent blocks. Basically, a System block, Chemical Detection System in our example, is unique and can have no ports.

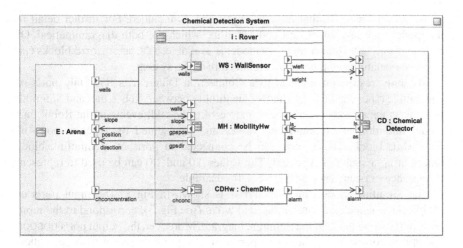

Fig. 4 Chemical detector connection diagram

An LComponent block, like Rover in Fig. 3, cannot have ports either. Since it is the EComponent blocks that represent multi-models, only them can contribute with inputs and outputs. For this reason, it does not make sense to include extra ports in an LComponent block, which just groups multi-models.

We recall that a cyber component models software aspects of the system. They should be specified using RoboChart. So, R3 requires that there is just one cyber component: the RoboChart module that is complemented by the Simulink diagrams. In our example, this is the ChemicalDetector block.

For simulation, parameters and inputs need an initial value as enforced by the restriction R4. For a parameter, this is the default value used in a simulation, unless an alternative value is provided. For the inputs, these are initial conditions that define the first set of outputs in the first step of the simulation. In our example, the initial values for position and direction, for instance, are (0.0,0.0) and (1.0,1.0). So, initially, the robot is stationary at a corner of the arena.

A controller can only ever sense or influence the environment using the sensors and actuators of the robotic platform. With R5, we, therefore, require that there is no direct connection between the controller and the environment. For example, Arena, representing a Simulink model of the environment, has an output port walls that identifies as a 4-tuple the distances from the current position to the walls in the directions left, right, front, and back. This port is connected to the input port of the same name in WallSensor. It is this component that provides ports wleft and wright connected to the input ports l and r of ChemicalDetector.

We note that FMI does not have vector (array) types. So, strictly speaking, instead of ports with vector types, we should have separate ports for each component of the vectors. The inclusion of vectors in the FMI standard is, however, expected. We, therefore, make use of them in our example.

We require with R6 that no POComponent is included. For further detail in the models, we use RoboChart and Simulink, which are both diagrammatical. Of course, if only a textual continuous model is available, POComponent blocks can improve readability of the overall architecture of the system.

The only restriction relevant to a Connection Diagram is R7. Only ports of compatible types can be connected; compatibility between RoboChart and Simulink types is as expected. On the other hand, as already said, events in the RoboChart model that do not communicate values are represented by typeless ports of its SysML block. These ports can be connected to ports of a Simulink block representing a signal of type real. The values 0.0 and 1.0 can be used to represent the absence or occurrence of the event, for example.

The Simulink model for MobilityHw is shown in Fig. 5. The input ports of MobilityHw, namely, ls, as, slope, and walls (see Fig. 3), correspond to the input ports of the same name in the Simulink diagram. Moreover, the output ports gpspos and gpsdir correspond to the output ports current_position and current_direction of the Simulink diagram.

The Simulink diagram consists of two main subsystems: rotate takes an angle and a vector as input and provides as output the result of rotating the vector by the given angle, and accelerate takes a linear speed (ls) and a slope and calculates the necessary acceleration profile to reach that velocity taking the slope into account. Essentially, given an initial_position and initial_direction, angular and linear speeds as and ls, a slope, and the distances walls to obstacles, the model calculates the movement of the robot. Restrictions over the speed are established by the block limit velocity. Restrictions over the position are described by the block Switch, which sets the speed to zero if there is a wall in front of the robot.

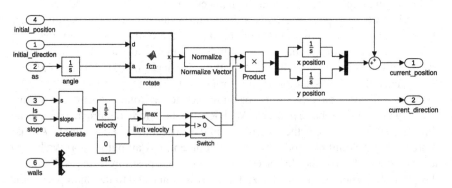

Fig. 5 MobilityHw Simulink diagram

3.3   Use of INTO-SysML with RoboChart

In addition to the proposed required changes to the INTO-SysML profile, there are some specific methodological issues to consider when defining a multi-model for RoboChart using the INTO-SysML profile. We outline these below.

Given a RoboChart module, the corresponding EComponent block has a particular form. First of all, it must have kind as cyber, the Platform as RoboChart, and the ModelType as discrete. This is illustrated in Fig. 3.

The variables of the RoboChart robotic platform become output ports. In our example, the variables ls and as of the Rover in Fig. 2 become output ports of ChemicalDetector in Fig. 3. The variables record the speeds required by the controller. This is used to define the behaviour of the mobility hardware.

The events of the RoboChart robotic platform are part of the visible behaviour of the RoboChart module. For this reason, they become flow ports in the cyber EComponent. In our example, we have events l, r, alarm, lightOn, and lightOff in the block ChemicalDetector of the Architecture Structure Diagram in Fig. 3, just like in the Rover of the module in Fig. 2.

In the RoboChart module, the definition of the direction of the events is from the point of view of the software controllers. In the Architecture Structure Diagram, the point of view is that of the hardware and the environment. So, their directions are reversed. For instance, the Rover in Fig. 2 can send the events l and r to the controller DetectAndFlagC indicating the presence of a wall on the left or on the right. In ChemicalDetector, however, these are input events. The relevant part of the hardware itself is modelled by the EComponent WallSensor, where the matching events wleft and wright are indeed outputs.

Operations of the RoboChart robotic platform, on the other hand, may or may not be part of the visible behaviour of the module. So, they are not necessarily included. For instance, move andLoadFlag are not in the EComponent Rover. On the other hand, ReleaseFlag is included in the ChemicalDetector to indicate that a call to this operation is visible: we can see the flag dropped.

The flow ports of the cyber EComponent can become flow ports also of one of the EComponent blocks that represent the robotic platform. It is possible, however, that there are extra flow ports for communication between the models of the robotic platform and of the environment. In our example, for instance, an extra flow port slope is used for the environment model Arena to inform the hardware model MobilityHw of the inclination of the floor, which has an effect on the hardware control of movement to achieve the targeted speed.

In the next section, we define a semantics for our extended profile. Given an INTO-SysML model, like that in Figs. 3 and 4, our semantics defines the FMI simulations that define inputs and outputs corresponding to the ports of the blocks in the AD and that, at each step of the simulation, connect these ports as described in the CD. This establishes a correctness criterion for (a model of) an FMI simulation, which includes extra components: a master algorithm and wrappers that allow communication between the FMUs and the master algorithm.

4 Semantics

A CSP semantics for INTO-SysML is already defined in [2]. Our semantics here is different in two ways: it considers extensions and restrictions described above, and it is based on events that represent calls to one of three functions of the FMI API— fmi2Set, fmi2Get, and fmi2DoStep. In contrast, the semantics in [2] identifies events with flows. It gives a simulation view of the model, where behaviour proceeds in steps, but a data flow is one interaction. In FMI, a flow is established by a pair of calls to fmi2Set and fmi2Get functions.

As a consequence of our approach here, our semantics is useful to define specifications for FMI simulations. In [9], we present a CSP semantics for such simulations that can be automatically generated from a description of the FMUs and their connections and a choice of master algorithm. The semantics presented here can be used, for example, to verify the correctness of those models.

A CSP specification is defined by a number of processes that communicate via channels. The system and each of its components are defined by a process. Communication is synchronous, atomic, and instantaneous.

The CSP process that defines the semantics of an INTO-SysML model uses communications on the following channels.

channel *fmi2Get* : *FMI2COMP* × *PORT* × *VAL* × *FMI2STATUSF*
channel *fmi2Set* : *FMI2COMP* × *PORT* × *VAL* × *FMI2STATUS*
channel *fmi2DoStep* : *FMI2COMP* × *TIME* × *NZTIME* × *FMI2STATUSF*

The types of these channels match the signature of the corresponding FMI API functions. *FMI2COMP* contains indices for each of the used instances of EComponent blocks, which represent FMUs in the INTO-SysML profile.

PORT contains indices, unique to each EComponent instance, to identify ports, which represent input and output variables of the FMU. *VAL* is the type of valid values; we do not model the SysML or the FMI type system. For ports corresponding to a RoboChart event, special values (perhaps just 0 and 1) represent absence or presence of an event occurrence. *VAL* must include these values.

In FMI, there is one fmi2Get and one fmi2Set function for each data type. For simplicity, however, we consider just one generic channel for each of them, since the overall behaviour of these functions is the same.

FMI2STATUS and *FMI2STATUSF* contain flags returned by a call to the API functions. In our model, all calls return the flag *fmi2OK*, indicating success. So, the scenarios that it defines do not cater for the possibility of errors.

Finally, the types *TIME* and *NZTIME* define a model of time, using natural numbers, for instance. In the case of *NZTIME*, it does not include 0, since fmi2DoStep does not accept a value 0 for a simulation step size.

For example, if we consider that the WallSensor FMU has index *WallSensor*, its port wleft has index *WSwleft*, and *VAL* includes the real numbers, then the communication *fmi2Get.WallSensor.WSwleft*.1.*fmi2OK* models the successful recording of the value 1 for the variable corresponding to the port wleft in the FMU for WallSensor. Similarly, *fmi2DoStep.WallSensor*.1.2.*fmi2OK* records a successful request for the same FMU to take a step at time 1, with a step size 2.

In what follows, we use the above channels to define CSP processes that correspond to EComponent instances (Sect. 4.1) and to co-simulations defined by a Connection Diagram for a System block (Sect. 4.2).

4.1 EComponent Instances

The process *EComponent(ec)* that defines the semantics of an EComponent block instance of index *ec* is specified in Fig. 6. We define a number of local processes *Init(setup)*, *TakeOutputs(outs)*, *DistributeInputs(inps)*, *Step*, and *Cycle* used to define the behaviour of *EComponent(ec)* as the initialisation defined by the process *Init*, followed by the process *Cycle*.

We use functions *Parameters*, *Inputs*, *Outputs*, and *Initials*, which, given an index *ec*, identify the parameters, input and output ports, and input ports with initial values, of the block instance *ec*. Instances of the same EComponent block have the same parameters, inputs, outputs, and input ports with initial values.

In *Init(setup)*, the parameters and the input ports identified in *setup* are initialised using values defined by a fifth function *InitialValues*, which, given a block *ec* and a parameter or input port *var*, gives the value of the parameter or the initial value of the port. Initialisation is via the channel *fmi2Set*. Each variable *var* in *setup* is initialised independently, so we have an interleaving ($\interleave$) of initialisations. Each initialisation is defined by a prefixing ($\rightarrow$) of a communication on *fmi2Set* to the process *SKIP*, which terminates immediately.

$EComponent(ec) = $ let

    $Init(setup) = $
        $(\ \interleave var : setup \bullet fmi2Set.ec.var.InitialValues(ec, var).fmi2OK \longrightarrow SKIP)$

    $TakeOutputs(outs) = $
        $sync \longrightarrow (\interleave var : outs \bullet fmi2Get.ec.var?x.fmi2OK \longrightarrow SKIP)$

    $DistributeInputs(inps) = $
        $sync \longrightarrow (\interleave var : inps \bullet fmi2Set.ec.var?x.fmi2OK \longrightarrow SKIP)$

    $Step = sync \longrightarrow fmi2DoStep.ec?t?ss.fmi2OK \longrightarrow SKIP$

    $Cycle = TakeOutputs(Outputs(ec));\ DistributeInputs(Inputs(ec));\ Step;\ Cycle$

within
    $Init(Parameters(ec) \cup Initials(ec));\ Cycle$

Fig. 6 CSP model of an EComponent block

Cycle defines a cyclic behaviour in three phases for an EComponent. It continuously provides values for its outputs, as defined by *TakeOutputs(Outputs(ec))*; takes values for its inputs, as defined by *DistributeInputs(Inputs(ec))*; and then carries out a step of simulation, as defined by *Step*. As already said, *fmi2Get* is a channel used to produce the values of the outputs, *fmi2Set* is used to take input values, and *fmi2DoStep* is used to mark a simulation step.

The process *TakeOutputs(Outputs(ec))* offers all the outputs *var* in the set *Outputs(ec)* via the channel *fmi2Get* in interleaving. The particular value *x* output is not defined (as indicated by the ? preceding *x* in the communication via *fmi2Get*). This value can be determined only by a particular model (in RoboChart or Simulink, for instance) for the EComponent. A synchronisation on a channel *sync*, that is, a communication without data passing, is used to mark the start of the outputting phase before the interleaving of communications on *fmi2Get*.

The process *DistributeInputs(Inputs(ec))* is similar, taking the inputs in the process *Inputs(ec)* via *fmi2Set*. Finally, the process *Step*, after accepting a *sync*, takes an input via *fmi2DoStep* of a time *t* and a step size *ss* and terminates.

In the next section, the semantics of a co-simulation uses the parallel composition ($[\![...]\!]$) below of instances of *EComponent(ec)* for each EComponent block instance. The processes *EComponent(ec)* synchronise on *sync* to ensure that they proceed from phase to phase of their cycles in lock step.

$$BlockInstances = ([\![\{sync\}]\!] \; ec : FMI2COMP \bullet EComponent(ec)) \setminus \{sync\}$$

The communications on *sync*, however, are hidden ($\setminus$). Therefore, as already indicated, the collective behaviour of the block instances is specified solely in terms of communications on the FMI API channels: *fmi2Get*, *fmi2Set*, and *fmi2DoStep*.

4.2 Co-simulation

A Connection Diagram for a System block instance characterises a co-simulation by instantiating blocks of the Architecture Diagram and defining how their ports are connected. This is captured by the CSP process *CoSimulation* defined in the sequel. We note that the instances of LComponent blocks play no role in the co-simulation semantics, since these blocks do not represent any actual component of a co-simulation, but just a logical grouping of co-models.

Besides *BlockInstances* above, *CoSimulation* uses the process *Connections* shown in Fig. 7. This is defined in terms of a parallel composition ($\|$) *Step* of processes *Connection(c)* that define each of the connections *c* in a Connection Diagram, identified by indices in a set *ConnectionIndex*.

The behaviour of *Connections* is defined by the sequential composition of the local processes *Init* followed by *Cycle*. *Init* initialises in interleaving the variables

Fig. 7 CSP model of a
connection diagram

$Connections = $ let

$Init = \; ||| ec : FMI2COMP \bullet$

$\quad (||| var : Initials(ec) \bullet fmi2Set.ec.var?x.fmi2OK \longrightarrow SKIP)$

$Step = \; || \; c : ConnectionIndex \bullet [AC(c)]Connection(c)$

$Cycle = Step; \; Cycle$

within
$\quad Init; \; Cycle$

corresponding to input ports of each component *ec* using the channel *fmi2set* as before. *Cycle* continuously behaves like *Step* described above.

A *Connection*(*c*) process takes an output from the source port of the connection and gives it to the target port. In our example, we can, for instance, give the connection between the ports wright of WallSensor and r of ChemicalDetector the index 3. In this case, *Connection*(3) is as follows, where *WallSensor* and *ChemicalDetector* are the indices in *FMI2COMP* for these EComponent block instances, and *WSwright* and *CDr* are variables corresponding to wright and r.

$$Connection(3) = fmi2Get.WallSensor.WSwright?x.fmi2OK \longrightarrow$$
$$fmi2Set.ChemicalDetector.CDr.x.fmi2OK \longrightarrow SKIP$$

Connection(3) ensures that the value *x* output via wright is input to the r port.

In the parallel composition in the process *Step*, each process *Connection*(*c*) is associated with an alphabet *AC*(*c*), which includes the communications over *fmi2Get* and *fmi2Set* that represent the connection it models. In our example, *AC*(3) contains all communications over *fmi2Get* with parameters *WallSensor* and *WSwright*, and over *fmi2Set* with parameters *ChemicalDetector* and *CDr*. The use of these alphabets in the parallelism that defines *Step* ensures that if there are several connections with the same source port, they share the output in the port by synchronising on that communication. In our example, the output *Awalls* of *Arena* is shared between the processes for the connections between Arena and WallSensor and between Arena and MobilityHw.

Finally, the semantics for the co-simulation defined by a Connection Diagram for a System instance is the parallel composition below.

$$CoSimulation = BlockInstances \; [\![\; FMIGetSet \;]\!] \; Connections$$

The processes synchronise on communications on the set *FMIGetSet* containing the union of the alphabets of the *Connection*(*c*) processes.

If there are ports that are not associated with a connection, their corresponding communications via *fmi2Set* or *fmi2Get* are not included in *FMIGetSet*. These communications are restricted only by the process *BlockInstances*. In our example, the ports lightOn and lightOff, for instance, are not connected to any other ports.

Their outputs are visible to the environment of the chemical detection system, but not connected to any other modelled components.

The behaviour defined by *CoSimulation* specifies a cyclic simulation whose steps contain three phases: all outputs are taken in any order, used to provide all inputs, also in any order, and then the time advances via a simulation step of each multi-model. As already said, a CSP semantics for an FMI co-simulation is available [9]. With that, *CoSimulation* can be used as a specification to validate an FMI co-simulation where the FMUs correspond to the EComponent block instances and must be orchestrated as indicated in the connection diagram.

5 Related Work

Another graphical domain-specific language for robotics is presented in [12]. It also supports design modelling and automatic generation of platform-independent code. It was defined as a UML profile, with all the advantages and problems entailed by this; reasoning about non-functional properties is envisaged.

Model-based engineering of robotic systems is also advocated in [38], where a component-based framework that uses UML to develop robotics software is presented. The communication between components is realised through a set of communication patterns such as *request/response* and *publish/subscribe*, which define the visibility of components. The goal of that work, however, does not include definition of a formal semantics for controllers, like we do for RoboChart.

Some domain-specific languages focus on a particular application (like programming self-reconfigurable robots [40] and service robots [7]). GenoM3 [27] supports the description of robotic applications in terms of its execution tasks and services. It has recently been given a timed behavioural semantics [17].

There are (famously) many different semantics for UML state machines [13]. Kuske et al. [24] give semantics for UML class, object, and state-machine diagrams using graph transformation. Rasch and Wehrheim [33] use CSP to give semantics for extended class diagrams and state machines. Davies and Crichton [10] also use CSP to give semantics for UML class, object, statechart, sequence, and collaboration diagrams. Broy et al. [6] present a foundational semantics for a subset of UML2 using state machines to describe the behaviour of objects and their data structures. RoboChart state machines have a precise semantics in CSP in the spirit of [33] and [10]; however, for the sake of compositionality, RoboChart state machines do not include history junctions and inter-level transitions.

UML 2.0 includes a timing diagram, a specific kind of interaction diagram with added timing constraints. The UML-MARTE profile [42] provides richer models of time based on clocks, including notions of logical, discrete, and continuous time. The Clock Constraint Specification Language (CCSL) provides for the specification of complex timing constraints, including time budgets and deadlines. This is accomplished with sequence and time diagrams; it is not possible to define timed constraints in terms of transitions or states like in RoboChart.

UML-RT [41] encapsulates state machines in capsules; inter-capsule communication is through ports and is controlled by a timing protocol with timeouts. More complex constraints, including deadlines, are specified only informally.

The work in [32] defines a semantics for a UML-RT subset in untimed *Circus* [45]. An extension to UML-RT is considered in [1] with semantics given in terms of CSP+T [46], an extension of CSP that supports annotations for the timing of events within sequential processes. The RoboChart timed primitives are richer and are inspired by timed automata and Timed CSP [39].

Practical work on master algorithms for use in FMI co-simulations includes generation of FMUs, their simulations, and hybrid models [3, 11, 14, 31]. FMUs can encapsulate heterogeneous models; Tripakis [44] shows how components based on state machines and synchronous data flow can be encoded as FMUs. In our approach, we have a hybrid co-simulation, but each EComponent is either discrete or continuous. Extensions to FMI are required to deal with that [5].

Savicks [36] shows how to co-simulate Event-B and continuous models using a fixed-step master algorithm. Savicks does not give semantics for the FMI API, but supplements reasoning in Event-B with simulation of FMUs within Rodin, the Event-B platform, applying the technique to an industrial case study [37]. The work does not wrap Event-B models as FMUs, and so it does not constitute a general FMI-compliant co-simulation. Here, we do not consider the models of FMUs, but plan to wrap CSP-based models of Simulink [8] and RoboChart [28] to obtain CSP-based FMU models that satisfy the specification in [9].

6 Conclusions and Future Work

In this chapter, we have extended and restricted the INTO-SysML profile to deal with robotic systems. For modelling the controller(s), we use RoboChart. For modelling the robotic platform and the environment, we use Simulink. The approach, however, applies to other languages of same nature: event-based reactive languages to define software and control-law diagrams. We have also given a behavioural semantics for models written in the profile using CSP. The semantics is agnostic to RoboChart and Simulink and captures a co-simulation view of the multi-models based on FMI.

Our semantics can be used in two ways. First, by integration with a semantics of each of the multi-models that defines their specific responses to the simulation steps, we can obtain a semantics of the system as a whole. Such semantics can be used to establish properties of the system, as opposed to properties of the individual models. In this way, we can confirm the results of (co-)simulations via model checking or, most likely, theorem proving, due to scalability issues.

As already mentioned, the CSP model is a front end for a UTP predicative semantics. It is amenable to theorem proving using Isabelle [16].

There are CSP-based formal semantics for RoboChart [28] and Simulink [8] underpinned by the UTP. Our next step is their lifting to provide an FMI-based view of the behaviour of models written in these notations. With that, we can use RoboChart and Simulink models as FMUs in a formal model of a co-simulation as suggested here and use CSP and the UTP to reason about the co-simulation. For RoboChart, for example, the lifting needs to transform inputs of values 0.0 and 1.0 on ports for typeless events to synchronisations. For Simulink, the notion of get and setting values and simulation steps is more directly recorded.

It is also relatively direct to wrap existing CSP semantics for UML state machines [10, 33] to allow the use of such models as FMUs in a co-simulation. In this case, traditional UML modelling can be adopted.

Secondly, we can use our semantics as a specification for a co-simulation. The work in [9] provides a CSP semantics for an FMI co-simulation; it covers not only models of the FMUs but also a model of a master algorithm of choice. The scenario defined by an INTO-SysML model identifies inputs and outputs and their connections. The traces of the FMI co-simulation model should be allowed by the CSP semantics of the INTO-SysML model. This can be verified via model checking.

As indicated in Fig. 1, currently there is no support to establish formal connections between a simulation and the state machine and physical models (of the robotic platform and the environment). The SysML profile proposed here supports the development of design models via the provision of domain-specific languages based on diagrammatic notations and facilities familiar to the engineering and robotics community for clear connection of models. Complementarily, as explained above, the profile semantics supports verification of FMI-based co-simulations.

There are plans for automatic generation of simulations of RoboChart models [28]. The semantics we propose can be used to justify the combination of these simulations with Simulink simulations as suggested above.

Acknowledgements This work is funded by the INTO-CPS EU grant and EPSRC grant EP/M025756/1. The authors are grateful to Wei Li, Pedro Ribeiro, Augusto Sampaio, and Jon Timmis for many discussions on RoboChart and simulation of robotic applications. No new primary data was created during this study.

References

1. Akhlaki, K.B., Tunon, M.I.C., Terriza, J.A.H., Morales, L.E.M.: A methodological approach to the formal specification of real-time systems by transformation of UML-RT design models. Sci. Comput. Program. **65**(1), 41–56 (2007)
2. Amálio, N.: Foundations of the SysML profile for CPS modelling. Technical Report D2.1a, INTO-CPS project (2015)
3. Bastian, J., Clauß, C., Wolf, S., Schneider, P.: Master for co-simulation using FMI. In: Modelica Conference (2011)
4. Broenink, J.F.: Modelling, simulation and analysis with 20-sim. Comput. Aided Control Syst. Des. **38**(3), 22–25 (1997)
5. Broman, D., Brooks, C., Greenberg, L., Lee, E.A., Masin, M., Tripakis, S., Wetter, M.: Determinate composition of FMUs for co-simulation. In: ACM SIGBED International Conference on Embedded Software. IEEE, New York (2013)

6. Broy, M., Cengarle, M.V., Rumpe, B.: Semantics of UML – towards a system model for UML: the state machine model. Technical Report TUM-I0711, Institut für Informatik, Technische Universität München (2007)

7. Bubeck, A., Weisshardt, F., Sing, T., Reiser, U., Hagele, M., Verl, A.: Implementing best practices for systems integration and distributed software development in service robotics-the care-o-bot® robot family. In: 2012 IEEE/SICE International Symposium on System Integration, pp. 609–614. IEEE, New York (2012)

8. Cavalcanti, A.L.C., Clayton, P., O'Halloran, C.: From control law diagrams to ada via Circus. Form. Asp. Comput. 23(4), 465–512 (2011)

9. Cavalcanti, A.L.C., Woodcock, J.C.P., Amálio, N.: Behavioural models for FMI Co-simulations. Technical Report, University of York, Department of Computer Science, York (2016). Available at www-users.cs.york.ac.uk/~alcc/CWA16.pdf

10. Davies, J., Crichton, C.: Concurrency and refinement in the unified modeling language. Form. Asp. Comput. 15(2–3), 118–145 (2003)

11. Denil, J., Meyers, B., De Meulenaere, P., Vangheluwe, H.: Explicit semantic adaptation of hybrid formalisms for FMI co-simulation. In: Spring Simulation Multi-Conference (2015)

12. Dhouib, S., Kchir, S., Stinckwich, S., Ziadi, T., Ziane, M.: RobotML, a domain-specific language to design, simulate and deploy robotic applications. In: Simulation, Modeling, and Programming for Autonomous Robots, pp. 149–160. Springer, Berlin (2012)

13. Eshuis, R.: Reconciling statechart semantics. Sci. Comput. Program. 74(3), 65–99 (2009)

14. Feldman, Y.A., Greenberg, L., Palachi, E.: Simulating rhapsody SysML blocks in hybrid models with FMI. In: Modelica Conference (2014)

15. FMI development group. Functional mock-up interface for model exchange and co-simulation, 2.0 (2014). https://www.fmi-standard.org

16. Foster, S., Zeyda, F., Woodcock, J.C.P.: Isabelle/UTP: a mechanised theory engineering framework. In: Naumann, D. (ed.) Unifying Theories of Programming. Lecture Notes in Computer Science, vol. 8963, pp. 21–41. Springer, Berlin (2015)

17. Foughali, M., Berthomieu, B., Dal Zilio, S., Ingrand, F., Mallet, A.: Model checking real-time properties on the functional layer of autonomous robots. In: Ogata, K., Lawford, M., Liu, S. (eds.) Formal Methods and Software Engineering, pp. 383–399. Springer, Berlin (2016)

18. Fritzson, P.: Principles of Object-Oriented Modeling and Simulation with Modelica 2.1. Wiley-IEEE, New York (2004)

19. Gibson-Robinson, T., Armstrong, P., Boulgakov, A., Roscoe, A.W.: FDR3 — a modern refinement checker for CSP. In: Tools and Algorithms for the Construction and Analysis of Systems, pp. 187–201 (2014)

20. Harel, D.: Statecharts: a visual formalism for complex systems. Sci. Comput. Program. 8(3), 231–274 (1987)

21. Hilder, J.A., Owens, N.D.L., Neal, M.J., Hickey, P.J., Cairns, S.N., Kilgour, D.P.A., Timmis, J., Tyrrell, A.M.: Chemical detection using the receptor density algorithm. IEEE Trans. Syst. Man Cybern. Part C Appl. Rev. 42(6), 1730–1741 (2012)

22. Hoare, C.A.R., Jifeng, H.: Unifying Theories of Programming. Prentice-Hall, Englewood Cliffs, NJ (1998)

23. Klein, J., Spector, L.: 3D Multi-agent simulations in the breve simulation environment. In: Artificial Life Models in Software, pp. 79–106. Springer, Berlin (2009)

24. Kuske, S., Gogolla, M., Kollmann, R., Kreowski, H.-J.: An integrated semantics for UML class, object and state diagrams based on graph transformation. In: Butler, M., Petre, L., SereKaisa, K. (eds.) Integrated Formal Methods. Lecture Notes in Computer Science, vol. 2335, pp. 11–28. Springer, Berlin (2002)

25. Larsen, P.G., Battle, N., Ferreira, M., Fitzgerald, J., Lausdahl, K., Verhoef, M.: The overture initiative – integrating tools for VDM. SIGSOFT Softw. Eng. Notes 35(1), 1–6 (2010)

26. Luke, S., Cioffi-Revilla, C., Panait, L., Sullivan, K., Balan, G.: Mason: a multiagent simulation environment. Simulation 81(7), 517–527 (2005)

27. Mallet, A., Pasteur, C., Herrb, M., Lemaignan, S., Ingrand, F.: Genom3: building middleware-independent robotic components. In: 2010 IEEE International Conference on Robotics and Automation, pp. 4627–4632 (2010)
28. Miyazawa, A., Ribeiro, P., Li, W., Cavalcanti, A.L.C., Timmis, J., Woodcock, J.C.P.: RoboChart: a state-machine notation for modelling and verification of mobile and autonomous robots. Technical Report, University of York, Department of Computer Science, York (2016). Available at www.cs.york.ac.uk/circus/publications/techreports/reports/MRLCTW16.pdf
29. Object Management Group: OMG Unified Modeling Language (OMG UML), Superstructure, Version 2.4.1 (2011)
30. OMG: OMG Systems Modeling Language (OMG SysML), Version 1.3 (2012)
31. Pohlmann, U., Schäfer, W., Reddehase, H., Röckemann, J., Wagner, R.: Generating functional mockup units from software specifications. In: Modelica Conference (2012)
32. Ramos, R., Sampaio, A.C.A., Mota, A.C.: A semantics for UML-RT active classes via mapping into Circus. In: Formal Methods for Open Object-based Distributed Systems. Lecture Notes in Computer Science, vol. 3535, pp. 99–114 (2005)
33. Rasch, H., Wehrheim, H.: Checking consistency in UML diagrams: classes and state machines. In: Najm, E., Nestmann, U., Stevens, P. (eds.) Formal Methods for Open Object-Based Distributed Systems. Lecture Notes in Computer Science, vol. 2884, pp. 229–243. Springer, Berlin (2003)
34. Rohmer, E., Singh, S.P.N., Freese, M.: V-rep: a versatile and scalable robot simulation framework. In: IEEE International Conference on Intelligent Robots and Systems, vol. 1, pp. 1321–1326. IEEE, New York (2013)
35. Roscoe, A.W.: Understanding Concurrent Systems. Texts in Computer Science. Springer, Berlin (2011)
36. Savicks, V., Butler, M., Colley, J.: Co-simulating event-B and continuous models via FMI. In: Summer Simulation Multiconference, pp. 37:1–37:8. Society for Computer Simulation International, San Diego (2014)
37. Savicks, V., Butler, M., Colley, J.: Co-simulation environment for Rodin: landing gear case study. In: Boniol, F., Wiels, V., Ameur, Y.A., Schewe, K.-D. (eds.) International Conference on Abstract State Machines, Alloy, B, TLA, VDM, and Z, pp. 148–153. Springer, Berlin (2014)
38. Schlegel, C., Hassler, T., Lotz, A., Steck, A.: Robotic software systems: from code-driven to model-driven designs. In: 14th International Conference on Advanced Robotics, pp. 1–8. IEEE, New York (2009)
39. Schneider, S.: Concurrent and Real-time Systems: The CSP Approach. Wiley, New York (2000)
40. Schultz, U.P., Johan, C.D., Stoy, K.: A domain-specific language for programming self-reconfigurable robots. In: Workshop on Automatic Program Generation for Embedded Systems (APGES), pp. 28–36 (2007)
41. Selic, B.: Using UML for modeling complex real-time systems. In: Mueller, F., Bestavros, A. (eds.) Languages, Compilers, and Tools for Embedded Systems. Lecture Notes in Computer Science, vol. 1474, pp. 250–260. Springer, Berlin (1998)
42. Selic, B., Grard, S.: Modeling and Analysis of Real-Time and Embedded Systems with UML and MARTE: Developing Cyber-Physical Systems. Morgan Kaufmann, Waltham (2013)
43. The MathWorks, Inc.: Simulink. www.mathworks.com/products/simulink
44. Tripakis, S.: Bridging the semantic gap between heterogeneous modeling formalisms and FMI. In: International Conference on Embedded Computer Systems: Architectures, Modeling, and Simulation, pp. 60–69. IEEE, New York (2015)
45. Woodcock, J.C.P., Cavalcanti, A.L.C.: *Circus*: a concurrent refinement language. Technical Report, Oxford University Computing Laboratory, Wolfson Building, Parks Road, Oxford (2001)
46. Zic, J.J.: Time-constrained buffer specifications in CSP + T and timed CSP. ACM ACM Trans. Program. Lang. Syst. **16**(6), 1661–1674 (1994)

Microservices: Yesterday, Today, and Tomorrow

Nicola Dragoni, Saverio Giallorenzo, Alberto Lluch Lafuente,
Manuel Mazzara, Fabrizio Montesi, Ruslan Mustafin, and Larisa Safina

Abstract Microservices is an architectural style inspired by service-oriented computing that has recently started gaining popularity. Before presenting the current state of the art in the field, this chapter reviews the history of software architecture, the reasons that led to the diffusion of objects and services first, and microservices later. Finally, open problems and future challenges are introduced. This survey primarily addresses newcomers to the discipline, while offering an academic viewpoint on the topic. In addition, we investigate some practical issues and point out a few potential solutions.

1 Introduction

The mainstream languages for the development of server-side applications, like Java, C/C++, and Python, provide abstractions to break down the complexity of programs into modules. However, these languages are designed for the creation of *single executable artefacts*, also called *monoliths*, and their modularisation abstractions rely on the sharing of resources of the same machine (memory, databases, files). Since the modules of a monolith depend on said shared resources, they are not independently executable.

N. Dragoni • A.L. Lafuente
Technical University of Denmark, Kgs. Lyngby, Denmark
e-mail: ndra@dtu.dk; albl@dtu.dk

S. Giallorenzo
Department of Computer Science and Engineering, INRIA/University of Bologna, Bologna, Italy
e-mail: saverio.giallorenzo@gmail.com

M. Mazzara (✉) • R. Mustafin • L. Safina
Innopolis University, Innopolis, Russia
e-mail: m.mazzara@innopolis.ru; r.mustafin@innopolis.ru; l.safina@innopolis.ru

F. Montesi
University of Southern Denmark, Odense M, Denmark
e-mail: fmontesi@imada.sdu.dk

© Springer International Publishing AG 2017
M. Mazzara, B. Meyer (eds.), *Present and Ulterior Software Engineering*,
https://doi.org/10.1007/978-3-319-67425-4_12

Definition 1 (Monolith) A monolith is a software application whose modules cannot be executed independently.

This makes monoliths difficult to use in distributed systems without specific frameworks or ad hoc solutions such as Network Objects [7], RMI [40], or CORBA [67]. However, even these approaches still suffer from the general issues that affect monoliths; below we list the most relevant ones (we label issues I|n):

I|1 large-size monoliths are difficult to maintain and evolve due to their complexity. Tracking down bugs requires long perusals through their code base.

I|2 Monoliths also suffer from the "dependency hell" [56], in which adding or updating libraries results in inconsistent systems that either do not compile/run or, worse, misbehave.

I|3 Any change in one module of a monolith requires rebooting the whole application. For large-sized projects, restarting usually entails considerable downtimes, hindering the development, testing, and maintenance of the project.

I|4 Deployment of monolithic applications is usually suboptimal due to conflicting requirements on the constituent models' resources: some can be memory-intensive, others computational-intensive, and others require ad hoc components (e.g. SQL-based rather than graph-based databases). When choosing a deployment environment, the developer must compromise with a one-size-fits-all configuration, which is either expensive or suboptimal with respect to the individual modules.

I|5 Monoliths limit scalability. The usual strategy for handling increments of inbound requests is to create new instances of the same application and to split the load amongst said instances. However, it could be the case that the increased traffic stresses only a subset of the modules, making the allocation of the new resources for the other components inconvenient.

I|6 Monoliths also represent a technology lock-in for developers, which are bound to use the same language and frameworks of the original application.

The *microservice* architectural style [34] has been proposed to cope with such problems. In our definition of microservice, we use the term "cohesive" [2, 6, 10, 25, 44] to indicate that a service implements only functionalities strongly related to the concern that it is meant to model.

Definition 2 (Microservice) A microservice is a cohesive, independent process interacting via messages.

As an example, consider a service intended to compute calculations. To call it a microservice, it should provide arithmetic operations requestable via messages, but it should not provide other (possibly loosely related) functionalities like plotting and displaying of functions.

From a technical point of view, microservices should be independent components conceptually deployed in isolation and equipped with dedicated memory persistence tools (e.g. databases). Since all the components of a microservice architecture are microservices, its distinguishing behaviour derives from the composition and coordination of its components via messages.

Definition 3 (Microservice Architecture) A microservice architecture is a distributed application where all its modules are microservices.

To give an example of a microservice architecture, let us assume that we want to provide a functionality that plots the graph of a function. We also assume the presence of two microservices: Calculator and Displayer. The first is the calculator microservice mentioned above; the second renders and displays images. To fulfil our goal, we can introduce a new microservice, called Plotter, that orchestrates Calculator to calculate the shape of the graph and that invokes Displayer to render the calculated shape. Below, we report (in black) a depiction of the workflow of such a microservice architecture.

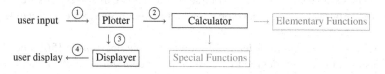

The developers of the architecture above can focus separately on implementing the basic microservice functionalities, i.e. the Calculator and the Displayer. Finally, they can implement the behaviour of the distributed application with the Plotter that ① takes the function given by a user, ② interacts with the Calculator to compute a symbolic representation of the graph of the function, and finally ③ requests the Displayer to show the result back to the user ④. To illustrate how the microservice approach scales by building on pre-existing microservice architectures, in the figure above we drew the Calculator orchestrating two extra microservices (in grey) that implement mathematical Elementary and Special Functions.

The microservice architectural style does not favour or forbid any particular programming paradigm. It provides a guideline to partition the components of a distributed application into independent entities, each addressing one of its concerns. This means that a microservice, provided it offers its functionalities via message passing, can be internally implemented with any of the mainstream languages cited in the beginning of this section.

The principle of microservice architectures assists project managers and developers: it provides a guideline for the design and implementation of distributed applications. Following this principle, developers focus on the implementation and testing of a few, cohesive functionalities. This holds also for higher-level microservices, which are concerned with coordinating the functionalities of other microservices.

We conclude this section with an overview, detailed in greater depth in the remainder of the chapter, on how microservices cope with the mentioned issues of monolithic applications (below, $S|n$ is a solution to issue $I|n$).

S|1 Microservices implement a limited amount of functionalities, which makes their code base small and inherently limits the scope of a bug. Moreover, since microservices are independent, a developer can directly test and investigate their functionalities in isolation with respect to the rest of the system.

S|2 It is possible to plan *gradual transitions* to new versions of a microservice. The new version can be deployed "next" to the old one, and the services that depend on the latter can be gradually modified to interact with the former. This fosters *continuous integration* [33] and greatly eases software maintenance.

S|3 As a consequence of the previous item, changing a module of a microservice architecture does not require a complete reboot of the whole system. The reboot regards only the microservices of that module. Since microservices are small in size, programmers can develop, test, and maintain services experiencing only very short redeployment downtimes.

S|4 Microservices naturally lend themselves to containerisation [56], and developers enjoy a high degree of freedom in the configuration of the deployment environment that best suits their needs (both in terms of costs and quality of service).

S|5 Scaling a microservice architecture does not imply a duplication of all its components, and developers can conveniently deploy/dispose instances of services with respect to their load [36].

S|6 The only constraint imposed on a network of interoperating microservices is the technology used to make them communicate (media, protocols, data encodings). Apart from that, microservices impose no additional lock-in and developers can freely choose the optimal resources (languages, frameworks, etc.) for the implementation of each microservice.

In the remainder of this chapter, in Sect. 2, we give a brief account of the evolution of distributed architectures until their recent incarnation in the microservice paradigm. Then, we detail the problems that microservices can solve and their proposed solutions in the form of microservice architectures. In Sect. 3, we detail the current solutions for developing microservice architectures and how microservices affect the process of software design, development, testing, and maintenance. In Sect. 4, we discuss the open challenges and the desirable tools for programming microservice architecture. In Sect. 5, we draw overall conclusions.

2 Yesterday

Architecture is what allows systems to evolve and provide a certain level of service throughout their life cycle. In software engineering, architecture is concerned with providing a bridge between system functionality and requirements for quality attributes that the system has to meet. Over the past several decades, software architecture has been thoroughly studied, and as a result software engineers have come up with different ways to compose systems that provide broad functionality and satisfy a wide range of requirements. In this section, we provide an overview of the work on software architectures from the early days to the advent of microservices.

2.1 From the Early Days to Object-Oriented Design Patterns

The problems associated with large-scale software development were first experienced around the 1960s [11]. The 1970s saw a huge rise of interest from the research community for software design and its implications on the development process. At the time, the design was often considered as an activity not associated with the implementation itself and therefore requiring a special set of notations and tools. Around the 1980s, the full integration of design into the development processes contributed towards a partial merge of these two activities, thus making it harder to make neat distinctions. References to the concept of software architecture also started to appear around the 1980s. However, a solid foundation on the topic was only established in 1992 by Perry and Wolf [70]. Their definition of software architecture was distinct from software design, and since then it has generated a large community of researchers studying the notion and the practical applications of software architecture, allowing the concepts to be widely adopted by both industry and academia.

This spike of interest contributed to an increase in the number of existing software architecture patterns (or generally called *styles*), so that some form of classification was then required. This problem was tackled in one of the most notable works in the field, the book *Software Architecture: Perspectives on an Emerging Discipline* by Garlan and Shaw [75]. Bosch's work [8] provides a good overview of the current research state in software engineering and architecture. Since its appearance in the 1980s, software architecture has developed into a mature discipline making use of notations, tools, and several techniques. From the pure, and occasionally speculative, realm of academic basic research, it has made the transition into an element that is essential to industrial software construction.

The advent and diffusion of object orientation, starting from the 1980s and in particular in the 1990s, brought its own contribution to the field of software architecture. The classic by Gamma et al. [37] covers the design of object-oriented software and how to translate it into code presenting a collection of recurring solutions, called *patterns*. This idea is neither new nor exclusive to software engineering, but the book is the first compendium to popularise the idea on a large scale. In the pre-Gamma era, patterns for object-oriented (OO) solutions were already used: a typical example of an architectural design pattern in object-oriented programming is the Model-View-Controller (MVC) [32], which has been one of the seminal insights in the early development of graphical user interfaces.

2.2 Service-Oriented Computing

Attention to *separation of concerns* has recently led to the emergence of the so-called component-based software engineering (CBSE) [77], which has given better control over design, implementation, and evolution of software systems. The last decade has seen a further shift towards the concept of service first [81] and the natural evolution to microservices afterwards.

Service-Oriented Computing (SOC) is an emerging paradigm for distributed computing and e-business processing that finds its origin in object-oriented and component computing. It has been introduced to harness the complexity of distributed systems and to integrate different software applications [51]. In SOC, a program—called a *service*—offers functionalities to other components, accessible via message passing. Services decouple their interfaces (i.e. how other services access their functionalities) from their implementation. On top of that, specific workflow languages are then defined in order to orchestrate the complex actions of services (e.g. WS-BPEL [66]). These languages share ideas with some well-known formalisms from concurrency theory, such as CCS and the π-calculus [57, 58]. This aspect fostered the development of formal models for better understanding and verifying service interactions, ranging from foundational process models of SOC [41, 50, 53] to theories for the correct composition of services [9, 45, 46]. In [86] a classification of approaches for business modelling puts this research in perspective.

The benefits of service-orientation are as follows:

- **Dynamism**—New instances of the same service can be launched to split the load on the system.
- **Modularity and reuse**—Complex services are composed of simpler ones. The same services can be used by different systems.
- **Distributed development**—By agreeing on the interfaces of the distributed system, distinct development teams can develop partitions of it in parallel.
- **Integration of heterogeneous and legacy systems**—Services merely have to implement standard protocols to communicate.

2.3 Second Generation of Services

The idea of componentisation used in service orientation can be partially traced back to the object-oriented programming (OOP) literature; however, there are peculiar differences that led to virtually separate research paths and communities. As a matter of fact, SOC at the origin was—and still is—built on top of OOP languages, largely due to their broad diffusion in the early 2000s. However, the evolution of objects into services, and the relative comparisons, has to be treated carefully since the first focus on encapsulation and information is hidden in a *shared-memory* scenario, while the second is built on the idea of independent deployment and *message passing*. It is therefore a paradigm shift, where both the paradigms share the common idea of componentisation. The next step is adding the notion of *business capability* and therefore focusing analysis and design on it so that the overall system architecture is determined on this basis.

The first "generation" of service-oriented architectures (SOA) defined daunting and nebulous requirements for services (e.g. discoverability and service contracts), and this hindered the adoption of the SOA model. Microservices are the second iteration on the concept of SOA and SOC. The aim is to strip away unnecessary levels of complexity in order to focus on the programming of simple services that effectively implement a single functionality. Like OO, the microservice paradigm needs ad hoc tools to support developers and naturally leads to the emergence of specific design patterns [74]. First and foremost, languages that embrace the service-oriented paradigm are needed (instead, for the most part, microservice architectures still use OO languages like Java and Javascript or functional ones). The same holds for the other tools for development support like testing suites, (API) design tools, etc.

3 Today

The microservice architecture appeared lately as a new paradigm for programming applications by means of the composition of small services, each running its own processes and communicating via light-weight mechanisms. This approach has been built on the concepts of SOA [51], brought from crossing-boundaries workflows to the application level and into the applications architectures, i.e. its service-oriented architecture and programming from the large to the small.

The term "microservices" was first introduced in 2011 at an architectural workshop as a way to describe the participants' common ideas in software architecture patterns [34]. Until then, this approach had also been known under different names. For example, Netflix used a very similar architecture under the name of *fine-grained SOA* [84].

Microservices now are a new trend in software architecture, which emphasises the design and development of highly maintainable and scalable software. Microservices manage growing complexity by functionally decomposing large systems into a set of independent services. By making services completely independent in development and deployment, microservices emphasise loose coupling and high cohesion by taking modularity to the next level. This approach delivers all sorts of benefits in terms of maintainability, scalability, and so on. It also comes with a bundle of problems that are inherited from distributed systems and from SOA, its predecessor. The microservice architecture still shows distinctive characteristics that blend into something unique and different from SOA itself:

- **Size**—The size is comparatively small wrt. a typical service, supporting the belief that the architectural design of a system is highly dependent on the structural design of the organisation producing it. Idiomatic use of the microservice architecture suggests that if a service is too large, it should be split into two or more services, thus preserving granularity and maintaining focus on providing only a single business capability. This brings benefits in terms of service maintainability and extendability.
- **Bounded context**—Related functionalities are combined into a single business capability, which is then implemented as a service.
- **Independency**—Each service in microservice architecture is operationally independent from other services, and the only form of communication between services is through their published interfaces.

The key system characteristics for microservices are as follows:

- **Flexibility**—A system is able to keep up with the ever-changing business environment and is able to support all modifications that is necessary for an organisation to stay competitive on the market.
- **Modularity**—A system is composed of isolated components where each component contributes to the overall system behaviour rather than having a single component that offers full functionality.
- **Evolution**—A system should stay maintainable while constantly evolving and adding new features.

The microservice architecture gained popularity relatively recently and can be considered to be in its infancy since there is still a lack of consensus on what microservices actually are. M. Fowler and J. Lewis provide a starting ground by defining principal characteristics of microservices [34]. S. Newman [64] builds upon M. Fowler's article and presents recipes and best practices regarding some aspects of the aforementioned architecture. L. Krause in his work [47] discusses patterns and applications of microservices. A number of papers have also been published that describe details of design and implementation of systems using microservice architecture. For example, the authors of [48] present development details of a new software system for Nevada Research Data Center (NRDC) using the microservice architecture. M. Rahman and J. Gao in [38] describe an application of behaviour-driven development (BDD) to the microservice architecture in order to decrease the maintenance burden on developers and encourage the usage of acceptance testing.

3.1 Teams

Back in 1968, Melvin Conway proposed that an organisation's structure or, more specifically, its communication structure constrains a system's design such that the resulting design is a copy of the organisation's communication patterns [22]. The microservices approach is to organise cross-functional teams around services, which in turn are organised around business capabilities [34]. This approach is also known as "you build, you run it" principle, first introduced by Amazon CTO Werner Vogels [39]. According to this approach, teams are responsible for full support and development of a service throughout its life cycle.

3.2 Total Automation

Each microservice may represent a single business capability that is delivered and updated independently and on its own schedule. Discovering a bug and/or adding a minor improvement does not have any impact on other services and on their release schedule (of course, as long as backwards compatibility is preserved and a service interface remains unchanged). However, to truly harness the power of independent deployment, one must utilise very efficient integration and delivery mechanisms. This being said, microservices are the first architecture developed in the post-continuous delivery era, and essentially microservices are meant to be used with continuous delivery and continuous integration, making each stage of delivery pipeline automatic. By using automated continuous delivery pipelines and modern container tools, it is possible to deploy an updated version of a service to production in a matter of seconds [52], which proves to be very beneficial in rapidly changing business environments.

3.3 Choreography over Orchestration

As discussed earlier, microservices may cooperate in order to provide more complex and elaborate functionalities. There are two approaches to establish this cooperation—orchestration [54] and choreography [69]. Orchestration requires a conductor—a central service that will send requests to other services and oversee the process by receiving responses. Choreography, on the other hand, assumes no centralisation and uses events and publish/subscribe mechanisms in order to establish collaboration. These two concepts are not new to microservices, but rather are inherited from the SOA world where languages such as WS-BPEL [66] and WS-CDL [82] have long represented the major references for orchestration and choreography, respectively (with vivid discussions between the two communities of supporters).

Prior to the advent of microservices and at the beginning of the SOA's hype in particular, orchestration was generally more popular and widely adopted, due to its simplicity of use and easier ways to manage complexity. However, it clearly leads to service coupling and uneven distribution of responsibilities, and therefore some services have a more centralising role than others. Microservices' culture of decentralisation and high degrees of independence represents instead the natural application scenario for the use of choreography as a means of achieving collab-

oration. This approach has indeed recently seen a renewed interest in connection
with the broader diffusion of microservices in what can be called the *second wave
of services.*

3.4 Impact on Quality and Management

In order to better grasp microservices, we need to understand the impact that this
architecture has on some software quality attributes.

3.4.1 Availability

Availability is a major concern in microservices as it directly affects the success
of a system. Given services independence, the whole system availability can be
estimated in terms of the availability of the individual services that compose the
system. Even if a single service is not available to satisfy a request, the whole
system may be compromised and experience direct consequences. If we take service
implementation, the more fault-prone a component is, the more frequently the
system will experience failures. One would argue that small-size components lead
to a lower fault density. However, it has been found by Hatton [42] and by Compton
and Withrow [21] that small-size software components often have a very high fault
density. On the other hand, El Emam et al. in their work [28] found that as size
increases, so does a component's fault proneness. Microservices are prevented from
becoming too large as idiomatic use of microservice architecture suggests that, as
a system grows larger, microservices should be prevented from becoming overly
complex by refining them into two or more different services. Thus, it is possible to
keep optimal size for services, which may theoretically increase availability. On the
other hand, spawning an increasing number of services will make the system fault-
prone on the integration level, which will result in decreased availability due to the
large complexity associated with making dozens of services instantly available.

3.4.2 Reliability

Given the distributed nature of the microservice architecture, particular attention
should be paid to the reliability of message-passing mechanisms between services
and to the reliability of the services themselves. Building the system out of small and
simple components is also one of the rules introduced in [72], which states that in
order to achieve a higher reliability, one must find a way to manage the complexities
of a large system: building things out of simple components with clean interfaces is
one way to achieve this. The greatest threat to microservices reliability lies in the
domain of integration, and therefore when talking about microservices reliability,
one should also mention integration mechanisms. One example of this assumption

being false is using a network as an integration mechanism and assuming network reliability is one of the first fallacies of distributed computing [73]. Therefore, in this aspect, microservices reliability is inferior to the applications that use in-memory calls. It should be noted that this downside is not unique only to microservices and can be found in any distributed system. When talking about messaging reliability, it is also useful to remember that microservices put restrictions on integration mechanisms. More specifically, microservices use integration mechanisms in a very straightforward way—by removing all functionality that is not related to the message delivering and focusing solely on reliable message delivery.

3.4.3 Maintainability

By nature, the microservice architecture is loosely coupled, meaning that there is a small number of links between services and services themselves being independent. This greatly contributes to the maintainability of a system by minimising the costs of modifying services, fixing errors, or adding new functionality. Despite all efforts to make a system as maintainable as possible, it is always possible to spoil maintainability by writing obscure and counterintuitive code [4]. As such, another aspect of microservices that can lead to increased maintainability is the above-mentioned "you build it, you run it" principle, which leads to a better understanding of a given service, its business capabilities and roles [20, 29].

3.4.4 Performance

The prominent factor that negatively impacts performance in the microservice architecture is communication over a network. The network latency is much greater than that of memory. This means that in-memory calls are much faster to complete than sending messages over the network. Therefore, in terms of communication, the performance will degrade compared to applications that use in-memory call mechanisms. Restrictions that microservices put on size also indirectly contribute to this factor. In more general architectures without size-related restrictions, the ratio of in-memory calls to the total number of calls is higher than in the microservice architecture, which results in less communication over the network. Thus, the exact amount of performance degradation will also depend on the system's interconnectedness. As such, systems with well-bounded contexts will experience less degradation due to looser coupling and fewer messages sent.

3.4.5 Security

In any distributed system, security becomes a major concern. In this sense, microservices suffer from the same security vulnerabilities as SOA [5]. As microservices use REST mechanism and XML with JSON as main data-interchange formats, particular attention should be paid to providing security of the data being transferred. This means adding additional overhead to the system in terms of additional encryption functionality. Microservices promote service reuse, and as such it is natural to assume that some systems will include third-party services. Therefore, an additional challenge is to provide authentication mechanisms with third-party services and ensure that the sent data is stored securely. In summary, microservices' security is impacted in a rather negative manner because one has to consider and implement additional security mechanisms to provide additional security functionality mentioned above.

3.4.6 Testability

Since all components in a microservice architecture are independent, each component can be tested in isolation, which significantly improves component testability compared to monolithic architecture. It also allows to adjust the scope of testing based on the size of changes. This means that with microservices, it is possible to isolate parts of the system that changed and parts that were affected by the change and to test them independently from the rest of the system. Integration testing, on the other hand, can become very tricky, especially when the system that is being tested is very large, and there are too many connections between components. It is possible to test each service individually, but anomalies can emerge from collaboration of a number of services.

4 Tomorrow

Microservices are so recent that we can consider their exploration to have just begun. In this section, we discuss interesting future directions that we envision will play key roles in the advancement of the paradigm.

The greatest strength of microservices comes from pervasive distribution: even the internal components of software are autonomous services, leading to loosely coupled systems and the other benefits previously discussed. However, from this same aspect (distribution) also comes its greatest weakness: programming distributed systems is inherently harder than monoliths. We now have to think about new issues. Some examples are how can we manage changes to a service that may have side effects on other services that it communicates with? How can we prevent attacks that exploit network communications?

4.1 Dependability

There are many pitfalls that we need to keep in mind when programming with microservices. In particular, preventing programming errors is hard. Consequently, building dependable systems is challenging.

4.1.1 Interfaces

Since microservices are autonomous, we are free to use the most appropriate technology for the development of each microservice. A disadvantage introduced by this practice is that different technologies typically have different means of specifying contracts for the composition of services (e.g. interfaces in Java, or WSDL documents in Web Services [19]). Some technologies do not even come with a specification language and/or a compatibility checker of microservices (Node.js, based on JavaScript, is a prime example).

Thus, where do we stand? Unfortunately, the current answer is informal documentation. Most services come with informal documents expressed in natural language that describe how clients should use the service. This makes the activity of writing a client very error-prone, due to potential ambiguities. Moreover, we have no development support tools to check whether service implementations actually implement their interfaces correctly.

As an attempt to fix this problem, there are tools for the formal specification of message types for data exchange, which one can use to define service interfaces independently of specific technologies. Then, these technology-agnostic specifications can be either compiled to language-specific interfaces—e.g. compiling an interface to a Java type—or used to check for well-typedness of messages (wrt. interfaces and independently of the transport protocol). Examples of tools offering these methodologies are Jolie [3, 55, 63], Apache Thrift [71], and Google's Protocol Buffers [80]. However, it is still unclear how to adapt tools to implement the mechanical checking (at compile or execution time) of messages for some widespread architectural styles for microservices, such as REST [30], where interfaces are constrained to a fixed set of operations and actions are expressed on dynamic resource paths. A first attempt at bridging the world of technology-agnostic interfaces based on operations and REST is presented in [61], but checking for the correctness of the binding information between the two is still left as a manual task to the programmer. Another, and similar, problem is trying to apply static type-checking to dynamic languages (e.g. JavaScript and Jolie), which are largely employed in the development of microservices [1, 31, 59].

4.1.2 Behavioural Specifications and Choreographies

Having formally defined interfaces in the form of an API is not enough to guarantee the compatibility of services. This is because, during execution, services may engage in sessions during which they perform message exchanges in a precise order. If two services engage in a session and start performing incompatible I/O, this can lead to various problems. Examples include a client sending a message on a stream that was previously closed; deadlocks, when two services expect a message from one another without sending anything; or, a client trying to access an operation that is offered by a server only after a successful distributed authentication protocol with a third-party is performed.

Behavioural types are types that can describe the behaviour of services and can be used to check that two (or more) services have compatible actions. Session types are a prime example of behavioural types [45, 46]. Session types have been successfully applied to many contexts already, ranging from parallel to distributed computing. However, no behavioural type theory is widely adopted in practice yet. This is mainly because behavioural types restrict the kind of behaviours that programmers can write for services, limiting their applicability. An important example of a feature with space for improvement is nondeterminism. In many interesting protocols, like those for distributed agreement, execution is nondeterministic and depending on what happens at runtime, the participants have to react differently [68].

Behavioural interfaces are a hot topic right now and will likely play an important role in the future of microservices. We envision that they will also be useful for the development of automatic testing frameworks that check the communication behaviour of services.

4.1.3 Choreographies

Choreographies are high-level descriptions of the communications that we want to happen in a system in contrast with the typical methodology of defining the behaviour of each service separately. Choreographies are used in some models for behavioural interfaces, but they actually originate from efforts at the W3C of defining a language that describes the global behaviour of service systems [85]. Over the past decade, choreographies have been investigated for supporting a new programming paradigm called Choreographic Programming [60]. In Choreographic Programming, the programmer uses choreographies to program service systems and then a compiler is used to automatically generate compliant implementations. This yields a correctness-by-construction methodology, guaranteeing important properties such as deadlock freedom and lack of communication errors [14, 15, 62].

Choreographies may have an important role in the future of microservices, since they shrink the gap between requirements and implementations, making the programmer able to formalise the communications envisioned in the design phase of a software. Since the correctness of the compiler from choreographies to distributed implementations is vital in this methodology, formal models are being heavily adopted to develop correct compilation algorithms [35]. However, a formalisation of how transparent mobility of processes from one protocol to the other is still missing. Moreover, it is still unclear how choreographies can be combined with flexible deployment models where nodes may be replicated or fail at runtime. An initial investigation on the latter is given in [49]. Also, choreographies are still somewhat limited in expressing nondeterministic behaviour, just like behavioural types.

4.1.4 Moving Fast with Solid Foundations

Behavioural types, choreographies, refinement types [78], and other models address the problem of specifying, verifying, and synthesising communication behaviours. However, there is still much to be discovered and developed on these topics. It is then natural to ask: do we really need to start these investigations from scratch? Or, can we hope to reuse results and structures from other well-established models in computer science?

A recent line of work suggests that a positive answer can be found by connecting behavioural types and choreographies to well-known logical models. A prominent example is a Curry-Howard correspondence between session types and the process model of π-calculus, given in [13] (linear logic propositions correspond to session types, and communications to proof normalisation in linear logic). This result has propelled many other results, amongst which are as follows: a logical reconstruction of behavioural types in classical linear logic that supports parametric polymorphism [83], type theories for integrating higher-order process models with functional computation [79], initial ideas for algorithms for extracting choreographies from separate service programs [16], a logical characterisation of choreography-based behavioural types [17], and explanations of how interactions amongst multiple services (multiparty sessions) are related to well-known techniques for logical reasoning [12, 18].

Another principle that we can use for the evolution of choreographic models is the established notion of computation. The minimal set of language features to achieve Turing completeness in choreographies is known [23]. More relevant in practice, this model was used to develop a methodology of procedural programming for choreographies, allowing for the writing of correct-by-construction implementations of divide-and-conquer distributed algorithms [24].

We can then conclude that formal methods based on well-known techniques seem to be a promising starting point for tackling the issue of writing correct microservice systems. This starting point gives us solid footing for exploring the more focused disciplines that we will need in the future, addressing problems like the description of coordination patterns amongst services. We envision that these patterns will benefit from the rich set of features that formal languages and process models have to offer, such as expressive type theories and logic. It is still unclear, however, how exactly these disciplines can be extended to naturally capture the practical scenarios that we encounter in microservices. We believe that empirically investigating microservice programming will be beneficial in finding precise research directions in this regard.

4.2 Trust and Security

The microservice paradigm poses a number of trust and security challenges. These issues are certainly not new, as they apply to SOA and in general to distributed computing, but they become even more challenging in the context of microservices. In this section, we aim to discuss some of these key security issues.

4.2.1 Greater Surface Attack Area

In monolithic architectures, application processes communicate via internal data structures or internal communication (for instance, socket or RMI). The attack surface is usually also constrained to a single OS. On the contrary, the microservice paradigm is characterised by applications that are broken down into services that interact with each other through APIs exposed to the network. APIs are independent of machine architectures and even programming languages. As a result, they are exposed to more potential attacks than traditional subroutines or functionalities of a large application, which only interacted with other parts of the same application. Moreover, application internals (the microservices) have now become accessible from the external world. Rephrasing, this means that microservices can in principle send the attack surface of a given application through the roof.

4.2.2 Network Complexity

The microservices vision, based on the creation of many small independent applications interacting with each other, can result in complex network activity. This network complexity can significantly increase the difficulty in enforcing the security of the overall microservices-based application. Indeed, when a real-world application is decomposed, it can easily create hundreds of microservices, as seen in the architecture overview of Hailo, an online cab reservation application.[1] Such an intrinsic complexity determines an ever-increasing difficulty in debugging, monitoring, auditing, and forensic analysis of the entire application. Attackers could exploit this complexity to launch attacks against applications.

---

[1]hailoapp.com.

4.2.3 Trust

Microservices, at least in this early stage of development, are often designed to completely trust each other. Considering a microservice trustworthy represents an extremely strong assumption in the "connectivity era", where microservices can interact with each other in a heterogeneous and open way. An individual microservice may be attacked and controlled by a malicious adversary, compromising not only the single microservice but, more drastically, bringing down the entire application. As an illustrative real-world example, a subdomain of Netflix was recently compromised, and from that domain, an adversary can serve any content in the context of netflix.com. In addition, since Netflix allowed all users' cookies to be accessed from any subdomain, a malicious individual controlling a subdomain was able to tamper with authenticated Netflix subscribers and their data [76]. Future microservices platforms need mechanisms to monitor and enforce the connections amongst microservices to confine the trust placed on individual microservices, limiting the potential damage if any microservice gets compromised.

4.2.4 Heterogeneity

The microservice paradigm brings heterogeneity (of distributed systems) to its maximum expression. Indeed, a microservices-based system can be characterised by a large number of autonomous entities that are not necessarily known in advance (again, trust issue); a large number of different administrative security domains, creating competition amongst providers of different services; a large number of interactions across different domains (through APIs); no common security infrastructure (different "Trusted Computing Base"); and, last but not least, no global system to enforce rules.

The research community is still far from adequately addressing the aforementioned security issues. Some recent works, like [76], show that some preliminary contribution is taking place. However, the challenge of building secure and trustworthy microservices-based systems is still more than open.

5 Conclusions

The microservice architecture is a style that has been increasingly gaining popularity in the last few years, both in academia and in the industrial world. In particular, the shift towards microservices is a sensitive matter for a number of companies involved in a major refactoring of their back-end systems [27].

Despite the fact that some authors present it from a *revolutionary* perspective, we have preferred to provide an *evolutionary* presentation to help the reader understand the main motivations that lead to the distinguishing characteristics of microservices and relate to well-established paradigms such as OO and SOA. With microservice architecture being very recent, we have not found a sufficiently comprehensive collection of literature in the field, so that we felt the need to provide a starting point for newcomers to the discipline and offer the authors' viewpoint on the topic.

In this chapter, we have presented a (necessarily incomplete) overview of software architecture, mostly providing the reader with references to the literature and guiding him/her in our itinerary towards the advent of services and microservices. A specific arc has been given to the narrative, which necessarily emphasises some connections and some literature, and it is possibly too severe with other sources. For example, research contributions in the domain of the actor model [43] and software agents [65] have not been emphasised enough, and still modern distributed systems have been influenced by these communities too. This calls for a broader survey investigating relationships along this line. For information on the relation between microservices and scalability, the reader may refer to [26].

Acknowledgements Montesi was supported by Choreographies for Reliable and efficient Communication software (CRC), grant no. DFF–4005-00304 from the Danish Council for Independent Research. Giallorenzo was supported by the EU EIT Digital project SMAll. This work has been partially funded by an Erasmus Mundus Scholarship. We would like to thank Daniel Martin Johnston who played a major role in proofreading the final draft of the chapter and improving the quality of writing.

References

1. Akentev, E., Tchitchigin, A., Safina, L., Mazzara, M.: Verified type-checker for Jolie. https://arxiv.org/pdf/1703.05186.pdf
2. Allen, E.B., Khoshgoftaar, T.M., Chen, Y.: Measuring coupling and cohesion of software modules: an information-theory approach. In: Proceedings Seventh International Software Metrics Symposium, pp. 124–134 (2001)
3. Bandura, A., Kurilenko, N., Mazzara, M., Rivera, V., Safina, L., Tchitchigin, A.: Jolie community on the rise. In: 9th IEEE International Conference on Service-Oriented Computing and Applications, SOCA (2016)
4. Bass, L.: Software Architecture in Practice. Pearson Education India, New Delhi (2007)
5. Bass, L., Merson, P., O'Brien, L.: Quality attributes and service-oriented architectures. Department of Defense, Technical Report September (2005)
6. Bieman, J.M., Kang, B.-K.: Cohesion and reuse in an object-oriented system. In: Proceedings of the 1995 Symposium on Software Reusability, SSR '95, pp. 259–262. ACM, New York (1995)
7. Birrell, A., Nelson, G., Owicki, S., Wobber, E.: Network objects. SIGOPS Oper. Syst. Rev. **27**(5), 217–230 (1993)
8. Bosch, J.: Software architecture: the next step. In: Software Architecture, pp. 194–199. Springer, Berlin (2004)
9. Bravetti, M., Zavattaro, G.: Towards a unifying theory for choreography conformance and contract compliance. In: Software Composition, pp. 34–50. Springer, Berlin, Heidelberg (2007)
10. Briand, L.C., Daly, J.W., Wüst, J.K.: A unified framework for coupling measurement in object-oriented systems. IEEE Trans. Softw. Eng. **25**(1), 91–121 (1999)
11. Brooks, F.P.: The Mythical Man-Month, vol. 1995. Addison-Wesley, Reading (1975)

12. Caires, L., Pérez, J.A.: Multiparty session types within a canonical binary theory, and beyond. In: Formal Techniques for Distributed Objects, Components, and Systems - 36th IFIP WG 6.1 International Conference, FORTE 2016, Held as Part of the 11th International Federated Conference on Distributed Computing Techniques, DisCoTec 2016, Heraklion, Crete, June 6–9, 2016, Proceedings, pp. 74–95 (2016)
13. Caires, L., Pfenning, F.: Session types as intuitionistic linear propositions. In: CONCUR, pp. 222–236 (2010)
14. Carbone, M., Montesi, F.: Deadlock-freedom-by-design: multiparty asynchronous global programming. In: POPL, pp. 263–274 (2013)
15. Carbone, M., Honda, K., Yoshida, N.: Structured communication-centered programming for web services. ACM Trans. Program. Lang. Syst. **34**(2), 8 (2012)
16. Carbone, M., Montesi, F., Schürmann, C.: Choreographies, logically. In: CONCUR, pp. 47–62 (2014)
17. Carbone, M., Montesi, F., Schürmann, C., Yoshida, N.: Multiparty session types as coherence proofs. In: CONCUR, pp. 412–426 (2015)
18. Carbone, M., Lindley, S., Montesi, F., Schürmann, C., Wadler, P.: Coherence generalises duality: a logical explanation of multiparty session types. In: Desharnais, J., Jagadeesan, R. (eds.) 27th International Conference on Concurrency Theory (CONCUR 2016). Leibniz International Proceedings in Informatics (LIPIcs), vol. 59, pp. 33:1–33:15. Schloss Dagstuhl–Leibniz-Zentrum fuer Informatik, Dagstuhl (2016). doi:10.4230/LIPIcs.CONCUR.2016.33, ISBN:978-3-95977-017-0. http://drops.dagstuhl.de/opus/volltexte/2016/6181
19. Christensen, E., Curbera, F., Meredith, G., Weerawarana, S., et al.: Web services description language (wsdl) 1.1 (2001)
20. Cohen, J., Brown, E., DuRette, B., Teleki, S.: Best Kept Secrets of Peer Code Review. Smart Bear, Somerville (2006)
21. Compton, B.T., Withrow, C.: Prediction and control of ADA software defects. J. Syst. Softw. **12**(3), 199–207 (1990)
22. Conway, M.E.: How do committees invent. Datamation **14**(4), 28–31 (1968)
23. Cruz-Filipe, L., Montesi, F.: Choreographies, computationally. In: CoRR, abs/1510.03271 (2015)
24. Cruz-Filipe, L., Montesi, F.: Choreographies, divided and conquered. In: CoRR, abs/1602.03729 (2016)
25. Dhama, H.: Quantitative models of cohesion and coupling in software. J. Syst. Softw. **29**(1), 65–74 (1995)
26. Dragoni, N., Lanese, I., Larsen, S.T., Mazzara, M., Mustafin, R., Safina, L.: Microservices: how to make your application scale. In: A.P. Ershov Informatics Conference (the PSI Conference Series, 11th edn.). Springer, Berlin (2017)
27. Dragoni, N., Dustdar, S., Larse, S.T., Mazzara, M.: Microservices: migration of a mission critical system. https://arxiv.org/abs/1704.04173
28. El Emam, K., Goel, N., Melo, W., Lounis, H., Rai, S.N., et al.: The optimal class size for object-oriented software. IEEE Trans. Softw. Eng. **28**(5), 494–509 (2002)
29. Fagan, M.: Design and code inspections to reduce errors in program development. In: Software Pioneers, pp. 575–607. Springer, Berlin (2002)
30. Fielding, R.T.: Architectural styles and the design of network-based software architectures. PhD thesis, University of California, Irvine (2000)
31. Flow: A static type checker for JavaScript. https://flowtype.org/
32. Fowler, M.: Patterns of Enterprise Application Architecture. Addison-Wesley Longman, Boston (2002)
33. Fowler, M., Foemmel, M.: Continuous integration. https://www.thoughtworks.com/continuous-integration (2006)
34. Fowler, M., Lewis, J.: Microservices. http://martinfowler.com/articles/microservices.html (2014)
35. Gabbrielli, M., Giallorenzo, S., Montesi, F.: Applied choreographies. In: CoRR, abs/1510.03637 (2015)

36. Gabbrielli, M., Giallorenzo, S., Guidi, C., Mauro, J., Montesi, F.: Self-reconfiguring microservices. In: Theory and Practice of Formal Methods, pp. 194–210. Springer, Berlin (2016)
37. Gamma, E., Helm, R., Johnson, R., Vlissides, J.: Design Patterns: Elements of Reusable Object-Oriented Software. Pearson Education India, New Delhi (1995)
38. Gao, J., Rahman, M.: A reusable automated acceptance testing architecture for microservices in behavior-driven development. In: Proceedings of the 2015 IEEE Symposium on Service-Oriented System Engineering (SOSE '15), pp. 321–325. IEEE Computer Society, Washington, DC (2015). doi:10.1109/SOSE.2015.55, ISBN:978-1-4799-8356-8. http://dx.doi.org/10.1109/SOSE.2015.55
39. Gray, J.: A conversation with Werner Vogels. ACM Queue **4**(4), 14–22 (2006)
40. Grosso, W.: Java RMI, 1st edn. O'Reilly & Associates, Inc., Newton (2001)
41. Guidi, C.: Formalizing languages for service oriented computing. Ph.D. thesis, University of Bologna (2007)
42. Hatton, L.: Reexamining the fault density-component size connection. IEEE Softw. **14**(2), 89–97 (1997)
43. Hewitt, C., Bishop, P., Steiger, R.: A universal modular actor formalism for artificial intelligence. In: Proceedings of the 3rd International Joint Conference on Artificial Intelligence, IJCAI'73, pp. 235–245. Morgan Kaufmann, Burlington (1973)
44. Hitz, M., Montazeri, B.: Measuring coupling and cohesion in object-oriented systems. Citeseer (1995)
45. Honda, K., Vasconcelos, V., Kubo, M.: Language primitives and type disciplines for structured communication-based programming. In: Proceedings of the 7th European Symposium on Programming: Programming Languages and Systems, pp. 22–138 (1998)
46. Honda, K., Yoshida, N., Carbone, M.: Multiparty asynchronous session types. J. ACM **63**(1), 9 (2016). Also: POPL, pp. 273–284 (2008)
47. Krause, L.: Microservices: Patterns and Applications, 1 edn. Lucas Krause, Paris (2014). 1 April 2015
48. Le, V.D., Neff, M.M., Stewart, R.V., Kelley, R., Fritzinger, E., Dascalu, S.M., Harris, F.C.: Microservice-based architecture for the NRDC. In: 2015 IEEE 13th International Conference on Industrial Informatics (INDIN), July 2015, pp. 1659–1664
49. López, H.A., Nielson, F., Nielson, H.R.: Enforcing availability in failure-aware communicating systems. In: Formal Techniques for Distributed Objects, Components, and Systems - 36th IFIP WG 6.1 International Conference, FORTE 2016, Held as Part of the 11th International Federated Conference on Distributed Computing Techniques, DisCoTec 2016, Heraklion, Crete, June 6–9, 2016, Proceedings, pp. 195–211 (2016)
50. Lucchi, R., Mazzara, M.: A pi-calculus based semantics for WS-BPEL. J. Logic Algebraic Program. **70**(1), 96–118 (2007)
51. MacKenzie, M.C., Laskey, K., McCabe, F., Brown, P.F., Metz, R., Hamilton, B.A.: Reference model for service oriented architecture 1.0. OASIS Standard, 12 Oct 2006
52. Mauro, T.: Adopting microservices at netflix: lessons for team and process design. http://nginx.com/blog/adopting-microservices-at-netflix-lessons-for-team-and-process-design/ (2015)
53. Mazzara, M.: Towards abstractions for web services composition. Ph.D. thesis, University of Bologna (2006)
54. Mazzara, M., Govoni, S.: A Case Study of Web Services Orchestration, pp. 1–16. Springer, Berlin, Heidelberg (2005)
55. Mazzara, M., Montesi, F., Guidi, C., Lanese, I.: Microservices: a language-based approach. In: Present and Ulterior Software Engineering. Springer, Berlin (2017)
56. Merkel, D.: Docker: lightweight Linux containers for consistent development and deployment. Linux J. **2014**(239), 2 (2014)
57. Milner, R.: A Calculus of Communicating Systems. Lecture Notes in Computer Science, vol. 92. Springer, Berlin (1980)
58. Milner, R., Parrow, J., Walker, D.: A calculus of mobile processes, I and II. Inf. Comput. **100**(1), 1–40, 41–77 (1992)

59. Mingela, B., Troshkov, N., Mazzara, M., Safina, L., Tchitchigin, A.: Towards static type-checking for Jolie. https://arxiv.org/pdf/1702.07146.pdf
60. Montesi, F.: Choreographic programming. Ph.D. thesis, IT University of Copenhagen. http://www.fabriziomontesi.com/files/choreographic_programming.pdf (2013)
61. Montesi, F.: Process-aware web programming with Jolie. Sci. Comput. Program. **130**, 69–96 (2016)
62. Montesi, F., Yoshida, N.: Compositional choreographies. In: CONCUR, pp. 425–439 (2013)
63. Montesi, F., Guidi, C., Zavattaro, G.: Service-Oriented Programming with Jolie. In: Web Services Foundations, pp. 81–107. Springer, Berlin (2014)
64. Newman, S.: Building Microservices. O'Reilly Media, Sebastopol (2015)
65. Nwana, H.S.: Software agents: an overview. Knowl. Eng. Rev. **11**, 205–244, 9 (1996)
66. OASIS: Web Services Business Process Execution Language. http://docs.oasis-open.org/wsbpel/2.0/wsbpel-v2.0.html
67. OMG: Common Object Request Broker Architecture. http://www.omg.org/spec/CORBA/
68. Ongaro, D., Ousterhout, J.K.: In search of an understandable consensus algorithm. In: 2014 USENIX Annual Technical Conference, USENIX ATC '14, Philadelphia, PA, 19–20 June 2014, pp. 305–319
69. Peltz, C.: Web services orchestration and choreography. Computer **36**(10), 46–52 (2003)
70. Perry, D.E., Wolf, A.L.: Foundations for the study of software architecture. ACM SIGSOFT Softw. Eng. Notes **17**(4), 40–52 (1992)
71. Prunicki, A.: Apache thrift (2009)
72. Raymond, E.S.: The Art of Unix Programming. Addison-Wesley Professional, Indianapolis (2003)
73. Rotem-Gal-Oz, A.: Fallacies of distributed computing explained, p. 20. http://www.rgoarchitects.com/Files/fallacies.pdf (2006)
74. Safina, L., Mazzara, M., Montesi, F., Rivera, V.: Data-driven workflows for microservices (genericity in Jolie). In: Proc. of The 30th IEEE International Conference on Advanced Information Networking and Applications (AINA) (2016)
75. Shaw, M., Garlan, D.: Software architecture: perspectives on an emerging discipline, vol. 1. Prentice Hall, Englewood Cliffs (1996)
76. Sun, Y., Nanda, S., Jaeger, T.: Security-as-a-service for microservices-based cloud applications. In: Proceedings of the 2015 IEEE 7th International Conference on Cloud Computing Technology and Science (CloudCom), CLOUDCOM '15, pp. 50–57. IEEE Computer Society, Washington, DC (2015)
77. Szyperski, C.: Component Software: Beyond Object-Oriented Programming, 2nd edn. Addison-Wesley Longman Publishing Co., Inc., Boston (2002)
78. Tchitchigin, A., Safina, L., Mazzara, M., Elwakil, M., Montesi, F., Rivera, V.: Refinement types in Jolie. In: Spring/Summer Young Researchers Colloquium on Software Engineering, SYRCoSE (2016)
79. Toninho, B., Caires, L., Pfenning, F.: Higher-order processes, functions, and sessions: a monadic integration. In: Programming Languages and Systems - 22nd European Symposium on Programming, ESOP 2013, Held as Part of the European Joint Conferences on Theory and Practice of Software, ETAPS 2013, Rome, March 16–24, 2013. Proceedings, pp. 350–369 (2013)
80. Varda, K.: Protocol buffers: Google's data interchange format. Google Open Source Blog, Available at least as early as July 2008
81. W3C: Web services architecture. http://www.w3.org/TR/ws-arch/
82. W3C: Web services choreography description language. https://www.w3.org/TR/ws-cdl-10/
83. Wadler, P.: Propositions as sessions. J. Funct. Program. **24**(2–3), 384–418 (2014). Also: ICFP, pp. 273–286 (2012)
84. Wang, A., Tonse, S.: Announcing ribbon: tying the netflix mid-tier services together, January 2013. http://techblog.netflix.com/2013/01/announcing-ribbon-tying-netflix-mid.html
85. Web Services Choreography Working Group et al.: Web services choreography description language (2002)

86. Yan, Z., Mazzara, M., Cimpian, E., Urbanec, A.: Business process modeling: classifications and perspectives. In: Business Process and Services Computing: 1st International Working Conference on Business Process and Services Computing, BPSC 2007, September 25–26, 2007, Leipzig, p. 222 (2007)

Microservices: A Language-Based Approach

Claudio Guidi, Ivan Lanese, Manuel Mazzara, and Fabrizio Montesi

Abstract Microservices is an emerging development paradigm where software is obtained by composing autonomous entities, called (micro)services. However, microservice systems are currently developed using general-purpose programming languages that do not provide dedicated abstractions for service composition. Instead, current practice is focused on the deployment aspects of microservices, in particular by using containerization. In this chapter, we make the case for a language-based approach to the engineering of microservice architectures, which we believe is complementary to current practice. We discuss the approach in general, and then we instantiate it in terms of the Jolie programming language.

1 Introduction

Microservices [3, 6, 18] is an architectural style stemming from Service-Oriented Architectures (SOAs) [10]. Its main idea is that applications are composed of small independent building blocks—the (micro)services—communicating via message passing. Recently, microservices have seen a dramatic growth in popularity, both in terms of hype and of concrete applications in real-life software [18]. Several companies are involved in a major refactoring of their backend systems [2] in order to improve scalability [4].

C. Guidi (✉)
italianaSoftware srl, Imola, Italy
e-mail: cguidi@italianasoftware.com

I. Lanese
Focus Team, University of Bologna/INRIA, Bologna, Italy
e-mail: ivan.lanese@gmail.com

M. Mazzara
Innopolis University, Innopolis, Russia
e-mail: m.mazzara@innopolis.ru

F. Montesi
University of Southern Denmark, Odense, Denmark
e-mail: fmontesi@imada.sdu.dk

© Springer International Publishing AG 2017
M. Mazzara, B. Meyer (eds.), *Present and Ulterior Software Engineering*,
https://doi.org/10.1007/978-3-319-67425-4_13

Current approaches for the development of server-side applications use mainstream programming languages. These languages, frequently based on the object-oriented paradigm, provide abstractions to manage the complexity of programs and their organization into modules. However, they are designed for the creation of single executable artifacts, called monoliths. The modules of a monolith cannot execute independently, since they interact by sharing resources (memory, databases, files, etc.). Microservices support a different view, enabling the organization of systems as collections of small *independent* components. Independent refers to the capability of executing each microservice on its own machine (if needed). This can be achieved because services have clearly defined boundaries and interact purely by means of message passing. Microservices inherit some features from SOAs, but they take the same ideas to a much finer granularity, from programming in the large to programming in the small. Indeed, differently from SOAs, microservices highlight the importance for services to be *small*, hence easily reusable, easily understood, and even easily rebuilt from scratch if needed. This recalls the single responsibility principle of object-oriented design [11].

Since it is convenient to abstract from the heterogeneity of possible machines (e.g., available local libraries and other details of the OS), it is useful to package a service and all its local dependencies inside a *container*. Container technologies, like Docker [12], enable this abstraction by isolating the execution of a service from that of other applications on the same machine. Indeed, in the literature about microservices, the emphasis is on deployment: since microservices live inside containers, they can be easily deployed at different locations. A major reason for this focus is that microservices are thought, since their inception as a style, to program in the cloud, where deployment and relocation play key roles. Even if microservices have now evolved well beyond cloud computing, the emphasis on deployment and containerization remains [6].

In this chapter, while supporting the current trend of microservices, we advocate for moving the emphasis from deployment to development, and in particular to the programming language used for development. We think that the chosen language should support the main mechanism used to build microservice architectures, namely, service composition via message passing communications. Furthermore, in order to master the related complexity, we support the use of well-specified interfaces to govern communication. Mainstream languages currently used for the development of microservices do not provide enough support for such communication modalities. In particular, service coordination is currently programmed in an unstructured and ad hoc way, which hides the communication structure behind less relevant low-level details.

While the idea of current methodologies for developing microservices can be summarized as "it does not matter how you develop your microservices, provided that you deploy them in containers," the key idea behind our methodology is "it does not matter how you deploy your microservices, provided that you build them using a microservice programming language." We describe our methodology in general and support the abstract discussion by showing how our ideas are implemented in the Jolie language [17, 21].

2 Language-Based Approach

The fine granularity of microservices moves the complexity of applications from the implementation of services to their coordination. Because of this, concepts such as communication, interfaces, and dependencies are central to the development of microservice applications. We claim that such concepts should be available as first-class entities in a language that targets microservices, in order to support the translation of the design of a microservice architecture (MSA) into code without changing domain model. This reduces the risk of introducing errors or unexpected behaviors (e.g., by wrong usage of bookkeeping variables).

What are then the key ingredients that should be included in a microservice language? Since a main feature of microservices is that they have a small size, realistic applications are composed by a high number of microservices. Since microservices are independent, the interactions among them all happen by exchanging messages. Hence, programming an MSA requires to define large and complex *message exchange structures*. The key to a "good" microservice language is thus providing ways to modularly define and compose such structures, in order to tame complexity. We discuss such ways in the rest of this section.

Interfaces In order to support modular programming, it is necessary that services can be deployed as "black boxes" whose implementation details are hidden. However, services should also provide the means to be composed in larger systems. A standard way of obtaining this is to describe via *interfaces* the functionalities that services provide to and require from the environment. Here, we consider interfaces to be sets of *operations* that can be remotely invoked. Operations may be either fully asynchronous or follow the typical request-response pattern. An operation is identified by a name and specifies the data types of the parameters used to invoke it (and possibly also of the response value).

Once we accept that interfaces are first-class citizens in microservices, it makes sense to have operators to manipulate them. Since interfaces are sets of operations, it is natural to consider the usual set-theoretical operators, such as union and intersection. For example, a gateway service may offer an interface that is the union of all the interfaces of the services that it routes messages to.

Ports Microservices may run in heterogeneous environments that use different communication technologies (e.g., TCP/IP sockets, Bluetooth, etc.) and data protocols (e.g., HTTPS, binary protocols, etc.). Moreover, a microservice may need to interact with many other services, each one possibly offering and/or requiring a different interface. A communication *port* concretely describes how some of the functionalities of a service are made available to the network, by specifying the three key elements above: interface, communication technology, and data protocol. Each service may be equipped with many ports, of two possible kinds. *Input ports* describe the functionalities that the service provides to the rest of the MSA. Conversely, *output ports* describe the functionalities that the service requires from the rest of the MSA. Ports should be specified separately from the implementation of a service, so that one can see what a service provides and what it needs without having to check its actual implementation. This recalls the use of type signatures for functions in procedural programming, with the difference that here the environment is heterogeneous and we thus need further information (communication medium, data protocol).

Example 1 Consider an online shopping service connected to both the Internet and a local intranet. This service may have 2 input ports, Customers and Admin, and 1 output port, Auth. Input port Customers exposes the interface that customers can use on the web, using HTTPS over TCP/IP sockets. Input port Admin exposes the administration controls of the service to the local intranet, using a proprietary binary protocol over TCP/IP sockets. Finally, output port Auth is used to access an authentication service in the local network.

Workflows Service interactions may require to perform multiple communications. For example, our previous Customers service may offer a "buy and ship" functionality, implemented as a structured protocol composed by multiple phases. First, the customer may select one or more products to buy. In the second phase, the customer sends her destination address and selects the shipment modality. Finally, the customer pays, which may require the execution of an entire sub-protocol, involving also a bank and the shipper. Since structured protocols appear repeatedly in microservices, supporting their programming is a key issue. Unfortunately, the programming of such *workflows* is not natively supported by mainstream languages, where all possible operations are always enabled. For example, consider a service implemented by an object that offers two operations, login and pay. Both operations are enabled at all times, but invoking pay before login raises an error. This causal dependency is programmed by using a bookkeeping variable, which is set when login is called and is read by method pay. Using bookkeeping variables is error prone; in particular, it does not scale when the number of causality links increases [14].

A microservice language should therefore provide abstractions for programming workflows. For example, one can borrow ideas from BPEL [19], process models [13], or behavioral types [9], where the causal dependencies are expressed syntactically using operators such as sequential and parallel compositions, e.g., login;pay would express that pay becomes available only after login. All the vast literature on business process modeling [22] can offer useful abstractions to this regard.

Processes A workflow defines the blueprint of the behavior of a service. However, at runtime, a service may interact with multiple clients and other external services. In our online shopping example, service Customers may have to support multiple users. Beyond that, the authentication service may be used both by service Customers and by other services, e.g., a Billing service. This is in line with the principle that microservices can be reused in different contexts. A service should thus support multiple executions of its workflow, and such executions should operate concurrently (otherwise, a new request for using the service would have to wait for previous usages to finish before being served).

A *process* is a running instance of a workflow, and a service may include many processes executing concurrently. The number of processes changes at runtime, since external parties may request the creation of a new process, and processes may terminate. Each process runs independently of the others, to avoid interference, and, as a consequence, it has its own private state.

3 The Jolie Language

Jolie [17, 21] is a language that targets microservices directly. Jolie was designed following the ideas discussed in Sect. 2. These were initially targeted at offering a language for programming distributed systems where all components are services, which later turned out to become the microservice paradigm.

Jolie is an imperative language where standard constructs such as assignments, conditionals, and loops are combined with constructs dealing with distribution, communication, and services. Jolie takes inspiration from WS-BPEL [19], an XML-based language for composing services, and from classical process calculi such as CCS [13] (indeed, the core semantics of Jolie is formally defined as a process calculus [8, 15]), but transfers these ideas into a full-fledged programming language. While we refer to [17, 21] for a detailed description of the Jolie language and its features, we discuss below the characteristics of Jolie that make it an instance of the language-based approach to microservices that we are advocating for.

The connection between Jolie and MSAs is at a very intimate level, e.g., even a basic building block of imperative languages like variables has been restructured to fit into the microservice paradigm. Indeed, microservices interact by exchanging data that is typically structured as trees (e.g., JSON or XML, supported in HTTP and other protocols) or simpler structures (e.g., database records). Thus, Jolie variables always have a tree structure [15], which allows the Jolie runtime to easily marshal and unmarshal data. It is clear that such a deep integration between language and microservice technologies cannot be obtained by just putting some additional library or framework on top of an existing language (which, e.g., would rely on variables as defined in the underlying language), but requires to design a new language from the very basic foundations.

A main design decision of the Jolie language is the separation of concerns between behavior and deployment information [16, 17]. Here with deployment information, we mean both the addresses at which functionalities are exposed and the communication technologies and data protocols used to interact with other services. In particular, as discussed in the previous section, each Jolie service is equipped with a set of ports: input ports through which the service makes its functionalities available and output ports used to invoke external functionalities. Thanks to this separation of concerns, one can easily change how a Jolie microservice communicates with its environment without changing its behavior.

Example 2 If the online shopping service of Example 1 is implemented in Jolie, its
`Customers` input port can be declared as:

```
1   inputPort Customers {
2     Location: "socket://www.myonlineshop.it:8000"
3     Protocol: https
4     Interfaces: CustomersInterface
5   }
```

The port declaration specifies the location where the port is exposed, which includes
both the communication technology, in this case a TCP/IP socket, and the actual
URL. Also, it declares the data protocol used for communication, in this case
HTTPS. Finally, the port refers to the interface used for communication, which is
described separately, and which can take, e.g., the form:

```
1   interface CustomersInterface {
2     RequestResponse: getList( void )( productIdList ),
3                      getPrice( productId )( double ),
4                ...
5   }
```

This interface provides two request-response operations, `getList` and
`getPrice`, and their signature. Types **void** and **double** are built-in, while
`productIdList` and `productId` are user defined; hence, their definition has
to be provided.

Having ports and interfaces as first-class entities in the language allows one to
clearly understand how a service can be invoked and which services it requires.
Furthermore, the same functionality can be exposed in different ways just by using
different input ports, without replicating the service. For instance, in the example
above, one can define a new port providing the same functionality using the SOAP
protocol. Finally, part of the port information, namely, location and protocol, can be
changed dynamically by the behavior, improving the flexibility.

Jolie also supports workflows [20]. Indeed, each Jolie program is a workflow: it
includes receive operations from input ports and send operations to output ports,
combined with constructs such as sequence, conditional, and loop. Notably, it
also provides parallel composition to enable concurrency and input-guarded choice
to wait for multiple incoming messages. Input ports are available only when a
corresponding receive is enabled; otherwise, messages to this port are buffered.

Example 3 Jolie also provides novel workflow primitives that can be useful in
practical scenarios. An example is the provide-until construct [14], which allows
for the programming of repetitive behavior driven by external participants. Using

standard workflow operators and provide-until, we can easily program a workflow for interacting with customers in our online shopping service from Sect. 2:

```
1  main {
2    login()( csets.sid ) { csets.sid = new };
3    provide
4      [ addToCart( req )( resp ) { /* ... */ } ]
5      [ removeFromCart( req )( resp ) { /* ... */ } ]
6    until
7      [ checkout( req )( resp ) { pay; ship } ]
8      [ logout() ]
9      }
```

The workflow above starts by waiting for the user to login (operation `login` is a request-response that returns a fresh session identifier `sid`, used for correlating incoming messages [15] from the same client later on). We then enter a provide-until construct where the customer is allowed to invoke operations `addToCart` and `removeFromCart` multiple times, until either `checkout` or `logout` is invoked. In the case for `checkout`, we then enter another workflow that first invokes procedure `pay` and then procedure `ship` (each procedure defines its own workflow).

From a single workflow, multiple processes are generated. Indeed, at runtime, when a message reaches a service, correlation sets [15] (kept in the special **csets** structure in the example above) are used to check whether it targets an already running process. If so, it is delivered to it. If not, and if it targets an initial operation of the workflow, a new process is spawned to manage it. Notably, multiple processes with the same workflow can be executed either concurrently or sequentially. This last option is mainly used to program resource managers, which need to enforce mutual exclusion on the access to the resource.

4 Conclusions and Related Work

We made the case for a linguistic approach to microservices, and we instantiated it on the Jolie language. Actually, any general-purpose language can be used to program microservices, but some of them are more oriented towards scalable applications and concurrency (both important aspects of microservices). Good examples of the latter are Erlang [5] and Go [7]. Between the two, Erlang is the nearest to our approach: it has one of the most mature implementations of processes, and some support for workflows based on the actor model (another relevant implementation of actors is the Akka framework [1] for Scala and Java). However, Erlang and Go do not separate behavior from deployment and more concretely do not come with explicitly defined ports describing the dependencies and requirements of services. WS-BPEL [19] provides many of the features we described, including ports, interfaces, workflows, and processes.

However, it is just a composition language and cannot be used to program single services. Also, WS-BPEL implementations are frequently too heavy for microservices.

Our hope is that other languages following the language-based approach would emerge in the near future. This would also allow one to better understand which features are key in the approach and which ones are just design decisions that can be changed. For instance, it would be interesting to understand whether language support for containerization would be useful and which form it could take. Such support is currently absent in Jolie, but it would provide a better integration with the classic approach focused on deployment. A related topic would be to understand how to improve the synergy between Jolie and microservices on one side and the cloud and IoT on the other side.

References

1. Akka (2017) http://akka.io/
2. Dragoni, N., Dustdar, S., Larsen, S.T., Mazzara, M.: Microservices: migration of a mission critical system (2017). https://arxiv.org/abs/1704.04173
3. Dragoni, N., Giallorenzo, S., Lluch-Lafuente, A., Mazzara, M., Montesi, F., Mustafin, R., Safina, L.: Microservices: yesterday, today, and tomorrow. In: Present and Ulterior Software Engineering. Springer, Berlin (2017)
4. Dragoni, N., Lanese, I., Larsen, S. T., Mazzara, M., Mustafin, R., Safina, L.: Microservices: how to make your application scale. In: A.P. Ershov Informatics Conference. The PSI Conference Series, 11th edn. Springer, Berlin (2017)
5. Erlang (2017) https://www.erlang.org/
6. Fowler, M., Lewis, J.: Microservices. ThoughtWorks (2014)
7. Go language (2017) https://golang.org/
8. Guidi, C., Lucchi, R., Gorrieri, R., Busi, N., Zavattaro, G.: SOCK: a calculus for service oriented computing. In: ICSOC. Lecture Notes in Computer Science, vol. 4294, pp. 327–338. Springer, Berlin (2006)
9. Hüttel, H., et al.: Foundations of session types and behavioural contracts. ACM Comput. Surv. 49(1), 3:1–3:36 (2016)
10. MacKenzie, M.C., et al.: Reference model for service oriented architecture 1.0. OASIS Standard, 12 (2006)
11. Martin, R.C.: Agile Software Development: Principles, Patterns, and Practices. Prentice Hall PTR, Englewood Cliffs (2003)
12. Merkel, D.: Docker: lightweight linux containers for consistent development and deployment. Linux J. 2014(239), 2 (2014)
13. Milner, R.: A Calculus of Communicating Systems. Lecture Notes in Computer Science, vol. 92. Springer, Berlin (1980)
14. Montesi, F.: Process-aware web programming with Jolie. Sci. Comput. Program. 130, 69–96 (2016)
15. Montesi, F., Carbone, M.: Programming services with correlation sets. In: ICSOC. Lecture Notes in Computer Science, vol. 7084, pp. 125–141. Springer, Berlin (2011)
16. Montesi, F., Guidi, C., Zavattaro, G.: Composing services with JOLIE. In: ECOWS, pp. 13–22. IEEE Computer Society, Los Alamitos (2007)
17. Montesi, F., Guidi, C., Zavattaro, G.: Service-oriented programming with Jolie. In: Web Services Foundations, pp. 81–107. Springer, Berlin (2014)

18. Newman, S.: Building Microservices. O'Reilly Media, Sebastopol (2015)
19. OASIS: Web Services Business Process Execution Language Version 2.0 (2007) http://docs.
    oasis-open.org/wsbpel/2.0/OS/wsbpel-v2.0-OS.pdf
20. Safina, L., Mazzara, M., Montesi, F., Rivera, V.: Data-driven workflows for microservices
    (genericity in jolie). In: Proceedings of the 30th IEEE International Conference on Advanced
    Information Networking and Applications (AINA) (2016)
21. The Jolie language website (2017) http://www.jolie-lang.org/
22. Yan, Z., Mazzara, M., Cimpian, E., Urbanec, A.: Business process modeling: classifications
    and perspectives. In: Business Process and Services Computing: 1st International Working
    Conference on Business Process and Services Computing, BPSC 2007, September 25–26,
    2007, Leipzig, p. 222 (2007)

Printed in the United States
By Bookmasters